Elmer Towns has opened the treasure house of wealth
in *Biblical Meditation for Spiritual Breakthrough*. This
is a little understood facet of Christian life that will
open new depths in our prayer lives.

CINDY JACOBS
COFOUNDER, GENERALS OF INTERCESSION
COLORADO SPRINGS, COLORADO

Meditation is a lost art in this media-dominated age when
people want to be entertained without thinking seriously.
Elmer Towns should be commended for providing
the Church this interesting challenge to an excellent
method of scriptural growth.

TIM LA HAYE
PRESIDENT, FAMILY LIFE SEMINARS, WASHINGTON, D.C.

Biblical Meditation for Spiritual Breakthrough is a refreshingly
informational and inspirational book that presents a thorough
study of the biblical principles that guide effective meditation.
Worksheets at the end of each chapter aid the reader in
making personal application from principles in each of the
10 biblical models. I know of no book on the subject of
meditation quite so practical and helpful as this one.

LARRY L. LEWIS
NATIONAL FACILITATOR, CELEBRATE JESUS 2000, MISSION AMERICA
LILBURN, GEORGIA

Biblical Meditation for Spiritual Breakthrough is a
practical book that bridges the gap between the word
"meditation" and its actual practice. This book will help
all of us experience God's transforming power.

DR. ERWIN W. LUTZER
SENIOR PASTOR, MOODY CHURCH
CHICAGO, ILLINOIS

Elmer Towns has done it again! *Biblical Meditation for Spiritual Breakthrough* is done in the classic Towns formula: choose a neglected topic of major importance to the spiritual life, examine it with encyclopedic thoroughness, and present that exhaustive study in a practical, easy-to-use format. This time his aim is to take the ancient practice of meditation, often the exclusive domain of the mystics, and make it attractive and available to all of us.

ROBERTSON MCQUILKIN
PRESIDENT EMERITUS, COLUMBIA INTERNATIONAL UNIVERSITY
COLUMBIA, SOUTH CAROLINA

Elmer Towns has performed a critical medical analysis for the Body of Christ and has discovered that the Body has lost its pulse. *Biblical Meditation for Spiritual Breakthrough* focuses on the problem and solution involved in the loss of mandated biblical meditation in the Church today. Buy this book and do it.

PAIGE PATTERSON
PRESIDENT, SOUTHEASTERN BAPTIST THEOLOGICAL SEMINARY
WAKE FOREST, NORTH CAROLINA

Elmer Towns has done it again with *Biblical Meditation for Spiritual Breakthrough*. With all the emphasis on fasting and seeking the face of God, Towns has given us the perfect companion for an extended fast. This book has revolutionized my devotional life. The unique arrangement makes it easy to find the meditation pattern you need. I love this book and intend to put it in our bookstore and promote it among our people.

DR. RON PHILLIPS
SENIOR PASTOR, CENTRAL BAPTIST CHURCH OF HIXSON
HIXSON, TENNESSEE

MORE PRAISE FOR

BIBLICAL MEDITATION for SPIRITUAL BREAKTHROUGH

Elmer Towns has done it again! He gets you meditating on
every page. This extensive commentary about life and
Scripture will jump-start your pondering process and help
you retreat from a speed-reading world. You'll think
more—and differently—about your Christian faith.

DOUG ROSS
PRESIDENT, EVANGELICAL CHRISTIAN PUBLISHERS ASSOCIATION
TEMPE, ARIZONA

Biblical Meditation for Spiritual Breakthrough is a must
read for every Christian. Elmer Towns has captured the
biblical reasons for meditating in a unique and inspiring
manner. Instead of using worldly models and symbols, he
has clearly lifted up biblical role models for this important
ritual in Christian experience. I intend to give every leader
in my local church a copy of this great book!

DR. STAN TOLER
AUTHOR AND INSTRUCTOR/INJOY MODEL CHURCH
SENIOR PASTOR, TRINITY CHURCH OF THE NAZARENE
OKLAHOMA CITY, OKLAHOMA

In *Biblical Meditation for Spiritual Breakthrough,*
Elmer Towns offers a blueprint for experiencing the
presence of God and His grace in everyday life. The
models and principles defined and illustrated in this book
provide methods of maintaining balance and living out the
Christlike life in a scriptural pattern of true discipleship.
This book has spoken to me in a very special way, and I
recommend it to all church leaders and laypeople as an
important tool for living the effective Christian life.

PAUL L. WALKER, PH.D
GENERAL OVERSEER, CHURCH OF GOD
CLEVELAND, TENNESSEE

BIBLICAL
MEDITATION
for
SPIRITUAL
BREAKTHROUGH

BIBLICAL
MEDITATION
for
SPIRITUAL
BREAKTHROUGH

ELMER TOWNS

Regal

A Division of Gospel Light
Ventura, California, U.S.A.

Published by Regal Books
A Division of Gospel Light
Ventura, California, U.S.A.
Printed in U.S.A.

Regal Books is a ministry of Gospel Light, an evangelical Christian publisher dedicated to serving the local church. We believe God's vision for Gospel Light is to provide church leaders with biblical, user-friendly materials that will help them evangelize, disciple and minister to children, youth and families.

It is our prayer that this Regal book will help you discover biblical truth for your own life and help you meet the needs of others. May God richly bless you.

For a free catalog of resources from Regal Books/Gospel Light please contact your Christian supplier or call 1-800-4-GOSPEL.

Cover Design by Barbara LeVan Fisher
Interior Design by Britt Rocchio
Edited by Virginia Woodard

ISBN 0-7394-1583-2

Rights for publishing this book in other languages are contracted by Gospel Literature International (GLINT). GLINT also provides technical help for the adaptation, translation and publishing of Bible study resources and books in scores of languages worldwide. For further information, contact GLINT, P.O. Box 4060, Ontario, CA 91761-1003, U.S.A., or the publisher.

CONTENTS

APPENDICES

DEDICATION

I could not think of just one person to whom to dedicate this book. Most of those who have deeper lives with God usually are not known for their strength in every area. Because every chapter presents a different kind of meditation, I have dedicated each chapter to those who best characterize its lesson.

> Those who meditate most on God,
> Quietly go on their daily search,
> So it's hard to know who meditates most,
> They don't talk about it much.

To Those I Appreciate

David Model: Harold Willmington, author of *Willmington's Bible Handbook* (Tyndale House), because of his majestic concept of God.
Mary Model: Mark Lowry, my former student, who wrote the words of a song, *Mary Did You Know That When You Kissed Your Baby Boy You Were Kissing the Face of God?*
Saint John Model: Wesley Afleck, the president before me of Winnipeg Bible College, Canada, who understood and loved Calvary.

Joshua Model: Ed Reis, a Navigator, who taught me the importance of Bible memory and application.

Saint Paul Model: Bill Greig Jr., president of Gospel Light, because he has a passion for the excellence of Christ.

Timothy Model: Charles Ryrie, my mentor at Dallas Theological Seminary, who taught me it was imperative to know my spiritual gifts.

Haggai Model: John Maxwell, a friend, who knows how to face and solve problems.

Asaph Model: Jerry Falwell, who constantly is delivered by God from attacks because he is never afraid to confront an immoral issue.

Malachi Model: John Morrison, a teacher who works for me, who has a passion to know the nature of God.

Korah Model: Laura Oldham, my wife's friend, who is intimate with God and exemplifies meditation.

FOREWORD

CALVARY CHAPEL WAS PLANTED IN 1981 BY
JOE FOCHT AND TODAY HAS 10,000 IN
ATTENDANCE EACH SUNDAY. IT IS THE LARGEST
CHURCH IN THE NORTHEASTERN UNITED
STATES AND IS STILL GROWING.

This book by Elmer Towns is an answer to the Midwestern religions' false teaching on meditation. I recommend it to any person who is experimenting with Near Eastern mysticism or false religious meditation.

Before I found Christ, I was playing guitar in a rock and roll band, traveling across the United States. I was typical of many in my generation; I was like a sheep without a shepherd. I was smoking pot and using cocaine. I put a blanket over my head and went into deep periods of meditation. I sat in front of an open window in the wintertime, not wearing a shirt, reading the Bible and searching to find God.

I went to the Eastern gurus and let the Maharaja blow into my ear, which was a symbol of placing thoughts or meditations into my head. Later, I came to realize he was just a little boy from India blowing into my ear.

Although I was embracing a search for meaning in mysticism, I saw a loophole in Christianity. There was a difference between a Savior and a guru. I had said that Jesus was my teacher, so I was reading the Bible and searching for truth. What I needed was Jesus as my *Savior*.

My best friend and fellow devotee, Harris Gordon, was irritated at me for claiming Jesus as my teacher instead of Maharaja. Harris and I had been discussing all night our search for God through meditation. He read 1 Corinthians 11 to me, how a man was not to pray having a veil cover his head. He was trying to prove the Bible and Jesus inconsistent with our Eastern mysticism.

Around three in the morning, the presence of the Lord filled the room. We both wept unashamedly before the Lord as we felt God's presence in our lives. We experienced the personage of the Holy Spirit in the room, and although He was not visible and we did not hear Him, we knew He was there. I hung my head and cried. I was ashamed of my sin, and I repented before God for all my transgressions. Then I felt wave after wave of love washing over me and cleansing me.

The next morning, I knew I had been saved. When I went outside, I noticed the sky was bluer and the birds' voices were sweeter—I had been transformed. I saw things in God's universe I had never seen before. I experienced the love of God I had never experienced before. When a friend asked me to come to his church and pray at the altar, I told him Christ had already saved me.

After reading this book, I realize Elmer Towns has found the secret of biblical meditation. The secret is not in an inner journey; the secret is in God. There are many ways to meditate on God, and I thank God for a book that will help people focus their meditation on Him.

I still call myself a mystic, but I am a biblical mystic. I ground my feelings on the Word of God, and let God's Word produce healing in me. I go to God in prayer, and let God speak to me through the Holy Spirit. Meditation is not something that comes out of my empty heart and soul; meditation is based upon the precepts I find in the Word of God, and I meditate upon the person of God.

Elmer Towns has given us illustrations of 10 people in the Bible and how they meditated differently. As I studied carefully what he wrote, I realized that all of us are different from each other, and we meditate on God differently. God never changes and His Word is eternal. When we bring our feelings to the Word of God, we meditate in different ways for different purposes.

I am concerned for many young people who don't know God. Many are following the pied pipers of their own generation, searching for God in the wrong places and in the wrong ways. They delve into transcendental meditation, or they begin following some Far Eastern mystic; but that is not the answer. The answer is in the Bible and in the God of the Bible.

May God use this book for His glory.

Joe Focht, Pastor
Calvary Chapel
Philadelphia, Pennsylvania

INTRODUCTION

I was converted to Christ on July 25, 1950. Since that evening, I have never once doubted the reality of my salvation. I knew intuitively the presence of Christ in my life, which I cannot explain except by the phrase "Christ lives in me" (Gal. 2:20).

On the first Easter Sunday after my conversion, I experienced a special sense of communion with God that I had not felt previously. At the time, I was discouraged. I knew I was saved and that Christ lived in me, but I still felt discouraged. About 9 o'clock that morning, I found myself waiting for a ride to take me to Capital View Community Chapel just outside Columbia, South Carolina. I was scheduled to teach a Sunday School class that morning, but my ride was late. While I waited for 30 minutes, I meditated on what the Bible meant for Christ to live in me.

> "I have been crucified with Christ; it is no longer
> I who live, but Christ lives in me; and the life
> which I now live in the flesh I live by faith in the
> Son of God, who loved me and gave Himself for me."
> —Galatians 2:20

I tried to determine what the two phrases meant, "I have been crucified with Christ," and the other phrase, "no longer I who live, but Christ lives in me." Then it dawned upon me that the real meaning of Easter was more than Christ dying for my sins—Jesus arose that first Sunday morning and now He lives—He lives in my heart. That day was the first Easter of my Christian life, and I felt His presence in my life as I was standing on that street corner. I had an overwhelming sense of His fullness. I experienced His presence at work in me.

As I stood in the warm morning sunlight, I renewed my commitment to Christ, yielding myself anew to God. I asked Jesus Christ to give me victory by living His faith through me. Jesus Christ had never been discouraged, and I wanted to rise above discouragement in my own life. I had been praying to God for my financial needs, but at that moment I wanted more. I wanted His faith to conquer my worry. I completely yielded to Jesus Christ and turned my life over to Him.

What I experienced that morning was very real. I did not kneel in prayer or close my eyes. I simply talked to Jesus and yielded everything to Him. I asked Him to live His life through me. That morning, for the first time, I experienced the meaning of the resurrection life. A year earlier, prior to my conversion, the Resurrection had been little more than a historical fact. Now, Easter was an inner reality. The risen Christ was alive in my life. I knew that inner sense of the presence of Christ would be tested, but that morning I did not have a care in the world. I was experiencing the faith of Christ.

Because of what I have experienced in my own life through the discipline of meditation, I wanted to write this book to help others experience their own spiritual breakthrough. I believe many Christians want a deeper and more meaningful relationship with Christ, but they have never been taught how to meditate on Jesus Christ. When they look for help to guide their thinking, little help is available. New believers tend to think the way they thought in their unsaved days. What controls their lives?

What Controls Our Thinking?

Financial pressure	Secularism
Promotion and advancement	Pleasure
Sex	Winning
Family concerns	Selfish pursuits

Although the discipline of meditation has been an important contribution to Christian living since the first days of the Church, very few meditate on Christian things today. I once asked a man what he thought of his church.

"I don't think about it much," was his answer.

That is probably an accurate description of most Christians. They don't think about their church very often, nor do they think much about Christ. Even when modern people read about meditation in a current magazine, it is not Christian meditation. Most of what we hear is based on Hindu and Buddhist mysticism.

New Age teachers instruct young people to assume the lotus position by crossing their feet and holding their fingers upward. They chant, "O-o-o-o-o . . .," and try to empty their minds of all thoughts . . . to become one with God . . . to experience moksha nirvana. They chant mantras or practice yoga, but these are not Christian practices.

Christian meditation is not about what methods you use, nor is it about what position you assume, nor is it about what you chant or how you focus. Christian meditation is about God. It is meditation that will change your life because you focus on God—and when you experience God, God changes you.

This book is an attempt to begin correcting the false ideas about meditation, without spending a lot of time studying all the false ideas. This book will focus on the positive biblical idea of meditation, and the positive ideas of God will expel the negative. In this book, I have tried to outline 10 key models for biblical practice of this discipline. Because people differ from each other, they think about God differently. This book examines 10 people from the Bible and how each meditated on God. All their approaches bear some similarity because there is only one God. I have attempted to outline the biblical principles that evolve from each of these 10 models and suggest practical steps to help you incorporate meditation into your life.

The David Model: Considering God's creation and majesty
The Mary Model: Pondering the person of Jesus
The Saint John Model: Thinking about the cross

The Joshua Model: Focusing on biblical principles
The Saint Paul Model: Becoming like Christ
The Timothy Model: Meditating on your calling and gifts
The Haggai Model: Considering your failures
The Asaph Model: Meditating on God's intervention
The Malachi Model: Meditating on God's name
The Korah Model: Contemplating intimacy with God

Christian meditation is much more than using the name of Jesus as a mantra or formula. Meditation is a dynamic process that changes your thought life as the first step in changing the rest of your life. Meditation will help you develop a deeper communion with God and will encourage your growth in character (i.e., the fruit of the Holy Spirit) and service.

What will you learn as you study the discipline of meditation?

"While we look for better methods," Matthew Henry once observed, "God looks for better men."

Learning the discipline of meditation is your key element to building a better life for His glory. Great Christian leaders throughout history have meditated and discovered their own spiritual breakthrough. I invite you to join me in my pursuit to join their ranks.

Thank you Doug Porter, a 17-year friend, for research and ideas. You are a model of one who knows Christ and walks with Him. Thank you Linda Elliott for typing and proofreading; you are a model of Christian service to all. I take responsibility for all the mistakes and omissions. May both you and God overlook them, and use what is usable for His glory.

Elmer L. Towns
Spring 1998
From my home at the foot
of the Blue Ridge Mountains of Virginia

~ 1 ~

THE LOST
ART OF
MEDITATION

A young boy frequently sat on the front porch of his home in a small New England town gazing at the large white rock on the other side of the valley. A man's face etched in the rock was called "Old Stone Face." The Indians had a legend that the white rock was the face of a man who would come to the valley someday and bring prosperity to all. The young boy studied every portion of the rock, looking for the eyes . . . the nose . . . the facial appearance. He thought,

I want to be the first to recognize the man who'll bring prosperity to my valley.

A salesman came into the valley, going door-to-door, selling a kitchen utensil to the ladies. The boy was sure he was the white face that would bring prosperity. He ran to town yelling,

"The man in the great stone face is here!"

The salesman's gimmick didn't bring prosperity, though. When the boy was proven wrong, he went back to study deeply the face in the rock.

A doctor came to town selling a miracle cure. This time the boy was sure this was Stone Face when he heard a rumor that someone was healed by the medicine. He ran through town yelling,

"The man in the great stone face is here!"

Again the boy was wrong. No healings occurred, and the doctor was a fraud; he was selling "snake oil." Again the boy studied Old Stone Face.

The boy grew into young manhood without discovering the man in the great stone face. He went to college, where he was converted to Christ. He went through seminary to prepare for the ministry. God put it upon his heart to return to his boyhood New England town to preach the gospel.

As he entered the town, he greeted the first lady he met, but she didn't speak. She just stared. The young minister thought,

She must be against preachers coming to her town.

When he went into a store, the clerk didn't wait on him; the clerk only stared at the young preacher. Everyone stared at the minister because he looked identical to the face in the great white rock. He had become the great stone face and the Indian myth came true; he brought prosperity to the town—spiritual prosperity.

> We become like
> the thing we constantly
> think about.

The boy in the story becomes like the "stone face," probably not in physical characteristics, but in inner spirit. The Bible calls this meditation. The word "meditate" is found almost two dozen times in Scripture. Why should God be concerned about what we think or how we meditate?

> "For as he thinketh in his heart, so is he."
> —Proverbs 23:7 (*KJV*)

Meditation is a beautiful Christian discipline; but like so many things in Christianity, the world and false religions are attempting to steal it. They take Christian actions such as prayer and fasting and fill them with non-Christian practices and anti-Christian goals. While writing this book, I saw an article about meditation in a women's magazine at the grocery store's checkout register. The article had nothing to do with Christianity. It was teaching modern women to gain inner peace through yoga.

Many forces compete for your mind. Television is compelling—the average American watches more than 25 hours a week. A large variety of newspapers and magazines are available everywhere. Our thoughts should be our own when we drive, but radios, audiocassettes, CDs, billboard advertising and other distractions vie for our attention. Having our houses located on the super-information highway of life makes it almost impossible to have private thoughts.

Some are rebelling against the data-crazed society; they retreat into yoga, transcendental meditation or some other form of contemplation (see appendix A). Some want to become like their god; Shirley MacLaine says she *is* God.

New Age seminars are available in large cities; the megabookstores, as well as the bookstores in shopping malls, include huge sections about New Age and Eastern religions. I watched a teenage girl at a Waldenbooks store in a mall in Myrtle Beach, South Carolina, pick up a New Age title and thumb through the pages. It was a book about contemplation. I was curious and I asked what she was looking for.

"I want some power over my friends," she answered.

When I tried to tell her I was a Christian, she was not interested in my answers.

"I want to make them do what I tell them to do," she responded.

People are curious about meditation for many reasons, and that is all right when they sincerely search for answers, and search in the right places. This book has some answers; it has biblical answers. The Bible gives us at least 10 ways to meditate, and at least 10 different results of meditation.

More Than One Way to Meditate
A time to think quietly about God the Creator
A time to think practically about God the Problem-Solver
A time to examine our principles

A time to look without at the world in wonder
A time to look at the past and remember
A time to look to the future and plan
A time to face our failures and do better
A time to examine our success and go on

I began telling a friend that I was writing a book about meditation. He scowled. I could see disapproval in his face, so I confronted him, wanting to know why he frowned.

"Meditation sounds mushy to me," he replied.

He thought meditation was something done by a medieval monk in a monastery . . . sitting in a cell all day . . . contemplating God. Then he added, "Meditation is what kids do at camp when they sit and watch the sun go down over the lake."

"Wrong!" I smiled at him.

Then to make sure I didn't alienate him, I explained that sometimes meditation was passive meditation, but at other times it was active problem-solving meditation that motivated us to make positive plans for the future. The Bible uses many other terms to describe meditation.

1. Remember
2. Think on these things
3. Ponder
4. Behold God's love
5. Muse on the work of thy hands
6. Meditate
7. Consider
8. Let the mind of Christ be in you
9. Set your mind on things above
10. Let the Word of Christ dwell in you richly

Not until you begin to meditate on God and His Word will you realize how much you have lost by trying to do it without God. Ralph Waldo Emerson said, "A man is what he thinks about all day long." If you think about food all day long, your life will revolve around food consumption. If you want to be more godly, you will have to begin thinking about God.

Meditation may help us gain such significant insight and understanding that we may surpass those who instruct us (see Ps. 119:99; 2 Tim. 2:7).

The Benefits of Meditation

1. You gain insight and instruction of truth (Ps. 119:99; 2 Tim. 2:7).
2. You get a positive outlook on life (Ps. 104:34).
3. You deepen your love for the Scriptures and God (Ps. 119:97).
4. You become prosperous as you apply the insights gained (Josh. 1:8).
5. You grow and become stable in the Christian life (Ps. 1:2,3; John 15:4).
6. You develop a strong prayer life (John 15:7).
7. You are motivated to ministry (1 Sam. 12:24; 1 Tim. 4:15).
8. You are motivated to repent and live better (Ps. 39:3; Rev. 2:5).
9. You find the peace of God (Phil. 4:8,9).
10. You get a clear focus to guide you in making decisions (Matt. 6:33; Col. 3:2).
11. You focus your life on Christ (Heb. 12:3; 1 John 3:1).
12. You worship God in His majestic glory (Deut. 4:39).

Most of us are busy. We talk on the phone, listen to news, read reports and chat with friends. Most people would tell me they have no time to meditate. If you don't think about and plan your life, however, you will be led about by the nose, by circumstances or by people who will think and plan your life for you.

When to Meditate

Commuting to work
Shaving or applying makeup
Waiting at the copier

> In the checkout line
> Waiting for a bus or taxi
> In bed before going to sleep
> Driving time
> Before the church service

Everyone meditates differently because personalities differ. Obviously, our minds function the same as other normal people, but what we think about and what we think is different. The optimistic businessman thinks positive thoughts. He has no pessimistic thought in his brain. The irresponsible worker who can't keep a job sees only the rain clouds; the person never expects to see the sun.

Henry J. Kaiser, the industrialist, at one time was supervising the building of a levy along a riverbank. A storm came through the area, and the riverbank flooded. All his earth-moving machinery was mired in mud and the work was destroyed. When he arrived at the work site, he found his workers sitting in despair.

"What's wrong?" Kaiser asked his workers. "Let's get started."

The workers pointed to all the machinery bogged down in mud. They were discouraged because all they had done had been destroyed.

"We can't work in this mud!" the foreman said to Kaiser.

"What mud?" Kaiser answered, "Look up, I don't see any mud in the sky. I see the sun." He explained that soon the sun would dry the mud. A clear blue sky would be a perfect day in which to work. "Soon the mud will be dry, you'll be able to move your machinery and we can start over again."

The way we think is one of the most powerful influences on the way we live. William James said, "The greatest discovery of my generation is that human beings can alter their lives by altering their attitude of mind." So it is possible to make a success of a failed life. First, we must change our way of thinking. We must get rid of the ideas that made us fail, and fill our minds with new, fresh, creative ways to succeed. Marcus Aurelius said, "A man's life is what his thoughts make of it."

This book is about the thoughts of 10 people in the Bible and how they meditated. Because their circumstances differed, they meditated differently from each other. Their problems and concerns also differed, so they thought differently from each other. Their occupation or task in life also influenced the way they thought. Read each meditation carefully; think about what they thought about and the way they meditated. You can learn from some of them, but because of the differences in people, all of the meditations may not appeal to you. Therefore, as you read this book, think carefully about what is said. Meditate deeply—this book can change your life.

The David Model: Considering God's creation and might
The Mary Model: Pondering the person of Jesus
The Saint John Model: Thinking about the cross
The Joshua Model: Focusing on biblical principles
The Saint Paul Model: Becoming like Christ
The Timothy Model: Meditating on your calling and gifts
The Haggai Model: Considering your failures
The Asaph Model: Meditating on God's intervention
The Malachi Model: Meditating on God's name
The Korah Model: Contemplating intimacy with God

Ten Ways to Practice Christian Meditation

The David Model is first because creation is where we all first encounter God. David, the young shepherd, spent many nights under the stars keeping watch over his father's flock. He learned, "The heavens declare the glory of God; and the firmament shows His handiwork" (Ps. 19:1). Before people ever read about God in the Scriptures, they can learn about God who reveals Himself through nature. The stars in the night sky were designed as signs (see Gen. 1:14), and special significance was attached to the rainbow after the Flood (see Gen. 9:13). Study the David Model to meditate on the majesty of God.

The one closest to Jesus on this earth was His mother, Mary. "Mary kept all these things and pondered them in her heart" (Luke 2:19). Throughout her life she reflected on His supernatural birth, life and death. She knew Him better than anyone, yet she wanted to know Him still better. Mary becomes our example of how to really know Christ.

When you apply the Saint John Model, you meditate on the cross and Christ's finished work. John was the only one of the 12 disciples to stand at the foot of the cross and witness the actual death of Christ. It forever changed his life. He urged his readers, "Behold what manner of love the Father has bestowed on us, that we should be called children of God!" (1 John 3:1). John and those who follow his example see the cross of Christ as a strong motivation to personal holiness (see v. 3), and a growing sense of Christian community (see 4:11).

Those who follow the Joshua example meditate on the scriptural principles for personal success. "This Book of the Law shall not depart from your mouth, but you shall meditate in it day and night, that you may observe to do according to all that is written in it. For then you will make your way prosperous, and then you will have good success" (Josh. 1:8). This approach to meditation is key to achieving success in every area of life.

Perhaps the fullest expression of Christian meditation is found in the Saint Paul Model: meditating on becoming like Christ. Paul urged the Colossians, "Set your mind on things above, not on things on the earth" (Col. 3:2). Some have mistakenly concluded that the Saint Paul example of meditation makes people so heavenly minded they can be no earthly good. Paul's way of thinking worked, though. He built churches and led people to Christ who then grew in grace. Writing to the Philippians, he urged, "Whatever things are true, whatever things are noble, whatever things are just, whatever things are pure, whatever things are lovely, whatever things are of good report, if there is any virtue and if there is anything praiseworthy—meditate on these things" (Phil. 4:8).

The Timothy Model of meditation reminds you to consider God's unique calling in your life and the way He has gifted you for Christian service. Paul urged Timothy, "Do not neglect the gift that is in you,....Meditate on these things; give yourself entirely to them, that your progress may be evident to all" (1 Tim. 4:14,15). By reflecting on his gifts and calling of God, Timothy could grasp a clear vision of God's mission for his life and achieve greater ministry effectiveness.

The Haggai Model calls us to look at our problems, failures and sins. Haggai uses the term "consider," telling the people of his day,

"Consider your ways" (Hag. 1:5,7). Haggai motivates us to look at our failures, change our thinking, then change our ways.

Asaph wrote 12 psalms that praise God for His interventions in his life. What God had done for him in the past was a key for his encouragement in difficult and discouraging times. "I will remember the works of the Lord; surely I will remember Your wonders of old. I will also meditate on all Your work, and talk of Your deeds" (Ps. 77:11,12). The Asaph Model encourages you to record significant answers to prayer so you can remember the unique ways of God.

The final book of the Old Testament describes the Malachi Model of meditation on the names of God. "Then those who feared the Lord spoke to one another, and the Lord listened and heard them; so a book of remembrance was written before Him for those who fear the Lord and who meditate on His name" (Mal. 3:16). The appendix of my book *The Names of the Holy Spirit* lists more than 1,000 names of God the Father, the Son and the Holy Spirit. Each name describes a unique character or task of God that teaches us more about Him. Meditating on God's name gives us a better understanding of who He is and how He relates to us. Practicing the Malachi Model inevitably draws us into a deeper relationship with Him.

The Korah Model focuses on knowing God intimately. Twelve psalms are attributed to the sons of Korah, who sang, "We have thought, O God, on Your lovingkindness, in the midst of Your temple" (Ps. 48:9). These writers longed to know God. They are different from Korah their patriarchal head, who was judged by God for refusing to come to the sanctuary of God. The sons of Korah cry out, "As the deer pants for the water brooks, so pants my soul for You, O God. My soul thirsts for God, for the living God" (Ps. 42:1,2). The sons of Korah were singers in the Temple and wrote, "My soul longeth, yea, even fainteth for the courts of the Lord" (Ps. 84:2, *KJV*), and "For a day in thy courts is better than a thousand" (v. 10, *KJV*).

What to Take Away

Kyle Duncan, associate publisher of Regal Books, has said my books are a unique blend of deeper life intimacy with God and user-friendly practicality. I hope this is true. I want you to know God intimately and to meditate on Him. Therefore, I have included several sections at the end of each chapter to make meditation easy to begin and to practice.

Perfume and Superglue

Perfume: I want you to delight in the experience of God's fragrance.
Superglue: I want you to make these practical ideas stick to your soul.

A young bride from the eastern United States married during wartime, and her husband was transferred to a U.S. Army base in the desert of California. Living conditions were marginal, the heat was unbearable, the desert constantly blew dust and sand into the house and her days were boring because her husband was gone most of the time. Their neighbors spoke only Spanish or were Native Americans from the reservation who did not speak English.

The young woman wrote to her mother that she was coming home because she couldn't take it anymore. Her mother responded by simply writing two lines:

Two men looked through prison bars:
one saw mud the other saw stars.

The young woman felt ashamed about her complaining attitude, and decided she would look to the stars. She made friends with the Indians, learned weaving, pottery making, and eventually learned everything she could about Indian history and culture. Later in life she became an Indian history and culture expert and wrote a book about the area.

What you think,
is a product of what you are.
And what you are,
is a product of what you think.

~ 2 ~

THE
DAVID MODEL:

Considering God's
Creation and Majesty

"LET THE WORDS OF MY MOUTH AND THE
MEDITATION OF MY HEART BE ACCEPTABLE
IN YOUR SIGHT, O LORD, MY STRENGTH
AND MY REDEEMER."

Psalm 19:14

David sat on a mound of green grass overlooking his sheep, which were grazing in the late afternoon sun. Young David had much time to meditate because a shepherd doesn't have a lot to do. He just has to make sure the sheep don't wander off—they tend to stray. David must protect the sheep from the threat of a wolf or a bear. Something about the tender vulnerability of sheep attracted predators. As David meditated on his task as a shepherd, he thought of its similarity to God's protection in his life.

> The Lord is my shepherd,
> I shall not want.

David's sheep didn't have to worry about a thing; he made sure they had good pasture for eating grass. Often David compared the role of the Lord to a shepherd. What David did for his sheep, the Lord did for His people. David meditated.

> The Lord makes His sheep lie down,
> In lush green pastures.
> The Lord leads His sheep beside still waters,
> To restore their parched souls.
> The Lord leads His sheep in right paths,
> For the sake of His nature.

The sheep had been grazing in this field all day. They had eaten abundantly; now much of the grass was gone. David looked around and saw a distant field, as green as this pasture had been that morning. To get from this field to that one, though, he had to lead the sheep through a narrow valley where wolves had been seen. David walked the valley first to make sure no wolves were waiting to prey on the sheep. Then, gathering the sheep close to him, David led them through danger.

> The Lord leads me through valleys of death,
> I will fear no danger.
> The Lord has a rod and staff to protect me,
> I am safe with Him.

On the other side of the valley the sheep spread out to eat, feeling neither fear nor worry. David found a spot under a tree to watch them. In the shade of a bay tree, David meditated on God's provision.

> The Lord prepares food for me to eat.
> My enemies, the wolves, watch from afar.
> The Lord anoints me with oil of prosperity,

I will dwell in His presence forever.
—Psalm 23, author's translation

David saw a storm churning over a nearby hill. He ran to herd the sheep together. The sheep were slow to respond because they couldn't sense the imminent danger. Lightning cracked on a distant mountain. The sound of thunder rumbled down the valley. Although threatened by danger, David could still meditate.

The voice of the Lord comes with the storm,
The God of glory thunders.
The voice of the Lord breaks cedar trees,
The power of God is in the wind.
The voice of the Lord shakes the wilderness,
The force of the Lord is majestic.
The voice of the Lord makes the streams
flood their banks,
The Lord gives peace in the storm.
—Psalm 29, author's translation

David sat on a small ledge, surveying the results of the afternoon storm. It was early evening; the overhanging branches of a bay tree protected him from the damp evening dew. The young shepherd studied the stars as each one began to twinkle in the darkening sky. The moon slowly rose over the hills, casting its early evening shadows. David meditated.

The heavens declare the glory of God,
The sky is a result of His handiwork.
The daylight reveals God's creative power,
The night shows God's creative plan.
—Psalm 19:1,2, author's translation

David wondered why all people didn't worship God when they saw His creative power in the moon and stars. David tried to count the stars, and to his limited sight in the Holy Land, he could only see hundreds upon hundreds of stars. He magnified God for the vast number of stars. If David could have gazed into the heavens through the amplified power of the Hubble telescope, the young shepherd would have found out that 50 billion galaxies exist (most of them more vast than our Milky Way), and each galaxy has more than 200 million burning stars. Trillions upon trillion of stars float around in the heavens . . . and why did God create so many stars? Because a limitless God declares His infinity by creating more stars than any of His created beings can fathom or comprehend. Young David meditated,

"God must like stars."

The meditation of young David led to worship of his Creator, just as God had planned it. In David's mind, he understood the God who had created him yet was interested in him personally.

> When I consider the heavens,
> The work of Your fingers,
> The sun, the moon, and the stars,
> Which You have ordained,
> What is the purpose of man
> That You are mindful of him?
> Or Your Son, who will become like man,
> And that You will visit Him?
> —Psalm 8:3,4, author's translation

David's meditation on nature never led him to worship things, nor did it motivate him to carve an idol that was like created things. When David observed the greatness of the sun, moon and stars, he worshiped God who created them. God was the originator of all things.

David's mediation led him to understand his place in life. He knew the role of humanity was to praise God, serve God and obey God.

> You have created man to magnify You,
> Lower than ministering angels that serve You,
> You have made man
> To glorify You and bring honor to You.

> You gave life to man,
> To have dominion over Your creation.
> You have glorified Yourself with
> Cattle, wild beasts, sheep, all fish and birds,
> You created all things,
> To be used by man for Your purpose.
> —Psalm 8:5-7, author's translation

David's meditation began as a shepherd boy when he observed God's created world. Later, David spent 13 years as a fugitive in the mountains and woods, running from Saul. He fellowshipped with God (see Ps. 139). In the palace, an older David never forgot his Creator (see Ps. 19).

What Meditation Did for David

1. It reminded him of God.
2. It motivated him to worship God.
3. It helped him understand his role in life.
4. He sought forgiveness of God.
5. He learned about God.
6. He fellowshipped with God.

David's meditation never focused only on creation, or ended with the wonders of the physical world. David was not a naturalist who simply worshiped nature. He was not just a subjective poet who meditated on the universe about him. He was a biblical poet and his observations of creation demanded that he meditate on the Creator, the Lord of heaven, who also created heaven.

Looking for Fingerprints

When people begin to meditate on God, they usually begin to think about God as they see Him in the natural world around them. Modern people begin to think about God, just as David the shepherd did. They see the majesty of nature, and think about creation.

An outstanding place to begin your meditation is the creative power of God. You can see the "fingerprints" of God in the world He has created; however, not everything about God is seen in creation. Many other things about God can't be understood by meditation. "The secret things belong to the Lord our God, but those things which are revealed belong to us and to our children forever, that we may do all the words of this law" (Deut. 29:29).

In the New Testament, the writer of Hebrews begins by stating, "God spoke to His people in the past at various times, in various ways, but in these last times, God has spoken to us through His son, who created the world, and who is the ruler of all things" (Heb. 1:1,2, author's translation). This statement suggests at least three other significant facts about how we can know God.

First, God has chosen to reveal Himself to us "in various ways" throughout history. He used visions, dreams, poetry, biographies, sermons, face-to-face conversations, miracles, parables and He even wrote on stone tablets.

Second, the ultimate expression of knowing God is through the physical birth and life of Jesus. "The Word became flesh and dwelt among us, and we beheld His glory" (John 1:14). To know and understand God, we must look at Jesus Christ.

Third, God tells us about Himself through the creation of the world. The first event in measurable time is summarized in the statement, "In the beginning God created the heavens and the earth" (Gen. 1:1).

In the act of creation, God has left His fingerprints everywhere. Just as a good detective collects evidence at the scene of a crime, so you can use God's created world as a starting point in your meditation about God. Meditation is not just a passing glance across a field or looking at a well-groomed garden, or scanning the night sky. Rather, meditation is searching through the natural world to see God. Your meditation's success is not measured by the beauty of nature—although it is beautiful and you should enjoy it—but the validity of meditation is always measured by the object of your meditation, who is God Himself.

If God's primary means of revealing Himself is in His creation, it is reasonable to assume two things. First, we can begin meditation by contemplating nature, but the second object of revelation is God. Certainly that appears to have been the case with David. Although his psalms suggest he used many experiences to meditate on God, his early psalms suggest he began focusing on the fingerprint of God in creation. For that reason, thinking about God because of his power in creating the universe is called "the David Model." A closer look at some of David's early psalms reveal how meditation or nature helps us grow in our understanding of God.

How David Practiced Meditation

Among those psalms usually attributed to the early years of David is Psalm 8. As a shepherd keeping watch over his father's flocks in the fields, David had a lot of time to consider the natural world around him. In this psalm, David makes specific mention of the moon, the stars, both domesticated and wild animals, birds and fish, describing each of them as the work of God's hands and fingers. Some commentators even see a reference to ocean currents in David's reference "the paths of the seas" (v. 8).

David's use of astronomy to meditate and learn about God is consistent with God's purpose in creating the moon and stars. When God made the sun, moon and stars on the fourth day, He said, "Let there be lights in the firmament of the heavens to divide the day from the night; and let them be for signs and seasons, and for days and years" (Gen. 1:14). The word "signs" suggests we look at a billboard or directional sign to learn something. The stars are God's "signs" to teach us something about Him, and perhaps gain direction for our lives. The complex mathematical formula involved in space flight today reveals something of the immense knowledge God used when He placed celestial bodies in their places.

Wildlife is also identified in Scripture as a specific means by which God has chosen to reveal Himself.

"But now ask the beasts, and they will teach you; and the birds of the air, and they will tell you; or speak to the earth, and it will teach you; and the fish of the sea will explain to you. Who among all these does not know that the hand of the Lord has done this, in whose hand is the life of every living thing, and the breath of all mankind?" (Job 12:7-10).

In the New Testament, Jesus often pointed to God's care of birds as evidence of God's greater concern for people (see Matt. 6:26; Luke 12:24).

David's meditation on God's created world gave him greater insight into the character of God Himself. As a result of thinking about the power of God in creation, David said, "O Lord, our Lord, how excellent is Your name in all the earth!" (Psalm 8:9). God's own commentary on His finished creation was that it was "very good" (Gen. 1:31). Although that "very good" creation has since been marred by sin, those who discover the fingerprints of God as they meditate on the natural world around them can't help but conclude, "God does all things well."

Psalm 19 is another of David's early psalms that reveal his interest in the created world as the starting point in his meditation. "The heavens declare the glory of God; and the firmament shows His handiwork" (v. 1). Although the most natural interpretation of this verse suggests David's meditation began with his thinking about the night sky, the verses following suggest that such things as clouds, birds and perhaps even insects visible in "the firmament" during the day may have given him cause to think further about God.

Psalm 19 is unique in that it shows the relationship between God's two kinds of revelation. First we see God in the natural world, and second we see God in His written Word. As people begin meditating about God in the context of natural revelation, it motivates them to learn more about God through His special revelation. In this psalm, David's thoughts about the natural world around him (see vv. 1-6) leads him to consider how God has revealed Himself in greater detail in the Scriptures (see vv. 7-11).

> **The Revelation of God in Psalm 19**
> God revealed in nature, vv. 1-6
> God revealed in Scripture, vv. 7-11

David's thoughts about God as revealed in nature caused him to recognize the great gulf between God and man. "What is man that You are mindful of him, and the son of man that You visit him?" (Ps. 8:4). His meditation apparently helped him recognize God's desire to bridge that gulf.

The best known of David's psalms are also a result of his early years of meditating on God. As a young shepherd boy he meditated on the natural world. Bible teachers are divided about just when Psalm 23 was written, but all agree it was David's experience as a shepherd watching over his father's flocks that prompted these insights into our relationship with God. He saw in the sheep many needs similar to those in his own life. Just as his sheep needed David's help, so it became clear that he, too, needed a Shepherd to care for him. As he summarized these thoughts about *Jehovah Rohi*—the Lord my Shepherd—David produced what is probably the best-known and most often memorized chapter in all of Scripture.

If David's thoughts of God as revealed in creation helped him recognize the greatness of God, his further thoughts about God as the Shepherd of his people helped him gain insights into the compassion and benevolence of God. Love is the starting point in faith. First, God loves us, then we must respond in faith.

> But without faith it is impossible to please Him, for he who comes to God must believe that He is, and that He is a rewarder of those who diligently seek Him (Heb. 11:6).

David's meditation on God as seen in the created world also gave him insights into the incredible power of God. He describes this aspect of God's being as "the voice of the Lord" in Psalm 29. In this psalm, David describes God's power in the context of tides, thunder, wind storms, birthing, fires, earthquakes and the flood. This incredible power of God calls even those who are recognized as mighty among their peers to humble themselves and "Give unto the Lord the glory due to His name; worship the Lord in the beauty of holiness" (v. 2). It is also the basis of God's promise to protect His people. "The Lord will give strength to His people; the Lord will bless His people with peace" (v. 11).

From time to time, circumstances arise in our lives that make us question the compassionate character of God. Things go bad and we suffer reverses in life, then we agonize inwardly. In moments of discouragement, we find ourselves asking: Does God really care about me? When we ask that question, we have identified a tension that can become our first step in using the David Model in meditation to achieve a spiritual breakthrough.

Although we can learn many things about the awesome power and design of God in nature by meditating on His fingerprints in creation, one thing that becomes readily apparent is His concern for the people He has created. Walk through the woods in spring and you will see abundant evidences of God's concern for those who have eyes to see. In His Sermon on the Mount, Jesus pointed to wild flowers growing in the fields, then said:

> "So why do you worry about clothing? Consider the lilies of the field, how they grow: they neither toil nor spin; and yet I say to you that even Solomon in all his glory was not arrayed like one of these" (Matt. 6:28,29).

What is true of lilies is also true of the other mosses, grasses, herbs, flowers, bushes and trees we encounter in our walk, but God's ultimate concern is with people, specifically you.

Following the logic implied in Jesus' comments, think through the following. If God goes to such effort to create beauty in these flowers, beauty that dies each fall, God is much more concerned about the welfare of people, specifically you. God has made you to live much longer than flowers and grasses. It is His intent that you live with Him throughout eternity. For some people, following the David Model in meditation and knowing God loves them more than anything in nature should help them break free of any depression.

Using the David Model in Meditation

People have followed the David Model in meditation throughout history. Prior to David's meditation example, others also meditated on God while observing nature. God told Abraham to walk in the fields and count the stars in heaven and count the grains of sand on the beach. His son Isaac also went into the fields to meditate about his concerns. "And Isaac went out to meditate in the field in the evening; and he lifted his eyes and looked, and there, the camels were coming" (Gen. 24:63). Isaac is the first person to be described in the Bible as meditating. Both before and after David meditated, nature has drawn people closer to God and motivated them to meditate on God.

Perhaps the best known example among the Early Church leaders who meditated about God in nature is St. Francis of Assisi. He often went into the fields and forests to commune with God and meditate on His providential care. One of Assisi's better known hymns, "All Creatures of Our God and King," is still sung in many churches today. In that hymn, St. Francis demonstrates he had thought long and hard about the natural world.

The Protestant Reformation inaugurated the great age of science and discovery. Most of the early scientists were Christians who believed God had created the world in which we lived. Men such as Isaac Newton, Galileo Galilei and Robert Boyle viewed science as a means of gaining further insight into the nature of God and the wonders of the world He had made.

Sir Francis Bacon once described his purpose in life by writing the following words:

> I am but a trumpeter, not a combatant. Nor is mine a trumpet which summons and excites men to cut each other to pieces...but rather to make peace between themselves, and

turning with united forces against the Nature of Things, to storm and occupy her castles and strongholds, and extend the bounds of human empire, as far as God Almighty in his goodness may permit.

George Washington Carver is said to have begun his study of the peanut by praying, asking God to show him all the wonderful things He had hidden in the peanut.

A survey of a typical church hymnal will reveal many great hymns of the faith born from a time of meditation. Thomas Chisholm, an insurance salesman in Warsaw, Indiana, drove to the shore of Winona Lake to have his devotions before going to work in the 1930s. As he saw the sun rise over the beautiful lake, he wrote the words to "Great Is Thy Faithfulness."

Wrong Uses of the David Model

Some abuses can be associated with the David Model in meditation. Some have begun meditating on nature, but have failed to look beyond creation to the Creator. Some even see God as everything (pantheism) rather than seeing God as the Creator of everything. Much of the Eastern meditation found in Hinduism and New Age thinking makes "God" no more than the force or the spirit found in nature. The focus of meditation, then, becomes the process of meditation. They want to become one with God. Christian meditation always distinguishes the worshiper from the One who is worshiped. The Christian focus of meditation is on God, not the one who is doing the meditating. The difference between Christian and non-Christian expressions of meditation is discussed further in appendix A.

The second abuse that hinders the David Model in meditation is anti-supernaturalism. Some simply deny the existence of God and the supernatural. Some say there is no God, because they find no evidence of Him. They are guilty of circular reasoning, not unlike the blind man who denies the existence of the sun because he has never seen it. They deny other evidences of the sun such as warmth, the testimony of others or the result of the energy of the sun on growing plants.

The Process of Doing Theology

Martin Luther once described meditation as one of the three steps in the process of doing theology.

First, we must study the Scriptures to know what is there. The more we study and the more widely we study the better will be our theology (i.e., belief about God). The more we know about God, the better we can believe in Him.

Luther's second step was meditation—we must "fit" all our facts about God together. We must think long and think often, fitting together all we know about God. In this second step of meditation, we must give ourselves time to see, to understand and to accept.

The third step is writing down what we have learned; Luther called the results of his writing "theology" or "doctrine." Later, you will be asked to write down what you think is a spiritual discipline. It will be called "journaling." This is nothing more than keeping a diary of your meditations.

Ten Steps to Apply the David Model

1. Observe nature. The David Model of meditation begins by carefully observing the work of God in the world around us. As noted, this is the essence of the natural sciences. In previous generations, many of the pioneer scientists in the various fields were really pastors and missionaries who did science in their spare time. Virtually any branch of the natural sciences can be a starting point in our meditation about God.

I worship God by reading the *National Geographic* magazine, learning about the 50 billion galaxies, each surrounded by approximately 200 million stars. A vastly bigger God than anyone imagines created a vastly bigger universe than anyone imagines. I read NASA's report about the awesome size of burning suns, compared to our small earth, and I worship God. A total of one million, three hundred thousand earths could fit into our sun. A total of 64 million of our suns could fit into the star Antares in the constellation Scorpius and 110 million Antareses could fit into one of the stars in the Hercules constellation, and several million of these Hercules stars could fit into Epsilon, the largest star we have discovered thus far. Epsilon is so large that the human mind can hardly comprehend it. A gigantic God created trillions of gigantic stars because God is bigger than gigantic. He is INFINITE—without limits.

2. Read the observations of others. One of the best tools to help you begin following the David Model in meditation involves reading the fruit of meditation by others. The writings of others help us worship God.

Michelangelo was exiled high in the mountains of Italy. His government in Florence was searching to arrest him. The Pope had banished him. Without family, friends or home, Michelangelo meditated long on the care of God. Sitting in the raw wind, he observed an approaching storm front. He saw the power of wind . . . lightning . . . and he felt the fury of the storm. In the hurricane's anger Michelangelo saw the judgment of God, but he saw the hand of God reaching from heaven to man. In return, he saw man's hand reaching out for God. What he saw in his mind that day became the picture he painted on the Sistine Chapel ceiling—perhaps the most famous painting reflecting Christianity. It came from his meditation on God's power in creation.

3. Sing the hymns of the Christian faith celebrating "the fingerprint of God on His creation." I keep a hymnbook on my desk at home, and during my devotions I sing about God and I sing to God. The statements in these hymns help guide our thoughts as we meditate the work of God in nature all around us. The following list of hymns is derived from some popular church hymnals in the hopes that several may be included in your meditation.

Hymns Celebrating the David Model

All Creatures of Our God and King (St. Francis of Assisi)

All Things Bright and Beautiful (Cecil F. Alexander)

Fairest Lord Jesus (Seventeenth Century German Hymn)

For the Beauty of the Earth (Folliott S. Pierpoint)

God Moves in a Mysterious Way (William Cowper)

God of Everlasting Glory (John W. Peterson)

Great Is Thy Faithfulness (Thomas O. Chisholm)

How Great Thou Art! (Carl Boberg/Stuart K. Hine)

I Believe in Miracles (Carlton C. Buck)

I Sing the Mighty Power of God (Isaac Watts)

It Took a Miracle (John W. Peterson)

Joy to the World! (Isaac Watts)

Joyful, Joyful, We Adore Thee (Henry van Dyke)

Morning Has Broken (Eleanor Farjeon)

O Worship the King (Sir Robert Grant)

Praise to the Lord, the Almighty (Joachim Neander)

The Great Creator (David George Ball)

The Heavens Declare Thy Glory (Isaac Watts)

The Spacious Firmament (Joseph Addison)

This Is My Father's World (Maltbie D. Babcock)

4. Sing the modern praise choruses. The David Model in meditation is a common theme in many of the newer praise and worship choruses of the Church. Because of the Church's positive response to this music, new songs are being released daily. The following list of popular praise and worship choruses identifies many that celebrate what God has done in creation. As you consider this list, other choruses may come to mind that may be more familiar to you. Try singing one or two of these choruses as you prepare to incorporate the David Model into your personal meditation time.

Choruses Celebrating the David Model

Ah Lord God (Kay Chance)

Come Let Us Worship and Bow Down (Dave Doherty)

God Owns the Cattle on a Thousand Hills
(John W. Peterson)
He's Everything to Me (Ralph Carmichael)
He's Got the Whole World in His Hands (Negro Spiritual)
Holy, Holy, Holy Is the Lord of Hosts (Nolene Prince)
How Excellent Is Thy Name (Paul Smith/Melodie Tunney)
How Majestic Is Your Name (Michael W. Smith)
In Him We Live (Randy Speir)
Mighty Is Our God
(Eugen Greo/Cerrit Gustafson/Don Moen)
More Precious Than Silver (Lynn DeShazo)
Psalm 136 (Brenda Barker)
The Trees of the Field (Steffi Geiser Rubin)
Thou Art Worthy (Pauline M. Mills)
We Bow Down (Twila Paris)

5. Ask questions. The more we observe about the world around us, the greater our insights into the character and nature of God. Kipling's six serving men become helpful tools in observing all there is to see. These "men" include the questions, (1) Who? (2) What? (3) Where? (4) When? (5) Why? and (6) How? Asking these questions will guide us as we think about God as revealed in nature.

6. Write down observations about God. Often we begin by writing statements about God's nature and character (i.e., God is faithful, mighty, wonderful, etc.). As we continue the process, these initial statements can be expanded to include areas in which God is faithful, times when God has been faithful to us and how that faithfulness may influence our lives.

7. Apply thoughts to practical expressions. Although some thoughts about God may not be measurable in our limited context, others must be applied. How would you verify God's faithfulness, might, wonder, etc. in your life? Adapting that question to the specific focus of your meditation will help you discover specific ways you can confirm the validity of your initial conclusions about God. Sometimes that involves taking inventory of evidence you have already collected in your life.

8. Move from meditation to prayer supplication. After you have formulated some thoughts about God, begin praying that God would begin applying these qualities to your life. Call on God to accomplish a specific work in your life, or to take away character defects (sins) that are not honoring to God. Remember, God's refusal to intervene on our behalf may demonstrate His sovereignty over us. Sometimes in the things we ask God to do He may in silence remind us that it is our responsibility to grow in certain character qualities.

9. Write in a journal of your meditation and growth. Many Christians keep a spiritual journal in which they record new insights about God and what God is doing in their lives. This is a good place to record the lessons you learn in your "experiment" with God.

10. Start a prayer list about your attitudes, values and personality. A prayer list or accountability report may also be a place where experimental data is recorded. When you collect data about your walk with God, it is important to analyze it carefully. Even when it appears to confirm your opinions, care should be taken to ensure that what you see is a correct interpretation of what is there. Bad opinions can confirm your wrong ideas and can lead you away from truth. Therefore, state what the Bible states.

The goal of meditation involves arriving at true ideas about God. Most often, our meditation will take the form of a testimony. As a Christian, you are called to be a witness (see Acts 1:8). A witness shares what he or she has seen or heard. The insights about God you have gained through using the David Model in meditation should become part of your witness to others.

Suggested Scripture Passages for Meditating on God's Majesty

Job 37:1-24	Psalm 39:1-13
Psalm 8:1-8	Psalm 90:1-17
Psalm 19:1-14	Isaiah 40:1-31
Psalm 29:1-11	Isaiah 44:1—45:25

Prayer	Praise
1. That I may see God's power in His creation.	1. Praise God for His plan and purpose for the earth, the heavens, and how this universe was created for humanity's use and to glorify God.
2. That I may accept God's record in Scripture of creation by faith (not humanity's explanation of evolution).	2. Praise God for His daily physical provision for people on the earth.
3. That I may grow in my understanding of God's power and purpose in creation.	3. Praise God for His laws that cause the universe to function perfectly.
4. That I may be prepared by my meditation to worship God more effectively.	4. Praise God that I can see His power and glory in the physical universe.
5. That I may praise and glorify God.	5. Praise God that He has taken away blindness so I can see Him in His universe.
6. That I may grow to spiritual maturity by meditation and worship.	6. Praise God that I can grow in understanding and worship Him.
7.	7.
8.	8.
9.	9.
10.	10.

Journaling

You will add discipline and direction to your meditation when you begin to write down your thoughts about God. Writing down your thoughts will help crystallize your thinking and focus your meditation. First, write down the meaningful things you think about God's creation and how those things focus your thoughts on God. Next, write your response to God in worship as a result of your meditation.

Now go back through your journal entry and classify your entries. You have written thoughts as they come to you. (1) Classify them into two columns: what you learned about creation and then what you learned about God. (2) Next, classify them in order of importance to you. (3) Finally, classify them by the order they are relevant in the Christian life (i.e., some thoughts are more meaningful to new believers, other thoughts become more relevant to those who have been believers longer).

Bible Study to Reflect on God's Creation

1. To properly meditate on God's creation, a person must do three things to prepare to get the most out of God's Word. What are these three steps?

> "Blessed is the man who walks not in the counsel of the ungodly, nor stands in the path of sinners, nor sits in the seat of the scornful; but his delight is in the law of the Lord, and in His law he meditates day and night."—Psalm 1:1,2

_____
_____
_____
_____

2. After separating yourself from three areas of evil influence, what two attitudes will help you get the most from meditation?

> "But his delight is in the law of the Lord, and in His law he meditates day and night."—Psalm 1:2

_____
_____
_____
_____

3. What are the results in the life of one who meditates on God? Focus your answer on explaining the meaning of *planted, wither, prosper.*

> "He shall be like a tree planted by the rivers of water, that brings forth its fruit in its season, whose leaf also shall not wither; and whatever he does shall prosper."—Psalm 1:3

_____
_____
_____
_____

4. How would you compare the creation of God's universe to the creation of people?

> "What is man that You are mindful of him, and the son of man that You visit him?"—Psalm 8:4

_____
_____
_____
_____

5. What can we know about God from His creative acts that produced the universe?

> "The heavens declare the glory of God; and the firmament shows His handiwork. Day unto day utters speech, and night unto night reveals knowledge."—Psalm 19:1,2

_____
_____
_____
_____

6. How often can we observe the universe so that we worship and glorify God?

> "Day unto day utters speech, and night unto night reveals knowledge."—Psalm 19:2

_____
_____
_____
_____

7. The phrases "their voice" and "their line" and "their words" are a reference to the message the universe gives us about God. Where is the message of God heard that is seen in creation?

> "There is no speech nor language where their voice is not heard. Their line has gone out through all the earth, and their words to the end of the world."—Psalm 19:3,4

_____

_____

_____

_____

8. The sun is pictured as sleeping in a tent, then emerging to run a race. What can we know about God from the message of the sun?

> "In them [the universe] hath he set a tabernacle for the sun, which is as a bridegroom coming out of his chamber, and rejoiceth as a strong man to run a race. His going forth is from the end of the heaven, and his circuit unto the ends of it: and there is nothing hid from the heat thereof."
> —Psalm 19:4-6 *(KJV)*

_____

_____

_____

_____

9. What does God know about our thought life?

> "O Lord, You have searched me and known me. You know my sitting down and my rising up; You understand my thought afar off."—Psalm 139:1,2

_____

_____

_____

_____

10. What should be our response to our thoughts about God?

> "Such knowledge is too wonderful for me; it is high, I cannot attain it."—Psalm 139:6
> "I will praise You, for I am fearfully and wonderfully made; marvelous are Your works, and that my soul knows very well."—Psalm 139:14

_____
_____
_____
_____

11. What should we do with the thoughts about God and His creative power?

"How precious also are Your thoughts to me, O God! How great is the sum of them! If I should count them, they would be more in number than the sand; when I awake, I am still with You."—Psalm 139:17,18

_____
_____
_____
_____

12. What is the prayer we should pray after we have understood and meditated on God's creative acts?

"Search me, O God, and know my heart; try me, and know my anxieties; and see if there is any wicked way in me, and lead me in the way everlasting."—Psalm 139:23,24

_____
_____
_____
_____

Verses to Memorize and Meditate

"Blessed is the man who walks not in the counsel of the ungodly, nor stands in the path of sinners, nor sits in the seat of the scornful; but his delight is in the law of the Lord, and in His law he meditates day and night."—Psalm 1:2,3

"O Lord, our Lord, how excellent is Your name in all the earth, who have set Your glory above the heavens! When I consider Your heavens, the work of Your fingers, the moon and the stars, which You have ordained, what is man that You are mindful of him, and the son of man that You visit him?"—Psalm 8:1,3,4

"For You have made him a little lower than the angels, and You have crowned him with glory and honor. You have made him to have dominion over the works of Your hands; You have put all things under his feet."—Psalm 8:5,6

"The heavens declare the glory of God; and the firmament shows His handiwork. Day unto day utters speech, and night unto night reveals knowledge."—Psalm 19:1,2

"Let the words of my mouth and the meditation of my heart be acceptable in Your sight, O Lord, my strength and my Redeemer." —Psalm 19:14

"Where can I go from Your Spirit? Or where can I flee from Your presence? If I ascend into heaven, You are there; if I make my bed in hell, behold, You are there. If I take the wings of the morning, and dwell in the uttermost parts of the sea, even there Your hand shall lead me, and Your right hand shall hold me."—Psalm 139:7-10

"I will praise You, for I am fearfully and wonderfully made; marvelous are Your works, and that my soul knows very well."
—Psalm 139:14

"How precious also are Your thoughts to me, O God! How great is the sum of them! If I should count them, they would be more in number than the sand; when I awake, I am still with You."
—Psalm 139:17,18

Photocopy and cut these verses into small cards to carry with you for memorization and meditation.

~ 3 ~

THE MARY MODEL:
Pondering the Person of Jesus

"BUT MARY KEPT ALL THESE THINGS AND
PONDERED THEM IN HER HEART." —*Luke 2:19*
"HIS MOTHER KEPT ALL THESE SAYINGS
IN HER HEART." —*Luke 2:51 (KJV)*

Every child is special, because each one leaves a unique memory with its mother. Jesus was no different, as He also left a unique unforgettable memory on Mary, His mother. The birth of Jesus, however, was not just something special; it was supernatural . . . one of a kind . . . a miracle . . . unforgettable.

There has never been another birth like Jesus' birth, so it is only natural His mother wouldn't forget Him, nor would she forget the details of that birth. She would spend the rest of her life pondering them.

When Mary was a young teenage girl, the angel Gabriel visited her as she was meditating on God's plan for her life. She didn't just begin thinking about God after the birth of Jesus; she meditated on Him all her life. One of the reasons Mary was chosen to be the mother of Jesus is that she was deeply reflective of spiritual things before she was chosen.

> What we do after God calls us
> is reflective of what we were doing
> when God called us.

Mary was engaged to Joseph when the angel appeared to her. She was probably praying about her coming marriage. The angel announced in his introduction to her that she was chosen because of her extraordinary qualities. "Greetings . . . you have been chosen by God because you are the most outstanding woman on earth. God will bless you and be with you" (Luke 1:28, author's translation).

Mary didn't understand the greetings, nor did she have any idea what lay in store for her. The angel told her,

"Do not be afraid, Mary, for you have found favor with God" (Luke 1:30).

The angel promised her that she would have a son. "You will conceive in your womb and bring forth a Son, and shall call His name Jesus" (Luke 1:31).

This was not yet a startling announcement. Mary probably expected to have children. As well, the name Jesus (Greek) was not an unusual name; it was the same name as Joshua (Hebrew). Many Jewish mothers in Jesus' day named their sons Joshua, which meant "Jehovah saves."

The angel promised Mary that her son would be called "The Son of the Highest" and that He would be a king like David, and would rule God's people. His kingdom would be without end. The angel's words were still not unusual; because both Mary and Joseph were born into the right families, they had David's blood running in their veins.

When Mary told the angel she was not yet married and had not known a man, an unusual declaration was made. Mary was told, "'The Holy Spirit will come upon you, and the power of the Highest will overshadow you; therefore, also, that Holy One who is to be born will be called the Son of God'" (Luke 1:35).

Only Mary heard the angel's prophecy, and only Mary knew her Son was the Son of God. She could never forget His birth. Although

Mary had at least six other children later in life (see Matt. 13:55,56), she would never forget this one. She would ponder it for the rest of her life.

> ### The Mary Model
> Meditating on Jesus, who He is,
> how He came into this world,
> and what influences He has on our lives.

An angel appeared to Joseph after he learned Mary was pregnant. He planned to be gentlemanly and dismiss Mary quietly, thinking the baby was conceived out of wedlock. The angel, Gabriel, appeared to him, telling Joseph the same thing he told Mary. The angel told Joseph to name the child Jesus, "For He will save His people from their sins" (Matt. 1:21). Joseph was also told the boy would be called "Immanuel, which is translated, God with us" (v. 23)

The place of Jesus' birth was special. God's providence upset the entire civilized world to arrange for Jesus to be born in Bethlehem, the city of King David's birth. The Roman Caesar decreed that all people had to return to the city of their births to be registered for taxation purposes. Caesar Augustus wanted no one overlooked.

Mary and Joseph had to travel from Nazareth approximately 100 miles south to Bethlehem. In the providence of God, Mary delivered her firstborn son in a stable because the inns were full. She wrapped baby Jesus in swaddling clothes and laid Him in the manger they found in the stable. Then Mary meditated on the nature of her Son who was predicted to be a king.

That night, a multitude of angels visited some shepherds in a nearby field. The angel of the Lord told the shepherds that their Savior and Deliverer was born in a stable in Bethlehem. The shepherds came immediately to worship the baby Jesus. Mary pondered the meaning of their visit, trying to understand the supernatural events surrounding the birth of her Son.

As Mary and Joseph took baby Jesus into the Temple to be dedicated, God's providence once again intervened. Elderly Simeon was told by God he would not die until he saw God's Messiah. The old saint met Mary and Joseph in the Temple, and blessed the child. Because Jesus was special, not just any priest could bless baby Jesus, so God chose Simeon to dedicate baby Jesus. Simeon predicted Jesus would bring light to the Gentiles: "Joseph and His mother [Mary] marveled at those things which were spoken of Him" (Luke 2:33).

As events progressed, wise men from the East followed a star to Bethlehem. A supernatural star guided them to the exact house where they found the baby Jesus. It was not just any star; it was called "His star." The wise men said, "We have seen His star in the East and have come to worship Him" (Matt. 2:2). Mary couldn't forget those influential men as they honored her Son's birth, the same as they would honor a king's birth. They brought expensive gifts, and the income from these gifts enabled Mary, Joseph and the baby Jesus to escape to Egypt, while Herod slaughtered all the babies in Bethlehem. Mary pondered God's providential care of her Son.

When Jesus reached the age of 12, Mary, Joseph and Jesus journeyed to Jerusalem for the annual feast of Passover. Jesus was admitted to adulthood there, and probably went through the rituals of bar mitzvah (i.e., He became a son of the law). As Joseph and Mary were returning home, they realized they had lost Jesus. After searching for Him three days, they found Him in the Temple, where Jesus was teaching the doctors and scholars. "They found Him in the temple, sitting in the midst of the teachers, both listening to them and asking them questions" (Luke 2:46). Jesus was a brilliant child prodigy, but Mary knew He was more than just an intellectual giant. "His mother kept all these sayings in her heart" (Luke 2:51, *KJV*).

Just as today a person can devote an entire life to studying Jesus and never fully understand Him because Jesus is the unfathomable God, so Mary never fully understood her Son. She pondered on Jesus' sayings and the experiences of His birth, trying to know more about her Son.

Who Ponders?

The term "ponder" is an old word seldom used today. The old dictionaries defined it to mean, "To weigh in the mind, to put one thing against another, to review mentally, i.e., to think about, to examine carefully."

To Ponder

1. To remember the past
2. To separate things for examination
3. To compare one thing with another

When you meditate on Jesus, you are following the Mary Model. You focus on Jesus to know more about Him and to understand Him. To truly meditate on Jesus and learn about Him, you will need the following qualities found in Mary.

1. Mary was yielded. We cannot just form our own thoughts and ideas about Jesus. Who Jesus is today corresponds to how Jesus came into the world, and how He grew up as a boy. We cannot make Jesus into something we "want" Him to be, nor can we redesign our Savior into someone we "think" He should be. We must study the Scriptures to know and understand this Jesus. We must yield our preconceptions, and meditate on what we read about Him in Scripture.

When the angel told Mary she would be the mother of Jesus, she had to surrender her ideas for a marriage and family. She had to suffer the suspicion and gossip of others who thought she had conceived out of wedlock. Her yieldedness is described in her prayers, "'Let it be to me according to your word'" (Luke 1:38).

2. Mary was humble. To follow the Mary Model of meditation, we must not only surrender our preconceptions, but we must also surrender our egos, our self-interests and our pride. Mary wanted God's will in her life. She prayed, "For he [God] hath regarded the low estate of his handmaiden" (Luke 1:48, *KJV*). Our true prayer is found in the words of John the Baptist, "He must increase, but I must decrease" (John 3:30).

3. Mary was forgiven. Many people have wrong thoughts about Jesus. They read the Bible, but miss the point. When a man writes a love letter, his sweetheart reads the words and understands what he says. She reads with her heart to understand the writer's heart.

Mary pondered with her heart to understand the heart of her Son. Ponder Jesus with your heart to understand His heart.

None of us realize what Mary thought. She gave birth to her Savior—the One who would save her from her sins was the little boy who sat at her dinner table. She prayed, "My spirit hath rejoiced in God my Saviour" (Luke 1:47, *KJV*). Some wrongly think Mary was sinless. If she were, she would have no need to pray to God, her Savior. Those who follow the Mary Model must ponder who Jesus is (i.e., He is our Savior). "He will save His people from their sins" (Matt. 1:21).

4. Mary was grateful. Those who follow the Mary Model must be grateful to God, as Mary prayed, "He [God] that is mighty hath done to me great things,...his mercy is on them that fear him from generation to generation" (Luke 1:49,50, *KJV*).

Those who can look back in gratitude are those who have great character. It takes unselfish people to realize that other people— good individuals—have made them what they are. As you meditate on Jesus, you will become more grateful for all He has done for you.

> Gratitude is the least remembered of all virtues,
> and
> Gratitude is the acid test of character.

5. Mary was committed to excellence. When God chose a woman to be the human instrument to give birth to His Son, not just any woman would do. She had to be from the tribe of Judah, because Jesus was born to rule Israel from the throne of David. God, however, didn't choose just any woman from Judah; God chose the best . . . an excellent woman. The angel Gabriel told Mary she was, "Highly favored...blessed...among women" (Luke 1:28). To be excellent, a person must be dedicated to excellence. Mary didn't become excellent in the moment God chose her (although God's choice elevated her to the most favored of all women). Mary was excellent because she had chosen excellence as a way of life. She sought excellence and became excellent in the process.

> We become excellent
> After we pursue a standard of excellence
> Because of our choice
> To live a life of excellence.

6. Mary was committed to her Son. Almost all mothers are committed to their children. What kind of mother would carry a child nine months in her body and not be committed to that child? What kind of mother going through the agonizing valley of the shadow of death to give birth to her child would not be committed to that child? These events alone should make a mother committed to her child. Mary also knew her Son was supernaturally conceived and miracles surrounded His birth. Because of that, she was committed to Jesus and would do nothing less than ponder His nature and purpose.

Later in life when attending the marriage feast in Cana, and the host had run out of wine, Mary instructed the servants, "Whatsoever he saith unto you, do it" (John 2:5, *KJV*). She was yielded to what Jesus would do. When you follow the Mary Model in meditation, you must commit/yield to do "whatsoever Jesus tells you to do."

7. Mary was satisfied. Those who follow the Mary Model in meditation about Jesus should also follow her example of satisfaction in God. She prayed, "He [God] has filled the hungry with good things" (Luke 1:53).

For some people, one life event defines their entire purpose in life. When they accomplish that purpose, they look back all their lives on that one event. They are satisfied being what they were called to become. Mary's main purpose in life was to be the mother of the Christ child. In response she prayed, "My soul doth magnify the Lord" (Luke 1:46, *KJV*).

During the allied invasion of Germany in World War I, my uncle Paul swam the Rhône River holding a rope over his shoulder. I remember his telling me the story several times when I was a boy. He told me he swam the frigid waters at night. He described the danger from enemy machine guns. I still vividly remember the story, as though that were the main reason Uncle Paul was born. To hear him tell the story, it was the only reason.

When you recall Jesus, you follow the model of Mary who pondered her Son. You focus on Jesus, but go beyond His physical life. You consider that He is God the Son, the second Person of the Triune God, the One by whom and for whom all things have been created, who sustains the very universe by His will (see Col. 1:15-17). You remember Jesus' death and resurrection for you. You ponder your conversion event. You ponder the great and awesome salvation God has given you.

> **You Ponder Jesus**
> 1. You meditate on Jesus' life.
> 2. You remember Jesus' death and resurrection.
> 3. You revisit your conversion experience.
> 4. You ponder your salvation.

How You Can Ponder Jesus

We should be meditating on many Christian themes, but the greatest theme is our Lord Jesus Christ. By following the Mary Model we can ponder this Jesus. Note the source of Mary's meditation. "But Mary kept all these things and pondered them in her heart" (Luke 2:19). She pondered in her heart, which is different from merely remembering them in the mind. Although the mind is part of the "heart," there is much more to the heart. In the Old Testament, the heart (Hebrew: *leb*) as a symbolic word was the seat of intellect, emotion and will, the source of self-direction and self-perception.

> **Ponder in Your Heart**
> The heart is the central seat of your intellect,
> emotion and will. It is the source of
> self-perception and self-direction.

When you ponder Jesus with your heart, your entire person embraces Him. You may have pleasant memories about your first date, but pondering Jesus is more than reviewing your memories. You ponder Jesus Christ because you love Him with all your heart, soul, mind and body. You may think about our first president, George Washington; but pondering Jesus is more than thinking about a historical person—you worship Jesus Christ.

Pondering Jesus with Your Mind

1. You observe. Go back to the Scriptures and read about Jesus to see Him again. The old hymn "Break Thou the Bread of Life" tells us, "Beyond the sacred page, I seek Thee, Lord." Before we can visit our memories, we must first meet Jesus and experience Jesus in the pages of the Bible. Our response must be like those on the Mount of Transfiguration. "When they had lifted up their eyes, they saw no man, save Jesus" (Matt. 17:8, *KJV*).

2. You store away. It is important to learn about Jesus and place information about Jesus in our memories. This involves memorizing facts about Jesus, but most importantly, memorizing Scriptures about Jesus. He commands us, "Take my yoke upon you, and learn of me" (Matt. 11:29, *KJV*).

How to Store Away Jesus Information

1. Read and reread Gospel accounts.
2. Compare Gospel events.
3. Learn facts about Jesus.
4. Memorize verses about Jesus.

---

3. You listen. You must listen to what your heart tells you about Jesus. What you have stored in your heart must be brought back to your thinking. Listening to your heart is a first step in pondering Jesus.

When we listen to hear what we have learned about Jesus,
Then we can ponder what we know about Jesus.

The disciples had many experiences with Jesus while He was alive. After His death and resurrection, they could only think back. "When He had risen from the dead, His disciples remembered that He had said this to them; and they believed" (John 2:22).

There is direction to pondering about Jesus. We don't remember Him simply to jog our memories or to increase our intelligence. We ponder to grow our faith in Jesus. "Then the disciples believed."

4. You recall. What we think directs what we desire and what we actually do. So all the things we have learned about Jesus must be brought out of our memories into our present awareness. This process is called "recalling." Throughout Scriptures, God exhorts His children to this task, as illustrated in God's command to Israel, "Remember that the Lord your God led you" (Deut. 8:2). When you recall Jesus, you remember all He has done for you and let Him direct your life.

The Lord doesn't want "blind obedience." That is obedience where we respond as robot machinery to a computer program. God wants you to know Him, and from your knowledge of God and His Word to respond in faith. On some occasions, however, "blind obedience" is better than "no obedience."

> As you know Jesus,
> So you follow Jesus.

Pondering Jesus with Your Emotions

Too much of Christianity involves no emotions. Many Christians follow Christ based on tradition and empty formalism. You are to worship and love God with all your heart . . . soul . . . and strength. Jesus reminds us, "Those who worship Him must worship in spirit and truth" (John 4:24). To worship in spirit, is to praise God with all our feelings or emotions. To worship in truth, is to praise God with our minds according to biblical principles. The Father wants both.

What emotions must have overwhelmed Mary when she pondered about her Son? Think of her love . . . her joy . . . her satisfaction . . . her gratitude. Mary must also have had some negative feelings when she pondered Jesus. When old Simeon dedicated Jesus to God, he said to Mary, "Yea, a sword shall pierce through thy own soul" (Luke 2:35, *KJV*). When Mary stood at the foot of the cross, seeing the sufferings of her Son, she suffered with her Son. A sword pierced her soul.

1. You open your heart. When you follow the Mary Model to ponder Jesus, you do more than think about Him. You open up your heart to feel all He wants to give you. The two disciples on the road to Emmaus were emotionally stirred. They testified, "Did not our heart burn within us?" (Luke 24:32).

2. You listen to your desires. Your heart has many desires. At times we have old voices of lust calling to us, as well as voices of the new nature calling out for obedience. When we become Christians, we ask Christ to enter our hearts. "That Christ may dwell in your hearts through faith" (Eph. 3:17). Therefore, when you ponder Jesus, you let Christ who dwells in your heart control the thoughts and direction of your heart.

David was "a man after His [God's] own heart" (1 Sam. 13:14). Just as the heart of David was committed to do God's will, so when you ponder Jesus in your heart, you let Him control your heart and life.

3. You open up your feelings. Jesus told His followers, "Thou shalt love the Lord thy God with all thy heart, and with all thy soul, and with all thy mind" (Matt. 22:37, *KJV*). This was the Great Commandment. When you ponder Jesus, you open up yourself to the love of Christ and, in return, you love Him with all your heart, soul and mind.

4. Your feelings reinforce your faith. We should never base our faith on our feelings. If we have deep faith in Christ because we have deep feelings of love, what happens when our feelings change? Feelings are the windows in the house that allow others to look in to see what is there. Windows also allow us to look out at others. What happens, though, when our feelings change? Some days we feel bad . . . we feel discouraged . . . we feel useless . . . we feel out of place. Feelings are wonderful when they make us feel happy, but our feelings are treacherous when they make us feel sad.

Don't base your Christianity on your feelings; base your faith at the foot of Calvary. Therefore, when you ponder Jesus, (1) begin with the facts of God's Word, (2) revisit the experience that gave you faith, (3) finally, realize your feelings will follow the first two.

A man wanted to cross a log bridge but didn't want to fall and get wet. He was not sure about the log. His feelings told him to go ahead, but the fact was the log was slippery. Where should he put his faith? This log bridge illustrates the confidence we seek about our relationship with Christ.

> Your feelings may falter,
> Your faith may lose its footing,
> But the facts of your conversion will never fail.

Pondering Jesus with Your Will

When you follow the Mary Model by meditating on Jesus, you let your enlightened will focus your emotions on Him. Some Christians seem to be all head; they are rational believers. Other Christians seem to be only heart; they are emotional believers. Finally, some focus only on their will; they are mechanical believers.

> **Excesses**
> Rational believers . . . dry up.
> Emotional believers . . . blow up.
> Mechanical believers . . . rust up.

Although we do not put all emphasis on our wills, we cannot escape its contribution to our meditation. A strong will can guide our thinking or guide our emotions. John Wesley gave an invitation for people to come to Christ. He held out his hand to the multitude and pleaded,

"If your heart is as my heart, then take my hand."

Wesley knew becoming a Christian involved more than knowledge or emotional stirring. It involved a choice; people had to exercise their wills to come to Christ.

When you follow the example of Mary to meditate on Jesus,

you must exercise your enlightened will to stir your feelings of love to Him.

1. Your will chooses what information to ponder. When you ponder Jesus, do not let your thoughts wander aimlessly, and do not let your passion run out of control. Direct your mind to thoughts about Jesus. Jeremiah knew the difficulty of controlling his thoughts. "O Lord, I know that the way of man is not in himself: it is not in man that walketh to direct his steps. O Lord, correct me, but with judgment; not in thine anger, lest thou bring me to nothing" (Jer. 10:23,24, *KJV*).

2. Your will gives reasons for your thoughts. When you ponder the direction for your life, look for God's reasons. Don't let your thoughts control you, but rather you control your thoughts. Whether answering outsiders or answering yourself, you should have reasons for what you do. "Sanctify the Lord God in your hearts: and be ready always to give an answer to every man that asketh you a reason of the hope that is in you" (1 Pet. 3:15, *KJV*).

3. Your will gives direction to your thoughts. When you ponder Jesus, let your enlightened will give direction to your meditation. In choosing what to think, always yield yourself to God. "A man's heart deviseth [chooses] his way: but the Lord directeth his steps" (Prov. 16:9, *KJV*).

4. Your will gives meaning and purpose to life. When you become a believer, you commit your life to God. Symbolize a blank sheet of paper representing your whole life and on it write a great big **YES**. Then every day take a sheet of paper representing that day and write a small **yes**. So daily your heart is committed to God's will for your life. In essence you are saying, "In all thy ways acknowledge him, and he shall direct thy paths" (Prov. 3:6, *KJV*). Then you prove the Bible promise, "A good man obtains favor from the Lord" (Prov. 12:2).

Ten Steps to Apply the Mary Model

1. Intentionally remember. When you read, study or listen to a sermon about Jesus, plan to remember everything about Him you can. You will remember more if you intend to remember more.

Jesus told His disciples, "These things have I told you." In essence, Jesus was reminding them to pay attention so that, "Ye may remember that I told you of them" (John 16:4, *KJV*).

2. Become a note taker. Matthew's Gospel probably derived from the notes he wrote down as he followed Jesus, listening to His sermons, observing His miracles and experiencing His compassion. Like Matthew, keep a notebook alongside your Bible to write down the things you learn about your faith; but especially, write down the things you learn about Jesus.

3. Make scrapbooks. Most mothers make scrapbooks of their children's mementos. These may include baby pictures, early school papers and memorable items. Mary probably didn't have a scrapbook, nor did she have a little box where she kept mementos from Jesus' childhood. She "kept all these things in her heart."

You can make a variety of scrapbooks. First, you could keep an actual pictorial and written record of your Christian life since conversion. If you can't make an actual scrapbook, make a mental scrapbook. Just as Mary kept things in her heart, so you can keep memorable things about Jesus in your heart.

4. Sing hymns about Jesus. Use your hymnbook to ponder Jesus. On many occasions, you will find the hymn writer will put your thoughts into words for you. Meditate on some of the following hymns:

Hymns Celebrating the Mary Model

Away in a Manger (Source unknown)

Christ Arose (Robert Lowry)

Crown Him with Many Crowns (Matthew Bridges, stanzas 1, 2, 4; Godfrey Thring, stanza 3)

In the Cross of Christ I Glory (John Bowring)

One Day (J. Wilbur Chapman)

Tell Me the Story of Jesus (Fanny J. Crosby)

The Old Rugged Cross (George Bennard)

Thou Didst Leave Thy Throne (Emily E. S. Elliott)

What a Friend We Have in Jesus (Joseph M. Scriven)

What Child Is This? (William C. Dix)

---

5. Sing praise choruses. The modern praise choruses focus on Jesus, and are usually sung to Jesus in worship and praise to Him. When you ponder Jesus, develop the habit of not only thinking *about* Jesus, but when you meditate, also *talk* to Jesus.

> Come Celebrate Jesus (Claire Cloninger)
> Emmanuel (Bob McGee)
> He Is Lord (Traditional)
> His Name Is Wonderful (Audrey Mieir)
> Jesus Is the Sweetest Name I Know (Lela B. Long)
> Jesus, Name Above All Names (Naida Hearn)
> Turn Your Eyes Upon Jesus (Helen H. Lemmel)

6. Memorize Scripture verses. At the end of this section, suggested Scripture verses will help you better ponder Jesus. Memorize these verses. Fill your mind with verses that will focus your attention on Jesus.

7. View art. The museums are filled with pictures of Jesus. Although each picture is the artist's conception of how he or she thinks Jesus looked, don't let someone else's concept distract your image of Him. However, you can "hitchhike" off someone's artwork to motivate you to ponder Jesus.

Remember, a physical description of Jesus is not mentioned in the Bible. Perhaps that is because God does not want us to relate to Jesus as He was in the flesh, but as He is today. Jesus is inside our hearts by faith (see Gal. 2:20), yet Jesus is also the man in the glory (see Heb. 7:24).

8. Display Christmas nativity scenes. Many churches display nativity scenes, especially now that they are not legally permitted on government or public property. Perhaps setting up a small nativity scene in your home at Christmas will center your mind on the real reason for Christmas. It is the celebration of His birth; but ponder more than the physical aspects of His birth. Remember, "When the fulness of the time was come, God sent forth his Son, made of a woman, made under the law, to redeem them that were under the law" (Gal. 4:4,5, *KJV*).

9. Think through His lifeline. A believer should do more than just read the Gospel accounts of the life of Jesus. Each believer should study carefully the events of His life from His birth right through to His death, resurrection and ascension. When you meditate on Jesus, you should be able to think sequentially through the life of Christ.

10. Practice journaling. When you keep a journal of your thoughts, you bring discipline to your thought life. By writing down what you think about Jesus, you add substance and direction to your meditation.

Suggested Scripture Passages
for Meditating on the Person of Jesus

Matthew 1:18—2:23	John 2:1-12
Matthew 3:13—4:11	John 13:1-35
Matthew 9:35—10:7	John 19:1-42
Matthew 16:13—17:13	Philippians 2:2-12
Luke 2:42-52	Hebrews 5:5-14
Luke 24:1-53	Revelation 1:9-20
John 1:1-18	Revelation 19:11-16

Prayer	Praise
1. That I may know more about Jesus and serve Him better.	1. Praise Christ for saving me and living in me.
2. That I may understand the love that God had for me in sending Jesus to become flesh and die for my sins.	2. Praise Christ for loving me enough to die for my sins.
3. That Christ may dwell in my life (see Eph. 3:17) and I may show Him to others.	3. Praise Christ for His birth, sinless life, death, resurrection and ascension back to heaven.
4. That I may abide in Christ and He may abide in me (see John 15:4).	4. Praise Christ that He lives in me and I can live in Him (see John 14:20).
5. That I may learn to ponder on Jesus as Mary did, and in my meditation become more like Him.	5. Praise Christ for helping me grow in the faith and giving me strength to live for Him.
6. That my meditation on Jesus Christ will help me grow as a Christian, solve my problems and give me more victories, and help me live for Him.	6. Praise Christ for the privilege of meditating on Him and growing daily in the knowledge of Him.
7.	7.
8.	8.
9.	9.

Journaling

When you ponder Jesus Christ, add discipline to your thoughts by writing them down. Many of your meaningful thoughts will be lost if you don't jot them down. Remember,

Short pencils are better
Than long memories.

1. Write down the story of your conversion, including the events that led up to and after receiving Christ.
2. Write down the ways you are grateful for the life and death of Christ (personal response).
3. Write down the things you are grateful for about the life and death of Christ (actual events).
4. Write a love letter to Jesus Christ.
5. Write down your prayer that worships Jesus Christ.
6. Write down Christ's answers to your prayers.

Bible Study to Ponder Jesus

1. One of the earliest doctrinal statements of the Early Church is found in 1 Timothy 3:16. What four things can we know about Jesus from this reference?

> "And without controversy great is the mystery of godliness: God was manifested in the flesh, justified in the Spirit, seen by angels, preached among the Gentiles, believed on in the world, received up in glory."—1 Timothy 3:16

_____
_____
_____
_____

2. What two supernatural things can we know about the birth of Jesus from Isaiah 7:14?

> "'Therefore the Lord Himself will give you a sign: Behold, the virgin shall conceive and bear a Son, and shall call His name Immanuel.'"—Isaiah 7:14

_____
_____
_____
_____

3. What is the difference between the "Child" and the "Son" in Isaiah 9:6?

> "For unto us a Child is born, unto us a Son is given; and the government will be upon His shoulder."—Isaiah 9:6

_____
_____
_____
_____

4. According to Luke 2:52, in what four areas did Jesus grow or increase?

> "And Jesus increased in wisdom and stature, and in favor with God and men."—Luke 2:52

---

5. What do we know about the perfection of Jesus Christ?

> "'Who committed no sin, nor was deceit found in His mouth.'"—1 Peter 2:22
> "And you know that He was manifested to take away our sins, and in Him there is no sin."—1 John 3:5

---

6. What is our example for attitudes and actions?

> "'Take My yoke upon you and learn from Me, for I am gentle and lowly in heart, and you will find rest for your souls.'"—Matthew 11:29
> "For to this you were called, because Christ also suffered for us, leaving us an example, that you should follow His steps."—1 Peter 2:21

---

7. What was the source of Jesus' power on earth and how did He use His power?

"God anointed Jesus of Nazareth with the Holy Spirit and with power, who went about doing good and healing all who were oppressed by the devil, for God was with Him."
—Acts 10:38

_____
_____
_____
_____

8. What was the source of Jesus' effectiveness in His preaching?

"Then Jesus returned in the power of the Spirit to Galilee, and news of Him went out through all the surrounding region. And He taught in their synagogues, being glorified by all."—Luke 4:14,15

_____
_____
_____

9. What was the primary purpose of Jesus coming to earth?

"The next day John saw Jesus coming toward him, and said, 'Behold! The Lamb of God who takes away the sin of the world!'"—John 1:29

_____
_____
_____

10. How do we know that the physical body of Jesus that died was actually raised from the dead?

"'Behold My hands and My feet, that it is I Myself. Handle Me and see, for a spirit does not have flesh and bones as you see I have.'"—Luke 24:39

"So they gave Him a piece of a broiled fish and some honeycomb. And He took it and ate in their presence."
—Luke 24:42,43

_____

_____

_____

_____

11. Where is the physical body of Jesus Christ today?

"But He, because He continues forever, has an unchangeable priesthood. Therefore He is also able to save to the uttermost those who come to God through Him, since He always lives to make intercession for them."
—Hebrews 7:24,25

_____

_____

_____

_____

12. Will we see Jesus again? When? How?

"For if we believe that Jesus died and rose again, even so God will bring with Him those who sleep in Jesus. For the Lord Himself will descend from heaven with a shout, with the voice of an archangel, and with the trumpet of God. And the dead in Christ will rise first."
—1 Thessalonians 4:14,16

_____

_____

_____

_____

Verses to Memorize and Meditate

"For unto us a Child is born, unto us a Son is given; and the government will be upon His shoulder."—Isaiah 9:6
"And the Word became flesh and dwelt among us, and we beheld His glory, the glory as of the only begotten of the Father, full of grace and truth."—John 1:14

"Though He was a Son, yet He learned obedience by the things which He suffered."—Hebrews 5:8

"Seeing then that we have a great High Priest who has passed through the heavens, Jesus the Son of God, let us hold fast our confession."—Hebrews 4:14

"Let us run with endurance the race that is set before us, looking unto Jesus, the author and finisher of our faith, who for the joy that was set before Him endured the cross, despising the shame, and has sat down at the right hand of the throne of God."—Hebrews 12:1,2

"'I am the vine, you are the branches. He who abides in Me, and I in him, bears much fruit; for without Me you can do nothing.'"—John 15:5

"'Where is He who has been born King of the Jews? For we have seen His star in the East and have come to worship Him.'"
—Matthew 2:2

"Come to Me, all you who labor and are heavy laden, and I will give you rest. Take My yoke upon you and learn from Me, for I am gentle and lowly in heart, and you will find rest for your souls. For My yoke is easy and My burden is light."—Matthew 11:28-30

Photocopy and cut these verses into small cards to carry with you for memorization and meditation.

～4～
—

THE SAINT
JOHN MODEL:
*Thinking About
the Cross*

"BEHOLD WHAT MANNER OF LOVE THE
FATHER HAS BESTOWED ON US, THAT WE SHOULD
BE CALLED CHILDREN OF GOD! THEREFORE
THE WORLD DOES NOT KNOW US, BECAUSE
IT DID NOT KNOW HIM."

—*1 John 3:1*

The island of Patmos was deserted. It contained rocks . . . dry thorn bushes . . . sand, and only a bare minimum of water. John was a prisoner, yet no barred cells, no locks and no guards were keeping him hostage. The island was a prison because it was not possible to leave the rocky atoll in the Aegean Sea.

Although John was a prisoner, no shackles bound his soul. He was free to think . . . to dream . . . to meditate. Jesus Christ had given him liberty. John was a young man when he heard Jesus say,

"You shall know the truth, and the truth shall make you free" (John 8:32).

John was a young man when he began following Jesus. To his credit, he was free of the sins and addictions of young men. As well, he had been released from his terrible temper, which had earned him the title, a "Son of Thunder." John had also experienced what Jesus had promised,

"If the Son makes you free, you shall be free indeed" (John 8:36).

Although John had to remain on the island, he was free to meditate. His memory traveled to the dusty Galilean road where he had walked with Jesus. He journeyed to the Sea of Galilee where Jesus had walked on water. John again walked to Jericho to revisit the experiences when Jesus had healed blind Bartimaeus.

Of all the places old man John revisited, his memory most often went back to the events of Calvary. He remembered the Last Supper where he had leaned on Jesus' breast—considered a privilege, but he was the disciple Jesus loved.

After the Last Supper, John remembers following Jesus to the Garden of Gethsemane, and in his youthful immaturity, he fell asleep. John followed Jesus from one trial to the next—from Caiaphas to Annas to the Sanhedrin to Pilate.

Although in reality John walked the dusty paths on Patmos, in his memory he rewalked the city trail of the Via Dolorosa, the path to the cross. When he closed his eyes, John could still hear the mocking crowd, the threatening Roman soldiers and the ring of the hammer on the nails that fastened Jesus to the cross. Then in agony, John heard the echo of the cross dropping into the hole chiseled into the rock.

John was the only disciple at the foot of the cross, for all the others ran away. He remembers looking up into Jesus' suffering face and hearing Him say to him,

"Behold thy mother!" (John 19:27, KJV).

Jesus knew He was dying, so He entrusted His mother into John's care. John was the youngest of the disciples, so he would have a long life to care tenderly for Mary. Then John remembers Jesus looking into the face of Mary. Jesus did not want to point out Mary to the ridicule of the crowd, so Jesus called her "woman." John knew whom he meant, though, and so did Mary. Jesus said to her,

"Woman, behold thy son!" (v. 26, *KJV*).

John meditated on the cross of Jesus and the love of God overwhelmed him: "How great is the love the Father has lavished on us, that we should be called children of God! And that is what we are!" (1 John 3:1, *NIV*).

Because these thoughts about the cross sustained John in his exile, he decided to write about them to his church in Ephesus. John believed that when other believers were despondent, they should remember the cross. He knew that meditation about the cross would give them victory and courage, even if they were in situations as impoverished as his.

Meditating on the Cross of Christ

When people think about Christianity, sooner or later they must think about the cross. The cross has become the universally recognized symbol of Christianity among Christians and non-Christians alike. Even a secular organization such as the Red Cross changes its name to the Red Crescent when working in Muslim nations to avoid offending those who are hostile to the Christian faith.

The cross has become the corporate logo of Christianity. I love to fly into Seoul, Korea, at night. As the plane descends into Seoul, I see hundreds of crosses . . . red neon crosses. Virtually every Christian church has a red neon cross on the side of the steeple. Even the churches that meet in commercial buildings erect a red neon cross on the roof. At night, the city becomes a sea of brightly lit crosses. In North America, crosses appear both inside and outside churches of various denominations. Many churches have even been designed and built in the shape of a cross, such as Westminster Abbey in London. The cross has also become a popular symbol incorporated into the jewelry worn by Christians, as well as those who endorse the Christian faith.

The cross is also a popular symbol in art history. Pictures of the suffering Savior on the cross are a common theme in the large stained-glass windows of cathedrals in paintings and in sculptures. The crucifix, a variation of the cross theme, is a popular icon in both the corporate and private worship of Roman Catholics. It appears on the walls of virtually every room in Catholic hospitals around the world.

Historically, ministers have referred to the cross when praying for healing, casting out demons, cleansing people from evil spirits and asking God for protection against the attacks of the evil one. The essence of the Christian faith is found in the message of the gospel and is expressed by the cross. In its simplest form, that message is summarized in Paul's statement, "We preach Christ crucified" (1 Cor. 1:23). In a more complete sense, the gospel is described: "That Christ died for our sins according to the Scriptures, and that He was buried, and that He rose again the third day according to the Scriptures" (1 Cor. 15:3,4). The message of the cross was so essential to the Christian faith that within 20 years of the death and resurrection of Christ, any change in the message was subject to divine judgment. "But even if we, or an angel from heaven, preach any other gospel to you than what we have preached to you, let him be accursed" (Gal. 1:8).

A quick survey of the four Gospels reveals that the death, burial and resurrection of Christ (His "passion") are the clear focus of each account. More verses are devoted to the last week of Christ's life leading up to His death and resurrection than to the entire 30 years previous. Yet despite the importance of the cross, most of those who followed Jesus did not witness His suffering. Most of the 12 disciples deserted Jesus, although He had quoted the Old Testament warning to His disciples, "I will strike the Shepherd, and the sheep of the flock will be scattered" (Matt. 26:31; see Zech. 13:7).

At Jesus' arrest, that prophecy was fulfilled as His disciples forsook Him. Later, Peter returned to the courtyard of Pilate. John, who had stayed, spoke to the gatekeeper to let Peter go near the fire. There, Peter denied Jesus three times. Before the end of the night, Peter had run away deep in sorrow. By the time the Roman soldiers had nailed Jesus to the cross, only John was present among the disciples to witness the events of the cross.

Watching Jesus die on the cross had a profound effect on the apostle John. Writing his Gospel account some 60 years after the fact, John recalls specific details about the event overlooked by others. His Gospel also tends to emphasize God's love for individual people more than the other Gospels. Obviously, John had meditated much about the cross during his many years of ministry. He described himself in his Gospel as "the disciple whom He [Jesus] loved" (John 19:26).

In John's first Epistle, he urged others to make the cross the starting point in their meditation. "Behold what manner of love the Father has bestowed on us, that we should be called children of God!" (1 John 3:1). Although some Christians may advocate meditating on the cross as an instrument, the Saint John Model exhorts us to meditate on the sacrifice of Christ for us and God's love to individuals.

How Saint John Practiced Meditation

The cross was widely recognized in the Early Church as an undeniable symbol of God's love. Paul summarized this love in his Epistle to the Romans. "But God demonstrates His love toward us, in that while we were His enemies, Christ died for us" (Rom. 5:8, author's translation). John emphasized the same love in the best-known verse in the Bible. "For God loved all people so much that He gave His only begotten Son to die for them, that whoever believes in Christ should not perish, but have everlasting life" (John 3:16, author's translation).

Writing to the Ephesians toward the end of his life, John tells others to meditate on God's love, using the cross as the starting point: "Behold what manner of love the Father has bestowed on us, that we should be called children of God! Therefore the world does not know us, because it did not know Him" (1 John 3:1). This verse suggests eight factors involved in practicing the Saint John Model of meditation.

1. Look back. The Saint John Model involves "beholding," a Greek word meaning calling something to your attention, which may be seen, heard or mentally remembered. John is calling Christians to think intensely about how much God loves them. The primary expression of God's love is seen in the cross where Jesus died for others. "The good shepherd [Jesus] gives His life for the [His] sheep" (John 10:11).

2. Remember the quality of Christ's love. The grammatical form used in the statement "what manner of love" is technically called a qualitative interrogative. Originally, a person was asked this question to find out the origin of his or her country or race. It is used on two other occasions in Scripture, which may help us feel John's emphasis.

After witnessing Jesus calming a violent storm on the Sea of Galilee, His disciples used this expression when they asked, "What manner of man is this, that even the winds and the sea obey him!" (Matt. 8:27, *KJV*). Peter used the same form later in one of his Epistles after describing the final destruction of the world in vivid detail. He then concluded with the question, "What manner of persons ought you to be in holy conduct and godliness?" (2 Pet. 3:11).

The quality of God's love is seen in the Greek word translated "love," which is the word *agape*. This word for love was a self-sacrificing love, such as a mother sacrificing for her child. In the New Testament, *agape* is used exclusively to describe God's love for people, the cross being the ultimate expression of that love, because Christ gave Himself for people. As great as that love was in the mind of the Greek language, God's love is greater, for it was not one human sacrifice for another; it was God sacrificing Himself for people.

3. Identify the source of demonstrated love. John uses the title "Father" to describe the first person of the Trinity. This is a uniquely Christian name for God. It was the title Jesus used most often to describe God and to describe the relationship between the Father and the Son. Unfortunately, not all fathers are what they should be, therefore, many have difficulty thinking positively about God as their heavenly Father. John calls us to meditate on God as our Father, not in terms of what our fathers may or may not have been, but in terms of what God the Father does for us.

The word "Father" is derived from a root describing one who is a nourisher, protector and upholder. This suggests at least three roles of our earthly fathers and our heavenly Father. First, our Father is a nourisher who provides for all we need to live the Christian life. Second, He is our protector. Jesus emphasized our protection by the Father when He taught His disciples to pray, "And lead us not into temptation, but deliver us from the evil one" (Matt. 6:13, *NIV*). Finally, He is our upholder. The Father encourages, supports and helps us in every aspect of our lives.

4. Recognize the results of God's love. For the word "bestowed," John uses a verb in the perfect active indicative to describe the completion of God's act of bestowing love on us. For many of us, we only love conditionally; but the Father's love is demonstrated unconditionally so we will respond to Him. God's love toward us is unconditional and complete. "While we were still sinners, Christ died for us" (Rom. 5:8). God loves us because He chose to love us, not because we deserve to be loved.

5. Receive God's love. As great as unconditional love is, it is even greater when we consider we are unworthy recipients. The thing that fascinated John most was that he was the recipient of God's love. As a young man, John was described as a "Son of Thunder." That meant he had a terrible temper; but Jesus changed him. Later, John is described as "The disciple whom He [Jesus] loved" (John 19:26).

It is unlikely Jesus loved John any more or less than He loved His other disciples. Even John understood that when he wrote, "Having loved His own who were in the world, He loved them to the end" (John 13:1). Rather, this statement tells us more about John's response to Jesus' unconditional love. Sixty years later, he still had not become used to the fact that Christ loved him and died for him. Perhaps if we meditated on John's insight on the cross we would also marvel at this unconditional love.

6. Be born into God's family. God's love results in our being called or named to His family. Just as Jesus was "called a Nazarene" (Matt. 2:23) because He lived in Nazareth, so we are called "children of God" because we are recipients of God's love. John uses the

Greek word *tekna* here, which describes us as God's children. We are loved as children of God.

7. Be confident in God's love. After meditating on the death of Christ, John came to the conclusion that a change had taken place in his own life. Notice the clarifying statement, "Beloved, now we are" (1 John 3:2). Therefore, it is likely that John wanted us to meditate on the cross, and remember we are the children of God . . . and we are. As we contemplate all Christ has accomplished on the cross for us, it becomes increasingly more difficult to realize we are indeed the recipients of all Christ has done. Using the cross as a starting point in our meditation results in a deeper confidence in our relationship with God.

8. Consider the implications of the cross. John continues, "Therefore the world does not know us, because it did not know Him" (1 John 3:1). Once again, when you learn to meditate, it provides a practical insight for life. John was writing to Christians who struggled to understand why their persecution was so intense. Considering the suffering of Christ, their persecution was probably not as intense as His, nor as intense as it could be. Given the way the world had responded to Christ, why should Christians expect any better treatment from a hostile world?

The Role of the Saint John Model in Meditation

The Saint John Model calls us to meditate on the work of Christ on the cross. Because the cross is at the heart of Christianity, when we practice this discipline we gain a greater understanding of our faith. The Epistles identify at least a half dozen accomplishments of the cross as they relate to the Christian life.

The Scriptures describe the death of Christ on the cross as a "substitution." Christ is our substitute for sin and He died in our place. Paul describes this, "Christ...loved me and gave Himself for me" (Gal. 2:20). Exactly what did He do in substitution?

The Old Testament describes it, "When You make His soul an offering for sin" (Isa. 53:10), just as God required the sacrifice of a lamb as a substitute for the sins of the people. Each year on the Day of Atonement, the high priest placed his hands on the heads of two goats, identifying the nation's sin with the animals. Symbolically, the animals bore the sins of Israel. One of the two goats was then offered in a sacrifice for the sins of the nation. The second goat was led out into the wilderness, illustrating how God had separated the sins of the people from Himself. All this was typical of another "Day of Atonement" when Christ would die as our substitute.

On the cross, God placed our sins upon Christ and accepted Him in our place. "For He [God] made Him [Christ] who knew no sin to be sin for us, that we might become the righteousness of God in Him" (2 Cor. 5:21). The substitutionary death of Christ is described in three contexts. First, He is a substitution for Christians (see Rom. 5:8). Second, Christ died for the Church (see Eph. 5:25). Ultimately, Christ died for everyone (see Heb. 2:9).

The second word to describe the cross in Scripture is "redemption." The word "redemption" means "to purchase." When Jesus died for our sins, He paid the price that satisfied the demands of God's holiness. The price of this redemption was the blood of Jesus (see 1 Pet. 1:18,19).

A third term used to describe the death of Christ in Scripture is "propitiation." This word means "satisfaction." The concept of propitiation involves God's satisfying wrath against our sin by Jesus' death (see Rom. 3:25,26). "[Jesus] is the propitiation for our sins: and not for ours only, but also for the sins of the whole world" (1 John 2:2, *KJV*). The term "propitiation" was used in Judaism to describe the mercy seat on the Ark of the Covenant. There the priest sprinkled blood on the Day of Atonement, hence it became symbolic of the judgment seat. This was the place where the justice of God was satisfied.

The death of Christ satisfied the "demands of the law." This is the fourth result of the cross. God's standard was offended when the human race fell into sin. One aspect of the gospel being so closely identified with the cross is that the demands of the law were nailed to the cross, making an end of the law (see Eph. 2:15,16; Col. 2:14,15). The law no longer condemns us. Christ's work on the cross satisfied all the punishment we should have had.

A fifth accomplishment of Christ's work on the cross was that He "reconciled" us to God. In this work, Christ brought God and humans together. The cross brought together two enemies and made them friends. "God was in Christ reconciling the world to Himself, not imputing their trespasses to them, and has committed to us the word of reconciliation" (2 Cor. 5:19). The work of reconciliation was accomplished by destroying the cause of hatred between God and people.

The cross is also described in the sixth action as the basis for "daily cleansing." It is sometimes said, "Christ died for our sin, past, present and future." Actually, all our sin was future in the historic context of the cross. When a believer sins, the cross remains the basis for cleansing. "But if we walk in the light as He is in the light, we have fellowship with one another, and the blood of Jesus Christ His Son cleanses us from all sin" (1 John 1:7). When we stumble out of the light, and thus sin, the solution to restore fellowship is found in 1 John. "If we confess our sins, He is faithful and just to forgive us our sins and to cleanse us from all unrighteousness" (1:9).

How can we respond to all Christ has done for us on the cross? At times, the very thought of what Christ accomplished in His death is overwhelming. Perhaps Paul best expressed our meditation response: "But God forbid that I should boast except in the cross of our Lord Jesus Christ, by whom the world has been crucified to me, and I to the world" (Gal. 6:14).

Because the cross is so central in the Christian faith, it is not surprising that the Saint John Model of meditation has been practiced by devout Christians throughout the centuries.

Wrong Uses of the Saint John Model

Some who meditated on the cross throughout the history of the Church degenerated into a variety of expressions never intended by God. One of the most dramatic of these is known as the "stigmata." Several mystics have claimed that they meditated so deeply on the cross that they began bleeding from the hands, side and/or feet. They claim this came as a result of prolonged meditation on the suffering of Christ on the cross. These mystics so identify with Christ in His suffering that they bear the marks of crucifixion in their own bodies.

Among Catholic mystics, a tradition has arisen stating that at any given time, only 12 people on earth experience the stigmata (i.e., one for each apostle). Actually, this phenomenon is much rarer and many claims cannot be substantiated. What can be said with some degree of certainty about this phenomenon is that God never intended it to be the norm in Christian experience.

Others have fallen into physical expressions of asceticism in their attempt to identify with Christ's sufferings. Through the years, some abuse has occurred in fasting, isolation and self-conflagration. Even today, in some predominantly Catholic nations such as Brazil and the Philippines, some will have themselves tied or nailed to crosses as part of their observation of Easter. Once again, these expressions were never intended as part of the normal Christian life.

A third more common expression growing out of a desire to meditate on the work of Christ on the cross involves the use of religious icons, including the crucifix, in prayer and meditation. God loves symbols—baptism and the Lord's Supper are outward expressions of inner meaning. Historically, many have used the symbol of the cross in their meditation of Christ's work on the cross. The intent appears to have been to remind believers of some aspect of Christ's work and/or suffering on the cross. Unfortunately, icons have become "Christian idols" in the minds of many. The cross in their hands (or on the wall) becomes more important than what Christ accomplished.

In some cultures, apparent conversions to Christianity have amounted to little more than exchanging the gods of a tribal religion for the gods represented by Christian icons. They give up an idol for a cross, but Christ is not in their hearts. Most evangelical believers avoid the use of icons for this reason.

Another common practice resulting from the Saint John Model through the years has been the use of the cross as a symbol. As noted earlier, the cross is a common symbol in religious art and church architecture. Various designs of the cross identified with

individual saints have become national symbols. The British flag—
the Union Jack—is based on the design of three separate crosses.
Others customarily "cross themselves" as an expression in prayer.
Often, this almost appears to be a kind of "good luck" expression,
such as when a batter comes to the plate during a baseball game.
Although some Christians find the symbol of the cross helps them
focus their thoughts, others are concerned because this practice
often borders on idolatry.

Because some have been distracted by outward things, this
should not discourage us from using the Saint John Model in our
personal meditation. In contrast to the previously mentioned
examples, Christians in every age, such as the apostle John, have
marveled at God's incredible demonstration of His love for us in
sending Jesus to die on our behalf.

Ten Steps to Apply the Saint John Model

1. **Sing Christian music.** The following list identifies a variety of
Christian hymns that have been used by a large cross-section of
faith groups. The common factor in each hymn is an emphasis on
the cross. That the emphasis is still prominent in the hearts of
many Christians is evidenced in that these hymns are still widely
sung in churches around the world today.

Hymns Celebrating the Saint John Model
At the Cross (Isaac Watts)
Beneath the Cross of Jesus (Elizabeth C. Clephane)
Blessed Redeemer (Avis Burgeson Christiansen)
Calvary Covers It All (Mrs. Walter G. Taylor)
Hail, Thou Once Despised (John Bakewell)
Hallelujah, What a Savior! (Philip P. Bliss)
I Saw the Cross of Jesus (F. Whitfield)
In the Cross of Christ I Glory (John Bowring)
Jesus Paid It All (Elvina M. Hall)
My Savior's Love (Charles H. Gabriel)
Near the Cross (Fanny J. Crosby)

O Sacred Head, Now Wounded (Bernard of Clairvaux)
The Old Rugged Cross (George Bennard)
There Is a Fountain (William Cowper)
There Is a Green Hill Far Away (Cecil Frances Alexander)
To God Be the Glory (Fanny J. Crosby)
What a Wonderful Savior! (Elisha A. Hoffman)
When I Survey (Isaac Watts)
Why? (John M. Moore)
Why Should He Love Me So? (Robert Harkness)

2. Practice beholding the cross. Set aside quality time to contemplate the suffering of Christ on the cross. Because most people today have never witnessed a crucifixion, it is difficult to visualize what it means. Read about a crucifixion in a Bible dictionary. Then "behold" it in your mind. Read the passages of Scripture that describe the cross death. (See list of Scriptures for meditation.)

3. View Christian art to help focus on the cross. For some, the image of a dying Christ portrayed on a stained-glass window or imprinted on a picture assists them in meditation. History warns us, however, of the danger of becoming too dependent upon works of art in our meditation and falling into the problem of idolatry.

4. Practice the ordinances. Jesus established two ordinances of the church that may focus on the cross as a corporate Christian community. Part of the symbolism in baptism is a reminder that Christ has indeed died for our sins. When the church gathers to observe the Lord's Supper, the focus on the death of Christ is even more specific. When the minister says, "Take, eat, this is my body," meditate on what Christ has done for you. When the minister says of the cup, "Drink ye all of it," meditate on the blood of Christ that was spilled for you. The symbols of the bread and wine are identified in Scriptures as symbols of the body and blood of Jesus.

5. Contemporary music can direct your thinking to the cross. Several traditional hymns of the faith celebrating the cross have already been identified. The work of Christ on the cross is also a common theme in many gospel choruses and praise music. Focus your thoughts as you sing one or more of these hymns and choruses.

> **Choruses Celebrating the Saint John Model**
> Behold the Lamb (Dottie Rambo)
> For God So Loved the World (Frances Townsend)
> I Am Crucified with Christ (John G. Elliott)
> I Know a Fount (O. Cooke)
> I Should Have Been Crucified (Dottie Rambo)
> I'm Forever Grateful (Mark Altrogge)
> Lamb of Glory (Greg Nelson/Phill McHugh)
> Lamb of God (Twila Paris)
> My Tribute (To God Be the Glory) (Andraé Crouch)
> O, How He Loves You and Me (Kurt Kaiser)
> Our God Reigns (Leonard W. Smith, Jr.)
> Take Me In (Dave Browning)
> There Is a Redeemer (Melody Green)
> Worthy Is the Lamb (Don Wyrtzen)
> Worthy the Lamb That Was Slain (Don Moen)

6. Meditate on the completeness of His death. As you think of Christ's finished work on the cross on your behalf, take time to realize it is complete. Christ announced, "It is finished!" (John 19:30). He meant many things were finalized. What exactly did God accomplish in your life through the cross? How many of His benefits have already been realized in your life? How much more do you need to grow? As you think about what God has done for you, remember, Christ will not suffer again, "It is finished!" (See list of Scriptures about meditation.)

7. Meditate on the Trinity. This means we consider the source of God's work on Calvary. The Bible describes all three members of the Trinity as being involved in the atoning work of Christ. First, our salvation was born in the heart of our heavenly Father. Our salvation was accomplished by the work of the Son on our behalf. Our salvation was applied to our lives through the regenerating work of the Holy Spirit. The Holy Spirit drew us to Christ and made us new creatures in Him. Perhaps you can begin your meditation by praising each member of the Trinity for their part in your salvation.

8. Look at the cross through God's eyes. Perhaps the love of God demonstrated on the cross is not fully realized until we look at it through God's eyes. What did we look like to God when He chose to send Jesus to die on our behalf? "While we were still sinners, Christ died for us" (Rom. 5:8). The more we recognize what God saw in the cross, the more overwhelming God's love for us becomes. Like John, we discover a truth from which we may never recover.

9. Apply the cross to a particular sin. Finally, as you continue meditating on the Saint John Model, begin identifying mistakes . . . faults . . . weaknesses . . . and sins in your life that need to be cleansed by the blood of Christ. There is power in the blood. Think of the places where you need strength, courage or victory. Apply the blood to your need. Perhaps you need to take up your cross daily to follow Christ. Perhaps you need to surrender your life to Him. Paul reminds us, "I have been crucified with Christ; it is no longer I who live, but Christ lives in me; and the life which I now live in the flesh I live by faith in the Son of God, who loved me and gave Himself for me" (Gal. 2:20).

10. Write down your thoughts about the cross. A journal can contain several things. You can write your testimony of your conversion, or you can list all the things Christ did for you on the cross. You can write about how Christ looked at the cross, and how the Father looked at the cross. Perhaps you want to write a letter of gratitude to Christ for what He did on Calvary for you. Others may want to make a list of the ways they have changed since they accepted Christ as Savior.

Suggested Passages for Meditating on the Cross

Isaiah 53:1-12	Ephesians 1:7; 2:13-18
John 19:16-37	Colossians 1:14; 2:9-15
Acts 4:10-12	Hebrews 9:11-28
Romans 3:21-26	1 Peter 1:18-23
1 Corinthians 11:23,34	

Prayer	Praise
1. That I may be grateful for the death of Christ for my sins.	1. Praise God that the Father planned my salvation, the Son bought it and the Holy Spirit delivered it to me.
2. That I may understand some of the enormous implications that God became flesh to die for me.	2. Praise God that He loves me unconditionally.
3. That I may apply the blood of Christ to my mistakes and sins, so I can be forgiven.	3. Praise God for the completion of my salvation, that truly, "It is finished!"
4. That I may grow in my Christian life as I meditate on the cross.	4. Praise God that Christ's blood takes away my sin: past, present and future.
5. That I will learn to worship the Trinity for what was done by each one for my salvation.	5. Praise God that I can walk in the light and know my sins are forgiven.
6. That my meditation on the cross of Christ will help me solve problems and cause me to be more like Christ.	6. Praise God I am growing in my understanding of the cross.
7.	7.
8.	8.
9.	9.
10.	10.

Journaling

We clarify our minds when we write down our thoughts. Write some of the following questions in your journal:

1. How were you converted?
2. What does the accomplishment of the cross of Christ mean to you?
3. Write down several of your verses about the cross and/or death of Christ. Describe what these verses mean to you. Why did you choose them?
4. How have you grown in your understanding of the cross because of the Saint John Model of meditation?
5. What changes in your life have resulted from knowing about the cross of Christ and applying its benefits to your life?

Bible Study to Think About the Cross

1. The death of Christ (Messiah) was predicted in the Old Testament. What was promised that the Messiah would do to Satan and what would Satan do to Him?

> "And I will put enmity between you and the woman, and between your seed and her Seed; He shall bruise your head, and you shall bruise His heel."—Genesis 3:15

_____
_____
_____
_____

2. What was predicted of Christ when He first began His ministry?

> "The next day John saw Jesus coming toward him, and said, 'Behold! The Lamb of God who takes away the sin of the world!'"—John 1:29

_____
_____
_____

3. Did the cross catch Jesus by surprise? How did He predict His death?

> "From that time Jesus began to show to His disciples that He must go to Jerusalem, and suffer many things from the elders and chief priests and scribes, and be killed, and be raised the third day."—Matthew 16:21
>
> "I am the good shepherd. The good shepherd gives His life for the sheep. No one takes it from Me, but I lay it down of Myself. I have power to lay it down, and I have power to take it again. This command I have received from My Father."
> —John 10:11,18

_____
_____
_____
_____

4. List those responsible for the death of Christ.

> "The kings of the earth took their stand, and the rulers were
> gathered together against the Lord and against His
> Christ."—Acts 4:26
>
> "Judas, who became a guide to those who arrested Jesus."
> —Acts 1:16

_____
_____
_____
_____

5. For whom did Christ die?

> "I have been crucified with Christ; it is no longer I who live,
> but Christ lives in me; and the life which I now live in the
> flesh I live by faith in the Son of God, who loved me and
> gave Himself for me."—Galatians 2:20;
>
> "Husbands, love your wives, just as Christ also loved the
> church and gave Himself for her."—Ephesians 5:25
>
> "But we see Jesus, who was made a little lower than the
> angels, for the suffering of death crowned with glory and
> honor, that He, by the grace of God, might taste death for
> everyone."—Hebrews 2:9

_____
_____
_____
_____

6. What is the currency used to purchase our salvation?

> "Knowing that you were not redeemed with corruptible
> things, like silver or gold, from your aimless conduct

received by tradition from your fathers, but with the precious blood of Christ, as of a lamb without blemish and without spot."—1 Peter 1:18,19

_____

_____

_____

_____

7. How was the cross of Christ predicted in the Old Testament?

"'If a man has committed a sin deserving of death, and he is put to death, and you hang him on a tree, his body shall not remain overnight on the tree, but you shall surely bury him that day, so that you do not defile the land which the LORD your God is giving you as an inheritance; for he who is hanged is accursed of God.'"—Deuteronomy 21:22,23 "Christ has redeemed us from the curse of the law, having become a curse for us (for it is written, 'Cursed is everyone who hangs on a tree')."—Galatians 3:13

_____

_____

_____

_____

8. What should be our attitude in sharing with others the message of the cross?

"For the message of the cross is foolishness to those who are perishing, but to us who are being saved it is the power of God."—1 Corinthians 1:18

_____

_____

_____

_____

9. What should be our general attitude about the cross?

> "'And I, if I am lifted up from the earth, will draw all peoples to Myself.' This He said, signifying by what death He would die."—John 12:32,33

_____

_____

_____

_____

10. The cross was a symbol of many things (i.e., self-denial, suffering and separation). What should be your daily attitude to the cross given to you?

> "Then He said to them all, 'If anyone desires to come after Me, let him deny himself, and take up his cross daily, and follow Me.'"—Luke 9:23

_____

_____

_____

11. The Christian life is described as co-crucifixion. We are described as having suffered with Christ when He died on the cross. What is the result of co-crucifixion in our daily lives?

> "I have been crucified with Christ; it is no longer I who live, but Christ lives in me; and the life which I now live in the flesh I live by faith in the Son of God, who loved me and gave Himself for me."—Galatians 2:20

_____

_____

_____

_____

12. Because of our co-crucifixion with Christ, what should be our attitude?

> "But God forbid that I should boast except in the cross of our Lord Jesus Christ, by whom the world has been crucified to me, and I to the world."—Galatians 6:14

_____

_____

_____

_____

Verses to Memorize and Meditate

"I have been crucified with Christ; it is no longer I who live, but Christ lives in me; and the life which I now live in the flesh I live by faith in the Son of God, who loved me and gave Himself for me."—Galatians 2:20

"The next day John saw Jesus coming toward him, and said, 'Behold! The Lamb of God who takes away the sin of the world!'"—John 1:29

"For He made Him who knew no sin to be sin for us, that we might become the righteousness of God in Him."—2 Corinthians 5:21

"But God demonstrates His own love toward us, in that while we were still sinners, Christ died for us."—Romans 5:8

"But if we walk in the light as He is in the light, we have fellowship with one another, and the blood of Jesus Christ His Son cleanses us from all sin."—1 John 1:7

"My little children, these things I write to you, so that you may not sin. And if anyone sins, we have an Advocate with the Father, Jesus Christ the righteous."—1 John 2:1

"Knowing that you were not redeemed with corruptible things, like silver or gold, from your aimless conduct received by tradition from your fathers, but with the precious blood of Christ, as of a lamb without blemish and without spot."—1 Peter 1:18,19
"But God forbid that I should boast except in the cross of our Lord Jesus Christ, by whom the world has been crucified to me, and I to the world."—Galatians 6:14

Photocopy and cut these verses into small cards to carry with you for memorization and meditation.

～ 5 ～

THE JOSHUA MODEL:
Focusing on Biblical Principles

"THIS BOOK OF THE LAW SHALL NOT DEPART FROM
YOUR MOUTH, BUT YOU SHALL MEDITATE IN IT
DAY AND NIGHT, THAT YOU MAY OBSERVE TO DO
ACCORDING TO ALL THAT IS WRITTEN IN IT. FOR
THEN YOU WILL MAKE YOUR WAY PROSPEROUS,
AND THEN YOU WILL HAVE GOOD SUCCESS."

—*Joshua 1:8*

"I can't do it," Joshua expressed his doubts to God. In prayer Joshua said, "I can't lead Israel as well as Moses did."

Joshua was in the tent praying on his face before God. He was scared of the future. He had followed Moses out of Egypt. At first, he was just another one of the million Jewish slaves Pharaoh had released. Then Moses asked Joshua to serve on the leadership staff because he was efficient . . . loyal . . . and brave.

Next, Moses appointed Joshua as his personal assistant. Joshua learned leadership from Moses, but the younger man was not sure he could take Moses' place. He remembered when Israel had been stuck on the other side of the Red Sea. Joshua had seen Moses lift the rod and the Red Sea had parted. Joshua worshiped the God of power who pushed back the Red Sea, but he didn't have Moses' faith or Moses' ability. Joshua prayed,

"I'm not as great as Moses."

Joshua remembered Moses going to the top of Mount Sinai to receive the Ten Commandments from God. Joshua had stayed at the bottom of the mountain. Joshua had seen Moses' face shine when he had came down from the mountain because Moses had seen God. Joshua, however, had not seen God.

"I'm not as great as Moses," Joshua criticized himself.

It had been 40 years since Israel had left Egypt to wander in the desert. All the older leadership had died. Only young people were left for Joshua to lead. They still didn't have a homeland and now Israel had to cross the mighty Jordan River.

"I don't have the faith of Moses," Joshua prayed to God. "I'll fail." Then Joshua heard the voice of God,

"Moses my servant is dead!"

Panic seized Joshua. What would he do without his leader.

"You will go over the River Jordan," God told Joshua. Then to make sure general Joshua understood its strategical implication, God added,

"You and all the people will cross Jordan. You will conquer this land. Every place that your foot treads upon, I will give it to you." Then God encouraged Joshua,

"As I was with Moses, so I will be with you."

On his face before God, Joshua was given the leadership of the 12 tribes—a million "chosen people" who had proven in the wilderness that they could be argumentative, stubborn and arrogant. How could Joshua persuade Israel—the Jewish people—to follow him? As a general, he knew his army had to fight as a unit. As a religious leader, he knew Israel had followed Moses because he was a miracle worker, but Joshua had not performed any miracles—yet.

"How can I do it?" Joshua asked God.

The answer God gave him was not the one he expected. God gave Joshua an answer that applies to everyone who has a task that is bigger than life. God's answer applies to everyone who is not a miracle worker. Although you may feel inferior to someone who has gone before you, God's answer applies to you today. God told Joshua,

"Follow My words of instruction that Moses wrote down." God reminded Joshua of the Scriptures He had given to Moses. "Think about these Scriptures . . . follow these Scriptures . . . obey these Scriptures."

Joshua was well versed in the Word of God. He had read the scrolls . . . many times. He wanted to obey God exactly so he would have the Lord's blessing on all he did. God told Joshua,

"If you meditate on my words of instruction day and night, you will do My will and you will be successful."

This was the secret Joshua needed; it was his advantage over his enemies. This was what Joshua needed to lead Israel. The Scriptures would reveal God's formula to successfully conquer the Promised Land.

Principles for Meditation That Will Make You Successful

Joshua was instructed to "meditate...on this Book of the Law" (see Josh. 1:8). The phrase "this Book" probably means he had access to the five books of Moses. To be successful, Joshua had to think about God's Word. Following the Joshua example of meditation is not going to a lake to watch the sun go down over the mountains so you can meditate on God. Following the Joshua Model is meditating on God's Word to be successful in the practical things in life.

Joshua's Model of Meditation

1. Think success—task goals.
2. Think plans—strategize.
3. Think actions—plan work.
4. Think prosperity—formalize priorities.

The Bible provides principles to live, work and grow as a person. God told Joshua to think about these principles of successful living so he could successfully conquer the land.

God knew that Joshua had all the fears any lieutenant faces when taking over from a great commander. So God reminded Joshua of the principle that would help him successfully conquer the Promised Land. To be a success in life, don't plan to reach that nebulous place called "success"; rather, plan to do successful things each day, and each day you will be successful. My good friend John Maxwell says in his book *The Success Journey,* "Success is a journey, not a destination."

Formula to Be Successful:
Don't plan to be successful,
Plan to do successful things.

The following 10 principles of my life derive from the Scriptures. I have included them to help you become successful in your life.

1. Be successful on the inside. Note that God didn't begin Joshua's training by telling him to gather soldiers, weapons or to develop a strategy to win. God didn't tell him to seek a goal of victory. God's first instructions were, "Be strong and of good courage" (Josh. 1:6). God told him the same thing three times (vv. 6,7,9).

If you win on the inside,
You win your first victory.
If you lose on the inside,
The battle is over.

You win a promotion when you prepare yourself for advancement, not when the boss gives it to you. You win that special mate in marriage when you make yourself worthy of his or her love. If Joshua had a "loser attitude," he would be a losing general. So God's first task with him was to make sure he was thinking straight; that is why God focused on his thinking . . . "meditate . . . you will make your way prosperous, and then you will have good success."

Notice Joshua didn't give excuses why he couldn't win the battle. Usually three kinds of excuses make people fail in their minds.

> ### Three Excuses for Failure
> 1. The competition is too big.
> 2. The circumstances are against me.
> 3. My background is inadequate.

a. The competition is too big. Joshua had been a spy in the land (see Num. 13:20—14:9). He knew Israel was outnumbered in fighting personnel, the enemy soldiers were physically superior and the enemy occupied fortresses. If our eyes expand the enemy and we make them bigger than life, we have lost before we have started. John Wooten, the most successful college basketball coach in history, never scouted the opposing team. He said, "My biggest problem is not my competitor, but myself." Wooten believed it was more important to encourage his team to focus on their game, not on the opposition. He believed focusing on the opposing team might frighten his players.

b. The circumstances are against me. As a general, Joshua knew he was fighting in unknown territory. The enemy would fight harder to defend its homeland. The Israelites were not trained soldiers, but had a history of slavery. Every circumstance seemed against Joshua.

c. My background is inadequate. Joshua's father was named Nun, named after the Egyptian moon god, implying his father could have been an idol worshiper. Perhaps Joshua didn't come from a strong Jewish home; he certainly didn't attend the best universities of Egypt as Moses had. He didn't even have the background of sheep leading as Moses had. Joshua grew up as a slave.

No matter who you are, what your background, the condition of your circumstances or the size of your task, God has the same command, "Be strong and of good courage; do not be afraid" (Josh. 1:9).

2. Take responsibility for your growth and future achievement.
God told him, "Arise, go over this Jordan, you and all this people"

(Josh. 1:2). Joshua couldn't make excuses. He had to take the responsibility of leadership.

> You acquire your greatest ability,
> When you begin taking responsibility.

When the boss oversees his employees, what does he think about them? Probably what you think about yourself is eventually what the boss thinks about you. When you think, *The boss can count on me*, and you demonstrate it day in and day out, eventually the boss will think, *I can count on you*.

> You start growing to become
> what you can be, When you take
> responsibility for what you can do.

3. Follow good role models. Joshua's role model for 40 years had been Moses. Now Moses was dead. Now Joshua had to do the things Moses had modeled. When my daughter was young, she wanted me to teach her the tune *Chopsticks* on the piano. I began to tell her about the eight notes in an octave and that every eighth note began a new octave. She responded, "I don't want to learn music, I just want to play *Chopsticks*." Most people don't want to learn the lessons of life—from anyone—they just want results. Success is no accident, though, and being successful cannot be separated from thinking success. "Meditate...then you will have success."

4. Commit yourself to your task. First, God told him, "Meditate...that you may...do." The secret of Joshua's conquest of the Promised Land was not in the size of his soldiers, but in their commitment to win. It was not their weapons, strategy, superior training or any other circumstance; it was their commitment to obey God. Your commitment to God should make you a better employee than any other person who works with you—if the qualifications are equal. Any commitment makes you stronger, and commitment to God amplifies that strength.

> You get strength to do
> when
> you make a commitment to do.

If you are lazy, however, you will not be any better by just committing yourself to God. You will just be a sanctified lazy employee. It takes commitment, training and hard work.

Couples do not stay together a lifetime just because they are compatible; it is their commitment to each other that makes a great marriage.

People who are committed to excellence do the best work . . . not those who are paid best, have the best surroundings or have the best perks. If you commit yourself to excellence, you will eventually earn more money.

> The world says, "Pay me more and I'll do more."
> You should say, "I'll do more, so you'll pay me more."

5. Learn to rise above your mistakes. It is hard to persuade a child to think like a responsible parent; it is even more difficult to persuade people who have failed for 40 years to think success. Joshua knew that Israel had disobeyed God 40 years earlier—they refused to enter the Promised Land because they were afraid they would be killed in battle. Sadly, during the next 40 years they died in the wilderness—in defeat. Now their children were given the same opportunity to obey God and enter the Promised Land.

> To refuse—because you think you'll fail;
> is
> To do nothing—and to actually fail.

Everyone makes mistakes. Falling down is part of the process of learning to walk, just as experimentation is part of the process of discovering a miracle cure for a disease. We must learn from our mistakes. A half century ago at a soap-making factory, a workman accidentally mixed the wrong amount of oxygen and the soap floated. Rather than firing him for a mistake, the company created a name brand that became a best-seller. The soap was advertised as "99 and 44/100% pure, it floats."

Learn obedience from every time you have doubted God. God promised Joshua, "I will not leave you nor forsake you" (Josh. 1:5). Let your mistakes be the tuition you pay for your education and advancement. Too many people give up when they drop the ball.

> 1. I tried before but failed.
> 2. I can't get started because I'll fail.
> 3. I can't work fast because I'll mess up.
> 4. I can't see myself successful because I've failed.
> 5. I can't keep up with others because I've failed.
> 6. I can't attain excellence because I've failed.
> 7. I can't be creative because I'll fail.

6. Do what you promise. Keeping your word and doing what you promise is a step in growing to maturity. When you start a new job, make yourself promises, and keep them. It is the path to advancement.

> 1. Promise yourself to clock in 10 minutes early and work at least 10 minutes beyond the time to clock out.
> 2. Promise yourself to do everything the boss tells you, plus a little more.
> 3. Promise yourself to do your best when no one is looking and when no one will know.
> 4. Promise yourself to do the extra things that will earn extra money for the company.
> 5. Promise yourself to act in a Christian way to everyone, and in response to everything at all times.

If you can't deliver, don't promise others, and don't promise yourself. It is best to promise to be a "3" and rise to a "4" than to promise someone you will be an "8" and come in as a "4." When you can't deliver, you lose respect, and you lose self-confidence.

If you promise yourself to be a "3" and you come in as a "4," then you have done a successful thing for that day. Enough successful things make you successful. To promise an "8" and come in as a "4" is to fail for that day. To fail too many times takes away your incentive.

Everyone fails once in a while. If you have been successful many times, people will forgive you for the occasional failure, so even when you fail once in a while, it does not make you a failure.

> I may have failed
> but
> I'm not a failure.

God told Joshua, "Arise, go over this Jordan" (Josh. 1:2). Next God promised, "Every place that the sole of your foot will tread upon I have given you" (v. 3). God promised to overcome obstacles, "No man shall be able to stand before you" (v. 5).

Joshua did what God promised and what he committed himself to do. "So Joshua took the whole land, according to all that the Lord had said" (Josh. 11:23).

7. Discipline yourself to do what you have to do. The first step to outward discipline is inward discipline. That is why God told Joshua, "Meditate...that you may...do."

> First you think about doing,
> Then you commit yourself to doing.

Many people live in a world called "I wish." They wish to be successful . . . to be rich . . . to be victorious. Many people "wish" to get a promotion, but successful people live in the world of "I will."

A salesman returned from a trip and reported, "I almost got to see the buyers, I almost sold 10,000 units, I almost got a new mailing list, I almost met the president, I almost got to be interviewed on television...." The truth is, he failed. Don't be an "almost Christian." If you don't make it, begin self-discipline by keeping your mouth closed. Maybe that is enough self-discipline to begin learning what you have to do next time to make the sale.

8. Prioritize your work and life. Not everyone can do everything, so learn what you can do, and what you do well. Begin where you have to begin. Don't be like children who eat their dessert first because they hate their vegetables. My mother gave me a rule in life, whether it was cutting grass, doing homework, delivering my paper route or going to Sunday School:

Do—what you have to do.

First, make a list of all the things you must do each day. Don't start at the beginning of the list and don't start with what you enjoy, and don't start with the biggest project. After you make your "To Do List," then put everything in priority of importance.

What Is Important
1. Time-dated task
2. Boss-directed task
3. Self-promised task
4. Expectation-by-others task
5. Self-growth task
6. Volume-producing task
7. Maintenance task

9. Give more to others than is expected. Parents know the great joy of seeing their children open their gifts on Christmas morning. The kids tear into their presents in eager anticipation. They are happy to receive things because they are kids—that is one of the characteristics of immaturity or babyhood—they need someone to give everything in life to them. Parents derive their happiness from giving—that is one of the characteristics of maturity—the satisfaction of adding value to someone else's life.

Don't judge each day by what you get,
Rather, judge each day by what you give.

Robert Louis Stevenson said, "Don't judge each day by the harvest you reap, but by the seeds you sow."

A good salesman knows that the more times he makes his sales presentation, the more likely his sales will grow. Probably when the number of sales presentations go down, so will his income. Jesus said,

> "Give, and it shall be given unto you; good measure, pressed down, and shaken together, and running over, shall men give into your bosom. For with the same measure that ye mete withal it shall be measured to you again."—Luke 6:38, *KJV*

10. Believe in yourself. When you believe in yourself, it is not self-belief that leads to salvation, nor is it belief in your ability to make yourself run faster by tugging on your sneaker strings. When you believe in yourself, you know your faith is in God, you know you have studied and practiced and you have covered all the bases. Belief in yourself means you know you are ready.

> Belief in yourself,
> is not what you possess.
> Belief in yourself,
> is what possesses you.

When the boss has to present a great motivational speech to get you going, you probably won't get to wherever he wants you to go. When you look deep within and know where you must go, however, you probably will get there. So God didn't have to give Joshua a motivational speech to go conquer the land. God commanded,

> "Meditate [think]...be strong and have courage, don't be afraid, nor be discouraged, for the Lord your God will go with you everywhere."—Joshua 1:8,9, author's translation

How Joshua Practiced Meditation

Although the book of Joshua does not describe Joshua's meditation practice in specific detail, God did promise success if he meditated.

The record of Joshua's many successes suggests Joshua followed these instructions and did indeed meditate on the law. To gain insight into Joshua's practice we must look back to the law itself, which was the focus of his meditation.

One of the most important statements of the law is recorded in Deuteronomy 6. "'Hear, O Israel: The Lord our God, the Lord is one! You shall love the Lord your God with all your heart, with all your soul, and with all your strength'" (Deut. 6:4,5). Rabbis refer to this passage as the *SHEMA*, taken from the first Hebrew word in the text, which means "hear." The *SHEMA* represents the heart of any success, because when a person properly loves God, his head is right, his feet are right and his heart is right.

In Hebrew liturgy, the *SHEMA* also includes the next few verses.

> "'Hear, O Israel: The Lord our God, the Lord is one! You shall love the Lord your God with all your heart, with all your soul, and with all your strength. And these words which I command you today shall be in your heart. You shall teach them diligently to your children, and shall talk of them when you sit in your house, when you walk by the way, when you lie down, and when you rise up.'"
> —Deuteronomy 6:4-7

Step one in Joshua's strategy for success is *meditation* and *memorization*. "And these words which I command you today shall be in your heart" (Deut. 6:6). You meditate on the Scriptures to understand them so you can memorize them. Then you memorize them for better meditation. This important discipline will benefit you: "The law of his God is in his heart; none of his steps shall slide" (Ps. 37:31). The psalmist also viewed Scripture memory as a key to victory over sin. "Your word I have hidden in my heart, that I might not sin against You" (119:11).

In the New Testament, Paul also urged memorization: "Let the word of Christ dwell in you richly in all wisdom, teaching and admonishing one another in psalms and hymns and spiritual songs, singing with grace in your hearts to the Lord" (Col. 3:16). The psalmist also memorized the Scriptures because of their life-giving nature. "I will never forget Your precepts, for by them You have given me life" (Ps. 119:93).

Some people struggle when memorizing Scripture, believing it is impossible for them to do so. Actually, the process of committing a verse to memory involves only two steps, *repetition* and *review*. Admittedly, some find it easier to remember than others, but we can commit a verse to memory if we are prepared to repeat it enough times and review it often. At first, you may have to repeat a verse many times, but the value in Scripture memory is worth it because you are meditating at the same time.

> To memorize—repeat the verse.
> To meditate—review the verse.

Step two in meditation includes *four times of review*. "'You shall teach them diligently to your children, and shall talk of them when you sit in your house, when you walk by the way, when you lie down, and when you rise up'" (Deut. 6:7). The four specific times identified in this verse suggest times when we are not engaged in activities that require a lot of thought. These times are as follows: (1) when we wake up in the morning, (2) when we go to sleep at night, (3) when we walk (drive) to work (4) and when we relax at home or wait in an office. What you think about in these four times during a typical day will influence your character.

> Your character—determines what you meditate.
> What you meditate—determines your character.

Step three is *decorating your home/office to enhance biblical meditation*: "'You shall write them on the doorposts of your house and on your gates'" (Deut. 6:9). To this day, many Jewish people attach a brass plate designed to remind them of the Ten Commandments to their front doors. Many Christians place a Bible in a prominent place or include Scripture texts as part of their household decorations. These symbols become subtle reminders to think about God and His plan for their lives.

Why Meditate on the Scriptures?

The process of meditating on the Scriptures helps achieve God's purpose for our lives. The opposite is also true. When we fail to meditate on the Scriptures, we rob ourselves of what God wants to do for us. Why meditate?

First, because the Bible reveals the secrets of our hearts. Many times moral codes and guides for living do not help us because of their cultural overtones. However, because God wrote the Bible, and He is the Savior of all humanity, it is only natural that He would reveal the sins that keep people away from Him (see Rom. 3:9-20).

After a missionary had been in China for some time, he finally finished translating the New Testament into the language of the people. When they read Romans, they challenged the missionary, "You told us your Book was very ancient; but it is very modern." They complained because the Bible revealed the evil thoughts of their minds. God, who knows the hearts of all people, has revealed our sinful nature in the Bible. You will be successful in life when you know your own heart well enough to know the hearts of others.

Second, the Scriptures reveal Jesus Christ to us. Jesus is the central theme of all Scripture (see John 5:39). He is the central theme of the final book of the Bible, "The Revelation of Jesus Christ" (Rev. 1:1). He is the glue that holds the Bible together and the theme of the whole Bible.

Third, the Bible shows us how to have eternal life and be assured of it. John's chief reason for writing his first Epistle was to ensure believers of the certainty of their salvation, "These things I have written...that you may know that you have eternal life" (1 John 5:13). Unlike other faiths where followers can never be assured of their eternal destiny, the Bible shows us how we can have personal assurance of our relationship to God.

A fourth benefit of Scripture is that it tells us God's expectations for our lives. The Bible gives us a standard by which to live. God revealed the law to Moses so that Israel would obey it (see Deut. 29:29). The Scriptures were provided to help Christians grow spiritually (see 2 Tim. 3:17). It is our Christian duty to do all that is commanded of us (see Luke 17:10). Our only biblical guarantee to success in the Christian life is tied to meditating and obeying the Scriptures (see Josh. 1:8).

Fifth; knowing the Scriptures makes us smart. Every Christian is encouraged to pray for wisdom (see Jas. 1:5). God, who is the source of wisdom, answers that prayer as we memorize and meditate on the Scriptures. The psalmist claimed, "You, through Your commandments, make me wiser than my enemies; for they are ever with me. I have more understanding than all my teachers, for Your testimonies are my meditation" (Ps. 119:98,99). One of the purposes of Scripture is found in "making wise the simple" (Ps. 19:7). The Christian who follows the Joshua Model as a personal discipline should be wiser concerning the decisions of life than those who do not know and apply the Scriptures to their lives (see Luke 16:8).

Finally, meditating on the Scriptures will provide spiritual power to keep us from sin. God revealed a way to help us live a clean life, knowing people would face the problem of sin (see Ps. 119:9-11). The Bible helps us overcome (see 1 Cor. 10:13). Jesus Himself used the Scriptures when He was tempted by Satan (see Matt. 4:1-11). In the flyleaf of his Bible, Dwight L. Moody wrote, "This Book will keep you from sin, or sin will keep you from this Book."

Ten Principles to Take Away

1. Begin by selecting a verse or verses for meditation. Several steps are involved in incorporating the Joshua Model into your personal meditation strategy. Begin by selecting a verse. The verse you select may be a pivotal verse in a book or chapter or a key verse in a particular doctrine. The verse will probably have some particular significance to you even before you begin meditating on it. Some Christians will select several verses, even a chapter, when following the Joshua Model. The longer the passage, the greater your time commitment involved in meditating on these verses.

How to Choose a Verse

1. Meets a need in your life
2. Caught your attention during Bible reading
3. A promise you want to claim
4. A thought you want to keep/memorize
5. A life you want to follow
6. An attitude you need in your life
7. A promise of victory over a problem/sin

2. Study the context and cultural background to get the meaning of the passage. Because you already may have some preconceived ideas about the meaning of the verse, apply your study skills to understand the meaning of the passage. If it is a promise, does the context suggest circumstances that may have a bearing on the relevance of that promise today? If it is a command, is there anything about the context that might modify its obedience today? Take time to understand the original meaning of the verse. Don't forget to study Bible commentaries and Bible dictionaries as well as other helpful resources.

3. Commit the verse to memory. The process of Scripture memorization involves repetition and review. Many people recite a verse five times each morning as they begin their day, and five times before going to bed. Many Scripture verses have been put to music, both in older hymns and the more contemporary Scripture choruses. For many years, the only hymns sung in churches were psalms (also called the Psalter). It was a wonderful way of memorizing the Scriptures.

4. Paraphrase the passage to capture its meaning in your own words. Before you write your own paraphrase, consult various other translations to help you as you look for creative ways to express the meaning of the passage.

5. Define key words and phrases to gain greater insight. Sometimes subtle emphases are implied by the author's choice of a particular word in the original language. These are usually explained in a good commentary or Bible dictionary.

6. Try to personalize the passage. This involves writing the first personal pronoun in the place of other names or pronouns used in the passage. These changes will apply the Scriptures to your life without changing the meaning. It is also a helpful tool to gain insight for meditation: "For God so loved ME that He gave ME His only begotten Son, that IF I believe in Him, I should not perish but rather I will have eternal life" (John 3:16, personalized).

7. Pray the passage to God. This is especially true of verses taken from the Psalms. If the verse was originally expressed as a prayer to God, it may prove to be a good way to express your own prayer to the Father. If the passage is not a prayer, make it a prayer: "Lord, I want to be as strong as Joshua, give me good courage and help me not be afraid of my enemies. Don't let me be discouraged and be with me wherever I go" (Josh. 1:9, personalized).

8. Think through the issues in the passage. Why are things described the way they are in your chosen passage? What are the implications of this verse as it relates to your various interests in life? Might other verses in Scripture give you greater insight into how to balance this passage in the broader teaching of Scripture?

9. Use the great historic hymns in meditation. The following chart lists hymns gathered from several hymnbooks. I keep a hymnbook on my desk at home and use hymns to sing, meditate and pray to God.

Hymns Celebrating the Joshua Model

Break Thou the Bread of Life (Mary A. Lathbury)
Holy Bible, Book Divine (John Burton)
How Firm a Foundation (Unknown)
In Times Like These (Ruth Caye Jones)
My Mother's Bible (M. B. Williams)
O Word of God Incarnate (William W. How)
Standing on the Promises (R. Kelso Carter)
Tell Me the Story of Jesus (Fanny J. Crosby)
The Old Book and the Old Faith (George H. Carr)
The Spirit Breathes Upon the Word (William Cowper)
Thy Word Have I Hid in My Heart (Earnest O. Sellers)
Thy Word Is Like a Garden, Lord (Edwin Hodder)
Wonderful Words of Life (Philip P. Bliss)

---

10. Learn the new praise choruses for meditation. The following brief list of popular choruses reflects an emphasis that values the Scriptures.

> **Choruses Celebrating the Joshua Factor**
> The B-I-B-L-E (Unknown)
> Every Promise in the Book Is Mine (Unknown)
> Thy Word (Amy Grant)

Using the Joshua Model in our personal meditation makes us apply the principle of successful living from the Word of God. When we spend much time meditating on the Scriptures, we cannot help but experience significant spiritual growth and success in life.

Suggested Scripture Passages for Focusing on Biblical Principles

Joshua 1:1-9	John 6:63-69
Psalm 19:7-14	Acts 17:11
Psalm 119:1-176	2 Timothy 3:14-17
Jeremiah 15:16	Hebrews 4:12

Prayer	Praise
1. That God will teach you the principles of how to continually be successful.	1. Praise God for giving you an inner drive to be successful and victorious.
2. That you would be continually victorious and be kept from the evil one.	2. Praise God for your strengths in certain areas that become a basis for growth and success in other areas.
3. That you will grow in Christ from victory to victory.	3. Praise God for past victories; these can become the basis for future victories.
4. That God will help you memorize verses on which you can claim victory.	4. Be thankful for family and friends who encourage you to be successful.
5. That God will not lead you into temptation, but will keep you victorious in the hour of temptation.	5. Be grateful for salvation that gives you eternal life and the indwelling Holy Spirit who keeps you daily.
6. That you can share with others the principles of success and victory.	6. Thank God for all the good things in your life.
7.	7.
8.	8.
9.	9.
10.	10.

Journaling

Writing in a journal will provide several benefits, particularly in the areas of learning to live the successful Christian life and learning how to victoriously face sin and problems. To achieve the most benefit, each day you will want to write down the lessons God is teaching you. The following suggestions will stimulate your thinking and guide your writing:

1. Make a list of the greatest victories in your Christian walk of faith. Seeing what God has done in the past will strengthen you, especially when you see what God has accomplished in your growth.
2. Write down the principles you follow to maintain a daily victorious walk with God. Leave space in your journal to come back and complete this list. It will probably take a lot of meditation to round out the list in every area of your life.
3. Think through the various problems you have/will face. Write down the principles you follow to gain victory when facing a problem/sin.
4. As you meditate on the Word of God, write down your thoughts about your fellowship with God.

Write down the lessons you learn from God. Write down the things you enjoy about being victorious over sin and how you enjoy His fellowship. The next time you face difficulties, reread this section to realize what you miss when you give in to sin or difficulties.

Bible Study for Successful Living

1. Before you can have victory over sin or live a successful life for God, you must realize sin exists. What victory is available to the believer? What specific victory do you want?

> "Now thanks be to God who always leads us in triumph in Christ, and through us diffuses the fragrance of His knowledge in every place."—2 Corinthians 2:14

_____

_____

_____

_____

2. Victory and success are ever present in the work of God. What promise does Paul offer to believers?

> "Therefore, my beloved brethren, be steadfast, immovable, always abounding in the work of the Lord, knowing that your labor is not in vain in the Lord."—1 Corinthians 15:58

_____

_____

_____

_____

3. God promises a "way of escape" for you to be victorious. How can you claim the way of escape?

> "No temptation has overtaken you except such as is common to man; but God is faithful, who will not allow you to be tempted beyond what you are able, but with the temptation will also make the way of escape, that you may be able to bear it."—1 Corinthians 10:13

_____
_____
_____
_____

4. God seems to suggest four principles to be an overcomer, (i.e., walks not, stands not, sits not and meditates). Rework these into four principles of success.

> "Blessed is the man who walks not in the counsel of the ungodly, nor stands in the path of sinners, nor sits in the seat of the scornful; but his delight is in the law of the Lord, and in His law he mediates day and night."—Psalm 1:1,2

_____
_____
_____
_____

5. Apply to your life the description of the successful person who overcomes problems.

> "He shall be like a tree planted by the rivers of water, that brings forth its fruit in its season, whose leaf also shall not wither; and whatever he does shall prosper."—Psalm 1:3

_____
_____
_____
_____

6. We are told to meditate on the Bible for success (see Josh. 1:8). What must we do *after* we meditate?

> "Have I not commanded you? Be strong and of good courage; do not be afraid, nor be dismayed, for the Lord your God is with you wherever you go."—Joshua 1:9

_____

_____

_____

_____

7. What will help us meditate on Scripture successfully?

"How can a young man cleanse his way? By taking heed according to Your word."—Psalm 119:9
"Your word I have hidden in my heart, that I might not sin against You."—Psalm 119:11

_____

_____

_____

_____

8. We can do certain things to prepare us for meditation from God's Word. What are these things?

"These were more fair-minded than those in Thessalonica, in that they received the word with all readiness, and searched the Scriptures daily to find out whether these things were so."—Acts 17:11

_____

_____

_____

_____

9. Jesus gave us an example of how to face temptation successfully. What did He do? What principles does that suggest for you?

"Jesus said to him, 'It is written again, You shall not tempt the Lord your God.'"—Matthew 4:7

10. Two things are offered to us by God when we face problems. What are they?

> "'My grace is sufficient for you, for My strength is made perfect in weakness.'"—2 Corinthians 12:9

_____
_____
_____
_____

11. We should never be arrogant because we are aware that God teaches us principles of success or Christ gives us victory over our weaknesses. What should be our attitude? What will be the result of arrogance?

> "Therefore let him who thinks he stands take heed lest he fall."—1 Corinthians 10:12

_____
_____
_____
_____

12. Sometimes it is difficult to learn success and sometimes we think we give up a lot of worldly pleasures or fleshly satisfaction to walk with God. What is promised to those who are victorious?

> "Blessed is the man who endures temptation; for when he has been approved, he will receive the crown of life which the Lord has promised to those who love Him."—James 1:12

_____
_____
_____
_____

Verses to Memorize and Meditate

"This Book of the Law shall not depart from your mouth, but you shall meditate in it day and night, that you may observe to do according to all that is written in it. For then you will make your way prosperous, and then you will have good success."
—Joshua 1:8

"Now thanks be to God who always leads us in triumph in Christ, and through us diffuses the fragrance of His knowledge in every place."—2 Corinthians 2:14

"Therefore, my beloved brethren, be steadfast, immovable, always abounding in the work of the Lord, knowing that your labor is not in vain in the Lord."—1 Corinthians 15:58

"No temptation has overtaken you except such as is common to man; but God is faithful, who will not allow you to be tempted beyond what you are able, but with the temptation will also make the way of escape, that you may be able to bear it."
—1 Corinthians 10:13

"Blessed is the man who walks not in the counsel of the ungodly, nor stands in the path of sinners, nor sits in the seat of the scornful; but his delight is in the law of the Lord, and in His law he meditates day and night."—Psalm 1:1,2

"Your word I have hidden in my heart, that I might not sin against You."—Psalm 119:11

"Blessed is the man who endures temptation; for when he has been proved, he will receive the crown of life which the Lord has promised to those who love Him."—James 1:12

"'My grace is sufficient for you, for My strength is made perfect in weakness.'"—2 Corinthians 12:9

Photocopy and cut these verses into small cards to carry with you for memorization and meditation.

~ 6 ~

THE SAINT PAUL MODEL:
Becoming Like Christ

"IF THEN YOU WERE RAISED WITH CHRIST,

SEEK THOSE THINGS WHICH ARE ABOVE, WHERE

CHRIST IS, SITTING AT THE RIGHT HAND OF GOD.

SET YOUR MIND ON THINGS ABOVE,

NOT ON THINGS ON THE EARTH."

—Colossians 3:1,2

Being arrested by Roman officials did not bother Paul. He was chained to a Roman guard, but many times the guard trusted Paul so that the shackles were removed to allow him to read, write and chat with friends. The believers in Rome had rented an apartment for Paul (see Acts 28:30), so he was not locked up in prison. Friends prepared Paul's meals so he wasn't forced to eat the swill other prisoners had to suffer.

Paul prayed daily for each church he established, and his concern this day was for the believers at Colossae. This church was located in the little town of Colossae near the sprawling commercial city of Ephesus. This church was dear to Paul's heart because they didn't have problems with fleshly sins, as the believers in Corinth did. Their problem was not a lack of doctrine as it was in Thessalonica; they knew biblical teaching. Paul knelt to pray,

"Lord, help the believers beware of vain philosophy" (see Col. 2:8).

Word had come to Paul in prison that the church in Colossae was being negatively influenced by some traveling philosophic preachers motivated by academic pride. They were not preaching the simplicity of belief in Christ Jesus, but their lofty intellectual sermons were filled with philosophy—the influence of Greek thinkers from Athens, Greece.

After prayer, Paul picked up a quill to write a letter to the Colossians to warn them. He wrote:

> "Beware lest any one spoil your walk in Christ by preaching Greek philosophy as a basis of your faith. They preach worldly philosophy and thinking because they are arrogant. This is nothing but the teaching of man's tradition and man's pride, it is not based on Christ."
> —Colossians 2:8, author's translation

Paul returned to intercession, "I pray that the Colossians may walk worthy of You Lord, and please You with fruits of good works" (1:10, author's translation).

Paul thought of what he could pray next,

"I pray the Colossians will be strengthened with Your power to patiently live simply for Christ" (v. 11, author's translation).

Paul thought about the Colossians' temptation to philosophic arrogance; then he bowed his head,

"I pray the Colossians may realize they have been delivered from the kingdom of Satan's darkness and have been translated into the kingdom of God's Son" (v. 13, author's translation).

Paul also heard that the Colossians were being led into false mysticism. They were told that good Christians did not eat meat and cakes, but had special diets that promised to give them intimacy with God. He picked up his pen and wrote to them:

> "Beware of those who are tricking you. They tell you to become one with God by going without sleep, abstaining from food, and dressing in rags to appear humble. They tell you to worship angels who fly to God. These people haven't seen the things they preach to you, but they lead you astray because they are puffed up by fleshly minds."
> —Colossians 2:23, author's translation

Meditating on the Excellency of Christ

Paul knew the Old Testament truth about the importance of what people think. The Proverbs taught, "For as he thinks in his heart, so is he" (23:7). Eventually, today's focus of our thinking will become tomorrow's lifestyle. It is only a matter of time.

> What's in your heart, influences what you think.
> What's in your mind, influences what you become.

The secular world has applied this principle to promote personal growth and/or business success. Business leaders are encouraged to first conceive their goals, then achieve their goals. The businessman may hang a motto on his wall,

> You cannot achieve
> What you cannot conceive.

Because unsaved people realize this truth works, they have strong ideas about their personal goals, and what they would like to have realized in their lives. They develop strategies to accomplish those goals. Positive thinking is an important part of the process in realizing significant behavioral change in our lives.

Years ago, Norman Vincent Peale, pastor of Riverside Church in New York City and a TV pastor, wrote a best-selling book titled *The*

Power of Positive Thinking. His thesis is that if you have positive thoughts about your life and plans for the future, you will most likely succeed. At a recent Gold Medallion Banquet for the Christian Booksellers Association, Mrs. Norman Vincent Peale told the audience how her husband's book had been published. Dr. Peale had submitted the manuscript to 14 publishers, mostly small Christian publishers. They all rejected the manuscript. He threw it into the wastebasket in disgust, although she protested. He was so angry that he told her,

"I forbid you to touch that manuscript!"

Mrs. Peale was obedient. Although Peale, who advocated positive thinking, had not sent it to the biggest publisher, and had given up after 14 rejection letters, she was the one exhibiting positive thinking. She picked up the wastebasket, manuscript untouched, and caught a cab to downtown New York and walked into the editor's office of one of the largest publishers in the nation.

"I can't touch it," she told the editor, "but this will be a best-selling book."

Mrs. Peale was right. The book became a best-seller and is still published decades later. The message of the book, however, is only half a truth. First, it is true that a positive attitude will help a person be successful in life. However, Peale did not include the second half of the truth—Christian truth—although he was a Christian minister. The second half is not about the power of your thoughts, but about the power of Christ. It is the power of Christ in us to change our lives. Paul told the Philippian church, "I can do all things through Christ" (Phil. 4:13) because "The good message of Jesus Christ is the power of God" (Rom. 1:16, author's translation).

The Colossian believers were being told there was power in philosophy. Paul wrote to them, "Beware of philosophy . . . for only in Jesus Christ do you get the fullness of God" (Col. 2:8,9, author's translation). Again he wrote, "Let no one beguile you with mysticism . . . because they do not hold on to Christ Jesus who is the head of the body of Christ . . . for the only way to grow is to grow in Him" (vv. 18,19, author's translation).

> By our faith, we get the life of God.
> By our faith, we daily live the life of God.

Paul wanted the Colossians to continue walking in faith. He wrote:

"Let no one defraud you of your reward, taking delight in false humility and worship of angels, intruding into those things which he has not seen, vainly puffed up by his fleshly mind, and not holding fast to the Head, from whom all the body, nourished and knit together by joints and ligaments, grows with the increase which is from God" (Col. 2:8,9, author's translation).

Paul wanted the Colossians to have faith in Christ, not in intellectual philosophy or experiential mysticism.

Faith is at the heart of what it means to be a Christian. "Without faith it is impossible to please Him [God]" (Heb. 11:6). One of the first descriptions of Christians in the Early Church was the expression "believers" (Acts 5:14). The kind of faith that impresses God and characterized early Christians, however, was a living faith (i.e., a faith that had life from God and produced a change in daily life). "For as the body without the spirit is dead, so faith without works is dead also" (Jas. 2:26). Biblical faith is best revealed in the way we live our lives.

Paul wanted the Colossians to think like Jesus Christ, not like their philosophy-driven teachers. He wanted them to live in Christ, and not to be influenced by their mystically driven preachers. He wrote:

> "If then you were raised with Christ, seek those things which are above, where Christ is, sitting at the right hand of God. Set your mind on things above, not on things on the earth. For you died, and your life is hidden with Christ in God."—Colossians 3:1-3

This was the same truth Paul earlier had told the Philippians, "Let this mind be in you which was also in Christ Jesus" (Phil. 2:5). He was concerned with the way Christians thought; for the way people think determines how they will live.

> When you have the mind of Jesus Christ,
> You want to live the example of Jesus Christ.

Christianity is a rational religion, different from all the religions of the world. First, you were created in the image of God (see Gen. 1:26,27), which means you are a reflection of God. You can never be equal with God because God was the Creator—you are the created one. God has a mind, so do you. God can think—He thinks without limitation—you think, but your thoughts are limited and are not perfect.

God made you to think; now He wants you to think about Him. He wants you to think correctly . . . to think completely . . . to think sincerely . . . and to think continually.

Some religions pursue God through their bodies by going on special diets and/or by fasting. Jesus tells us to begin with our minds, "Learn of me; for I am meek and lowly" (Matt. 11:29, *KJV*). Other religions seek to lose their identity through chanting, meditations and mantras. Jesus said to search for Him with our minds, "If any one wants to know true doctrine, if he willingly searches for truth, he shall know the doctrine that is of God" (John 7:16,17, author's translation).

Jesus challenged His followers to study, learn and know. "If you continue in my words, this proves you are my disciples. You will know the truth, and the truth will set you free" (John 8:31,32, author's translation).

The false religions think that by beginning with physical manipulation they can know God. Christianity believes in the opposite strategy. First you know God, then correct thinking will change your outward life. The following steps demonstrate the Christian path to a changed life.

Paul understood that our thought lives were foundational to our lifestyles. He knew the best way to change behavior was to begin by changing our thinking. His pattern was to first give his readers the content of Christianity to think about, followed by the second part of his letters, the practical application. Typically, his Epistles may be divided into two major sections. The first section may be described in terms of "doctrinal explanation." The second section may be described in terms of "practical exhortation." This division is illustrated in the following chart as it applies to three of Paul's most important doctrinal Epistles.

Doctrinal Explanation	Practical Exhortation
Romans 1—11	Romans 12—16
Ephesians 1—3	Ephesians 4—6
Colossians 1—2	Colossians 3—4

The Role of the Saint Paul Model in Changing Our Lives

Paul wanted his believers to follow the thinking of Christ. He told them to "Think on these things" and "Let this mind be in you which also was in Christ Jesus" and "Think on things above, not on things of this earth."

Paul's passion was Jesus Christ. He pleaded, "That I may know Him" (Phil. 3:10). Paul wanted to know Christ in three areas:

> To know the power of Christ's resurrection.
> To fellowship with the sufferings of Christ's death.
> To be conformed to Christ's character.
> —Philippians 3:10, author's translation

Notice the passion of Paul began with the intellect, or the mind. Paul wanted to know Christ, not to know facts about Him or to know the history of Him. Paul wanted to know Christ.

Because Paul was converted, when he said he wanted to "know Christ," it did not mean to initially know Christ in salvation. Paul wanted to know Christ in a daily experiential way. He wanted the person of Christ to be real to him.

> "I do not count myself to have arrived at a perfect level of living. I have not fully captured Christ in my life, like Christ captured me on the Damascus Road. This one thing I will do in life. I will forget what is past, and I will press toward the finish line to capture the goal of fully knowing Christ Jesus my Lord."—Philippians 3:10-14, author's translation

When we gain Christ, we have Him in our lives. Paul said, "Christ lives in me, and my life now lives by the faith of the Son of God" (Gal. 2:20, author's translation). To live for Christ is to develop Christian character, which is Christ's life shining through us. Paul described this life to the Colossians, "Which is Christ in you" (Col. 1:27). The following are steps to go from thinking about Christ to manifesting Christ in your character.

> ## Character Steps to Be Like Christ
>
> 7. Being like Christ
> 6. Repeating
> 5. Doing
> 4. Focusing
> 3. Desiring
> 2. Believing
> 1. Thinking

Character Step One—Thinking

The first step to a changed life begins with the mind: "When you change people's thinking, you change their beliefs." It is wrong to say it does not make any difference what people believe, as long as they are sincere. It does make a difference what we believe. In the Scriptures, belief is a commitment to a life of discipleship. Those who were first called believers were soon called disciples, as the watching world saw how their faith changed the way they lived their lives (see Acts). You first think the Bible before you live the Bible. An aged saint prayed, "May I think my thoughts after Thee, O God."

Character Step Two—Believing

What does it mean to believe in Jesus Christ?

1. Some treat belief as mere speculation, "I believe it will rain." They only speculate there is a God.
2. Some treat belief as mere historical awareness (i.e., "I believe that God created the world"). They only give mental assent that there is a God.
3. Some treat belief as the result of strong logical argument (i.e., "I accept the existence of God"). They only have a philosophical explanation of God.
4. Bible belief is deeper than knowing about God, feeling God or convincing our wills that God is true. When a person believes in God, he or she says, "I know there is a God and I know Him personally. Bible belief is certainty."

> I believe,
> therefore
> I know.

Faith is produced by the Scriptures, called "the word of faith" (Rom. 10:8). "So then faith comes by hearing, and hearing by the word of God" (v. 17). This means the Christian who wants to develop his or her faith in God must begin by learning the basic facts of Scripture. The knowledge of Scripture then becomes the basis upon which the Christian life is lived.

Character Step Three—Desiring

The next step is summarized in the statement, "When you change people's beliefs, you change their expectations." Our expectations or vision must come from God's Word. "Where there is no vision, the people perish: but he that keepeth the law, happy is he" (Prov. 29:18, *KJV*).

When you are converted, God gives you new desires. These new desires center on Christ. "If anyone is in Christ, he is a new creation" (2 Cor. 5:17). These new desires involve every area of life:

New Things
New home in heaven (see Rev. 21:1)
New desire to be godly (see Rom. 7:21,22)
New standards of living (see Rom. 8:2,3)
New inward power of living (see Gal. 2:20)
New relationship to God (see Rom. 8:14-16)
New identity (see Eph. 2:3-5)

Our new desires give us a new perspective of living for God—we have new dreams, new desires and new visions. We look at life differently after we have been saved. The way we see life is the way we live life.

Some people have difficulty living the Christian life because they don't view it correctly. People may have at least five different responses regarding the Christian life.

First, some never consider themselves as living for God. They have a *spiritual blindness problem.*

Second, others are aware of the Christian life, but don't understand it. They have a *mental problem.*

Third, still others know about the Christian life, but never pursue it. They have a *problem of the will.*

A fourth group endorses the Christian life, but never feels it. They have a *heart problem.*

The fifth group accepts the Christian life and through obedience achieves it. This final group has eyes to see, a heart to respond and a *will to choose Christ.*

What expectation has Scripture created in your life? God's vision for your life can be grasped in four ways. First, *look within* yourself to determine how God has enabled and gifted you.

Second, *look behind* yourself to see how God has used past events to shape you and prepare you for something greater. Third, *look around* yourself to find examples you can follow. I often tell people, "Tell me who your hero is and I'll tell you where you'll be in 10 years." Fourth, *look ahead* to determine where the Lord is leading in your life.

Character Step Four—Focusing

The fourth step toward achieving Christian character is summarized in the statement, "When you change people's expectations, you change their attitudes." People's attitudes are their predispositions to life's focus. Your life may be defined as the way you continually focus your attention. We are on a downward cycle when we develop a "hardening of the attitudes." In contrast, a positive attitude puts us on an upward cycle.

A new attitude develops new actions that change our lives. When I become tired of always being late, I decide to start being on time (step one, change of thinking). Thus, I know change is possible (step two, change of belief). I begin to see myself as an on-time person (step three, change of desires). As I dream of a new life, the desire produces new attitudes (step four, change of focusing). After I focus on new desires, I make changes to arrive on time (step five, change of doing). As I arrive on time more and more frequently, it is easier to be an on-time person and it becomes a habit (step six, change of repeating). I then change (step seven, being like Christ). The new habit helps shape character. I become an "on-time person."

We usually have to enter four doors to develop new attitudes. First, identify the problem you wish to address. In the illustration just provided, the problem was chronic lateness. The second door is knowing right thinking will lead to changing an emotional habit. A person decides to be on time. The third door is relating to positive people. We will think like those with whom we associate. If we want to become punctual, we should begin associating with people who tend to be punctual. The final door is to develop a plan that will encourage positive attitudes and help develop a new habit.

Begin by being on time for your next meeting, then the next one and so on. By being on time for one meeting at a time, you will eventually develop the habit of being on time and become known as a punctual person.

Character Step Five—Doing

The fourth step is summarized in the statement, "When you change your attitude, you change your actions." The dictionary defines an action as "anything done or performed."

My actions earn my reputation and communicate to others the kind of person I am. "Even a child is known by his deeds, whether what he does is pure and right" (Prov. 20:11). Jesus emphasized this truth when He said a tree is known by its fruit. "For every tree is known by its own fruit. For men do not gather figs from thorns, nor do they gather grapes from a bramble bush" (Luke 6:44). My actions are the fruit by which others determine what kind of person I am.

Character Step Six—Repeating

The fifth step is summarized in the statement, "When you change your actions, you change your habits." When we do something regularly, it is either a habit or an accomplishment. We use the word "accomplished" in a positive way when we say, "She is an accomplished pianist." The goal of the Scriptures is "that the man of God may be complete [accomplished], thoroughly equipped for every good work" (2 Tim. 3:17).

Character Step Seven—Being Like Christ

The final step is summarized in the statement, "When you change your habits, to do what Christ did, you develop inner character to be like Christ." Some people act like Christ around believers; but a famous man once said, "Your character is what you are when no one is looking." You don't want to just act like Christ; you want to be like Christ. Notice the process that makes us what we are. First, we think it. Then we know it. After that, we dream it. We begin to focus on it. Then we act on it. That leads us to accomplishing it habitually. Ultimately, we become it.

Building Character Through the Saint Paul Model

1. When you change your thinking, you change your beliefs.
2. When you change your beliefs, you change your expectations.
3. When you change your expectations, you change your attitudes.
4. When you change your attitudes, you change your actions.
5. When you change your actions, you change your habits.
6. When you change your habits, you change your character.
7. When you change your character, you become like Christ.

A young pastor preached through the entire book of Philippians during a period of several months. The congregation began to memorize the Epistle as they studied it together. Many church members accepted the challenge and joined their pastor in committing the entire Epistle to memory. Each week they encouraged each other, reciting the verses they had learned that week and sharing how the verses had helped them face various challenges.

One week, a lady told the following story about how the Scriptures had changed her thinking. The Sunday previously, the pastor's sermon was based on Philippians 4:8. The next morning, the lady diligently committed the verse to memory. She had taken longer than usual because she struggled with the eight virtues identified in that verse in their correct order.

Later that afternoon, the lady sat on her couch to begin watching some of her favorite afternoon television programs. As she began watching, her memory verse for the week came to mind.

Finally, brethren, whatever things are true, whatever things are noble, whatever things are just, whatever things are pure, whatever things are lovely, whatever things are of good report, if there is any virtue and if there is anything praiseworthy—meditate on these things (Phil. 4:8).

The lady realized what she was watching on the soap opera did not measure up to Paul's standard. She turned off the television. A half hour later, she began watching another program. Once again the verse came to mind and again the television was turned off. Throughout the week, the process was repeated. "I haven't been able to watch my soaps this week because of that verse," she shared with others. The Saint Paul Model in meditation changed her television viewing habits.

Ten Principles to Take Away for Meditation

1. **Make a checklist for change.** The process of following the Saint Paul Model in our personal meditation begins with a willingness to change our thinking. When we change our thinking, we begin changing our entire lives. For some of us, we need to begin where the lady who needed to change her television viewing habits began. The eight virtues listed in Philippians 4:8 provide the basis of an excellent checklist by which we can evaluate our thought lives.

The Saint Paul Model Checklist for Meditation

- Is it true?
- Is it noble?
- Is it just?
- Is it pure?
- Is it lovely?
- Is it of good report?
- Is there virtue in this?
- Is there anything praiseworthy in this?

---

2. Read the meditations of others. One tool to help us begin applying the Saint Paul Model involves reading the fruit of meditation by others. Diaries, devotional books and daily helps are readily available for your quiet time.

3. Sing and think about the historic hymns of the faith. Many Christian hymns reflect the deep yearning of the writer to become more like Jesus by drawing closer to Him. As you read and think about the statements in these hymns, they can help you focus your own thoughts on "things above" and acquire the mind of Christ in your own life.

Hymns Celebrating the Saint Paul Model

Be Thou My Vision (Mary E. Byrne/Eleanor H. Hull)

Channels Only (Mary E. Maxwell)

Christ Be Beside Me (James Quinn)

Fill All My Vision (Avis B. Christiansen)

Footsteps of Jesus (Mary B. C. Slade)

Higher Ground (Johnson Oatman, Jr.)

I Want a Principle Within (Charles Wesley)

I Want to Be Like Jesus (Thomas O. Chisholm)

I Would Be Like Jesus (James Rowe)

I Would Be True (Howard A. Walter)

Make Me a Blessing (Ira B. Wilson)

May the Mind of Christ, My Savior
(Kate B. Wilkinson)

More Like the Master (Charles H. Gabriel)

Nearer, My God, to Thee (Sarah F. Adams)

Nearer, Still Nearer (Lelia N. Morris)

Not I, But Christ (A. A. Whiddington)

Nothing Between (Charles A. Tindley)

O Love That Will Not Let Me Go (George Matheson)

O to Be Like Thee! (Thomas O Chisholm)

Savior, More than Life (Fanny J. Crosby)

Take My Life and Let It Be (Frances R. Havergal)

Take Time to Be Holy (William D. Longstaff)

---

4. Learn the new praise and worship choruses. The following list of popular praise and worship choruses raise our thoughts to a higher plain and help us acquire the mind of Christ. Try singing one or two of these choruses as you prepare to follow the Saint Paul Model in your personal meditation.

Choruses Celebrating the Saint Paul Model

All That I Need (Twila Paris)
As the Deer (Martin Nystrom)
Change My Heart, O God (Eddie Espinosa)
Cover Me (Andrew Culverwell)
Day by Day—A Prayer (Saint Richard of Chichester)
Here I Am (Chris A. Bowater)
In My Life, Lord, Be Glorified (Bob Kilpatrick)
Just a Closer Walk with Thee (Traditional Folk Song)
Let the Beauty of Jesus Be Seen in Me
(Albert W. T. Osborn)
Lord, I Want to Be a Christian (Traditional)
Make Me a Servant (Kelly Willard)
My Desire (Lillian Plankenhorn)
Reign in Me (Chris Bowater)
Seek Ye First (Karen Lafferty)
Take Me In (Dave Browning)
The Greatest Thing (Mark Pendergrass)
To Be Like Jesus (Traditional)
With Eternity's Values in View (Alfred B. Smith)

---

5. Make a list of positive traits you desire. First, realize you are not patient. Add patience to a list of things you want in your life. This list is important because you will never become what you don't desire to become.

6. Make a list of negative traits you want to eliminate. Usually, both negative and positive habits are inseparable. Recently, a friend told me how she had quit biting her fingernails. She repeatedly tried to stop biting her nails. Someone told her to replace a bad habit with a good habit. She began carrying a nail file and every time she was tempted to bite her nails, she testified, "I reached for my nail file and filed them." She proudly held up 10 beautiful nails and commented, "If you know of anyone who bites her nails, tell her to make her nail file her best friend."

7. Pray for supernatural help. It is one thing to change your thinking, but sometimes you need divine help. After listing patience as a virtue you want to possess, think about God's formula, "If any of you lacks wisdom, let him ask of God" (Jas. 1:5). God gives supernatural help, but sometimes God uses secondary things to accomplish the purpose. "Count it all joy when you fall into various trials...the testing of your faith produces patience" (Jas. 1:2,3).

8. Seek accountability help. Ask a fellow believer to pray with you about your project. When you are accountable to someone, you will be more responsible for yourself and more faithful to God.

> It is hard to do in life what you expect.
> It is easier to do in life what others inspect.

9. Develop your strengths. Don't begin by thinking about your problems, they may discourage you. Begin thinking about your strengths. Don't think of your new areas of strength as a strength you want to develop, rather, begin with the strongest area of your life. Take for example your intellect, your emotions or your will. Which is your strongest? Use it as leverage to work on your weakest areas. If the intellect is strongest, read a lot of Scripture, Christian books and other helps. If you have deep feeling, let your emotions direct your life. If you are disciplined, allow your will to control your life.

Checklist	Weakest	Strongest
Intellect—your thinking Emotions—your feelings Volition—your will power		

10. Begin writing down your progress. It is good exercise for Christians to keep a record of their journey of faith. Luke kept a journal of Paul's journey to the churches and his voyage across the Mediterranean Sea. Your life is enriched by these journal accounts. You can add quality to your life by keeping a journal (see Journaling section for help).

Conclusion

Changing the focus of our thinking to "things above" is of little value if we do not allow the process to change our entire lives. Changing our thinking will result in a change of beliefs. Changed beliefs will lead to changed expectations in life. Those changed expectations should result in changed attitudes. If our attitudes change, a change in our actions should follow. Changed actions establish changed habits, and changed habits change our character to be like Christ.

Suggested Scriptures Passages for Meditation to Become Like Christ

Galatians 2:19-21	1 Thessalonians 5:16-24
Philippians 2:5-12	2 Timothy 2:15
Colossians 1:14-23	Philemon 4-21
Colossians 3:1-11	

Prayer	Praise
1. That you would grow in your knowledge of Christ and become more like Him.	1. Praise God that Christ came into your life and lives within you.
2. That Christ would be magnified in your life and service.	2. Praise God for wisdom, strength and happiness you receive because Christ is in you.
3. That you would have "the mind of Jesus" in all your ways.	3. Praise God for His eternal salvation and all its benefits He planned and gave to you.
4. That you would learn to think about things that are true, noble, just, pure, lovely, of good report, virtuous and praiseworthy (see Phil. 4:8).	4. Thanks that you are not what you used to be before salvation.
5. That you would learn to "set your mind on things above."	5. Praise God for your growth in grace and the things He has taught you.
6. That you would share with others what you have learned about Christ.	6. Praise God for your single-mindedness to serve Christ and glorify Him with your life.
7.	7.
8.	8.
9.	9.
10.	10.

Journaling

When you begin to write down your thoughts about the indwelling Christ, you are doing what many others have done. As you write down your experiences, try not to emphasize physical results (that is for other journal entries), and do not go to the other extreme of writing only your feelings. Use the following guidelines:

1. Make a list of the positive traits you want for yourself. Then find a verse for each trait. As you pray to develop that trait in your life and meditate on its qualities, God will develop it within you.
2. Prioritize your list to give more direction to your growth.
3. Make a list of your negative traits you want to eliminate. Remember, it is easier to develop strong new habits that take the place of old negative habits than it is to just work on breaking nagging habits that enslave you.
4. Make a list of the strong traits/habits you now have. Making this list will give you confidence for growth and obtain victory over weak areas. Once you have written down this list of your strengths, assign a verse that characterizes each trait. You will gain more strength by meditating on the Word of God. You will go from "strength to strength" and from "victory to victory."
5. Write down the verses that challenge you to let Christ control your life, then pray these verses by personalizing them.

Bible Study for Spiritual Excellence

1. We must give Christ our total lives. Where does our spiritual journey begin?

> "Then he said to them all, 'If anyone desires to come after Me, let him deny himself, and take up his cross daily, and follow Me.'"—Luke 9:23

_____

_____

_____

_____

2. How can we continue walking with Christ once we begin the journey?

> "Then Jesus said to those Jews who believed Him, 'If you abide in My word, you are My disciples indeed.'"—John 8:31

_____

_____

_____

_____

3. What must we develop in our journey with Christ?

> "Therefore be imitators of God as dear children. And walk in love, as Christ also has loved us and given Himself for us, an offering and a sacrifice to God for a sweet-smelling aroma."—Ephesians 5:1,2

_____

_____

_____

_____

4. Upon conversion a person repents of known sin, which is turning from sin. On the journey with Christ, however, the

person must continually do a similar action. What is it?

> "Brethren, I do not count myself to have apprehended; but one thing I do, forgetting those things which are behind and reaching forward to those things which are ahead."
> —Philippians 3:13

_____

_____

_____

_____

5. As we journey with Christ, we must think His thoughts and meditate on Him. How can we do this?

> "Let this mind be in you which was also in Christ Jesus."
> —Philippians 2:5

_____

_____

_____

_____

6. The Christians were "in Colosse" (Col. 1:2) and "with Christ" (3:3). While on earth, they were to put their thoughts on heaven. What does this mean to you?

> "If then you were raised with Christ, seek those things which are above, where Christ is, sitting at the right hand of God. Set your mind on things above, not on things on the earth."—Colossians 3:1,2

_____

_____

_____

_____

7. What is the basis for "setting our minds on things above"?

> "For you died, and your life is hidden with Christ in God."
> —Colossians 3:3

_____
_____
_____
_____

8. What is the basis of hope for the believer?

> "Him we preach, warning every man and teaching every man in all wisdom, that we may present every man perfect in Christ Jesus."—Colossians 1:28

_____
_____
_____
_____

9. What was the controlling passion of Paul's life? In what three areas did this passion express itself?

> "That I may know Him and the power of His resurrection, and the fellowship of His sufferings, being conformed to His death."—Philippians 3:10

_____
_____
_____
_____

10. Paul knew he was not perfect, but he had a future goal. What was it?

> "Not that I have already attained, or am already perfected; but I press on, that I may lay hold of that for which Christ Jesus has also laid hold of me."—Philippians 3:12

_____
_____
_____
_____

11. Paul gave all his energy for his passion of "knowing Christ." How does this apply to your life?

"I press toward the goal for the prize of the upward call of God in Christ Jesus."—Philippians 3:14

_____
_____
_____
_____

12. Paul wanted to live for Christ. What would happen to him at death?

"For our citizenship is in heaven, from which we also eagerly wait for the Savior, the Lord Jesus Christ, who will transform our lowly body that it may be conformed to His glorious body, according to the working by which He is able even to subdue all things to Himself."
—Philippians 3:20,21

_____
_____
_____
_____

Verses to Memorize and Meditate

"For to me, to live is Christ, and to die is gain."—Philippians 1:21

"That I may know Him and the power of His resurrection, and the fellowship of His sufferings, being conformed to His death."—Philippians 3:10

"I press toward the goal for the prize of the upward call of God in Christ Jesus."—Philippians 3:14

"I can do all things through Christ who strengthens me." —Philippians 4:13

"Let this mind be in you which was also in Christ Jesus." —Philippians 2:5

"Finally, brethren, whatever things are true, whatever things are noble, whatever things are just, whatever things are pure, whatever things are lovely, whatever things are of good report, if there is any virtue and if there is anything praiseworthy—meditate on these things."—Philippians 4:8

"Him we preach, warning every man and teaching every man in all wisdom, that we may present every man perfect in Christ Jesus."—Colossians 1:28

"If then you were raised with Christ, seek those things which are above, where Christ is, sitting at the right hand of God. Set your mind on things above, not on things on the earth." —Colossians 3:1,2

Photocopy and cut these verses into small cards to carry with you for memorization and meditation.

~ 7 ~

THE TIMOTHY MODEL:
Meditating on Your Calling and Gifts

WRITTEN FROM PAUL TO TIMOTHY:
"DO NOT NEGLECT THE GIFT THAT IS IN YOU,
WHICH WAS GIVEN TO YOU BY PROPHECY
WITH THE LAYING ON OF THE HANDS OF
THE ELDERSHIP. MEDITATE ON THESE THINGS;
GIVE YOURSELF ENTIRELY TO THEM, THAT
YOUR PROGRESS MAY BE EVIDENT TO ALL."
—*1 Timothy 4:14,15*

As Timothy walked to the top of the hill, he looked down on the city of Ephesus. The young preacher was not sure he could do what he was asked to do. Timothy didn't doubt God; he knew God had saved him. He grew up in a Christian home; his grandmother, Lois, and his mother, Eunice (see 2 Tim. 1:5), had instructed him in the faith. Timothy didn't doubt God; he doubted himself. Timothy had been selected as the next pastor of the church at Ephesus. He knew God had called him, but it was intimidating to pastor a church the apostle Paul and the apostle John had previously pastored.

As Timothy walked into the outskirts of this vibrant commercial town, he knew he had to evangelize the unsaved there. He had been converted by the powerful preaching of Paul (see 1 Tim. 1:2), and he knew God could save the unsaved. Could God do it through him, though?

It was a scary thing to become pastor of one of the greatest churches in the Christian world. Timothy was not sure he could do it. He knew he was young, although Paul had told him, "Let no one despise your youth" (1 Tim. 4:12).

Timothy knew Paul had started the church: "He [Paul] came to Ephesus,....he himself entered the synagogue and reasoned with the Jews" (Acts 18:19). Timothy wondered how difficult it would be to pastor people who were converted by Paul. He could not preach as well as Paul, and he did not have the power or wisdom of Paul. However, Paul had reminded Timothy, "God has not given us a spirit of fear, but of power and of love and of a sound mind. Therefore do not be ashamed" (2 Tim. 1:7,8).

Timothy knew he was not a strong pulpiteer, and the people at Ephesus had the greatest orator preaching to them: "Apollos,....an eloquent man and mighty in the Scriptures, came to Ephesus. This man had been instructed in the way of the Lord; and being fervent in spirit, he spoke and taught accurately the things of the Lord" (Acts 18:24,25).

Timothy knew he could not hold a candle to Apollos. Paul told him, however, "You therefore, my son, be strong in the grace that is in Christ Jesus. And the things that you have heard from me among many witnesses, commit these to faithful men who will be able to teach others also" (2 Tim. 2:1,2).

When Timothy prepared to preach his first sermon, he remembered the church had experienced a great revival in Ephesus. Timothy wondered if his sermon would produce any spiritual results. Revival is defined as "God pouring His presence on His people." Timothy remembered when 12 disciples of John the Baptist were the cause of atmospheric revival. "When Paul had laid hands on them, the Holy Spirit came upon them, and they spoke with tongues and prophesied. Now the men were about twelve in all" (Acts 19:6,7).

On another occasion of revival, an exorcism of demons had occurred. "This was known to all the Jews and Greeks also dwelling at Ephesus; and fear fell on them all,....And many that believed came, and confessed,....Many of them also which used curious arts brought their books together, and burned them...So mightily grew the word of God and prevailed" (Acts 19:17-20, *KJV*).

Timothy was intimidated by these past revivals. He was a second-generation believer, whereas Paul, his mentor, was a first-generation founder of Christianity. Paul wisely counseled Timothy: "Wherefore I put thee in remembrance that thou stir up the gift of God, which is in thee" (2 Tim. 1:6, *KJV*). Paul also reminded Timothy of his ordination challenge from some great men: "Neglect not the gift...which was given thee by...the laying on of the hands of the presbytery" (1 Tim. 4:14, *KJV*).

Finally, Paul reminded Timothy of his responsibility . . . not to the past . . . not to others . . . but to God. Paul told Timothy, "Preach the word;...reprove, rebuke, exhort" (2 Tim. 4:2, *KJV*).

Often our zeal to accomplish something for Christ begins with the prayer, "Lord, what do You want me to do?" (Acts 9:6). When we are scared, we pray, "Lord, what do I have to do?"

As we find a place in ministry, we may experience either joy or frustration. Those who find themselves frustrated or fearful, as Timothy did, should realize fear comes from serving God in our own strength. Strength, however, comes in knowing our spiritual gifts and knowing God has called us to ministry. As we begin to understand our calling and spiritual gifts, we can achieve greater effectiveness and personal fulfillment in ministry.

Sometimes we find ourselves feeling unfulfilled in our service for Christ. God may be blessing our ministry, yet we sense that God has more in mind for us. This poses a new question: How can I know if God has called me into this ministry?

As a young man in ministry, Timothy most likely experienced each of these questions in his own life. His zeal for serving Christ had earned him a good reputation, so much so that the apostle Paul invited him to serve with him. Through the years, Timothy proved to be a faithful worker for the cause of Christ. Still, at times he had questions and experienced personal anguish. At this point in his Christian service, Timothy had to relearn important principles about his calling and gifts.

Paul knew Timothy was struggling. How could he encourage Timothy and give him a tool to strengthen his ministry? He wrote, "Do not neglect the gift that is in you, which was given to you by prophecy with the laying on of the hands of the eldership. Meditate on these things; give yourself entirely to them, that your progress may be evident to all" (1 Tim. 4:14,15).

> When you are frustrated in service,
> Remember your gifts and calling for service.

It is possible that many questions could be answered through proper meditation or thought patterns. Paul knew that if Timothy would change his thinking, Timothy could meet the challenge in the new church. Paul called Timothy to meditate on the gifts and calling of God in his life. Paul knew "the gifts and the calling of God are irrevocable" (Rom. 11:29). This means once we acquire them, God does not take them away from us. Paul wanted Timothy to remember how God had gifted and called him. That was the key to Timothy's discovering answers to the questions he struggled with in ministry. This is the essence of the Timothy Model for meditation.

How Timothy Practiced Meditation

Earlier in the Epistle, Paul had urged Timothy "to stir up the gift of God which is in you through the laying on of my hands" (2 Tim. 1:6). From their years of association, Paul knew Timothy had spiritual potential that would make him effective in his own ministry.

So if Timothy could revive and activate his gifts in ministry, his ministry would be more effective to accomplish results.

One of the things Jesus did when He ascended into heaven was to grant spiritual gifts or abilities to people (see Eph. 4:8). These abilities to serve God are identified by a variety of names in Scripture. They are called *talents, gifts, abilities, spirituals* (original language), *works* and *operations*. When Paul addressed the Corinthians about the subject, he used five Greek words to describe the nature of these gifts (see 1 Cor. 12:1-7). Each of these words tends to emphasize a separate aspect of the Christian's spiritual ability.

First, Paul used the word *pneumatikon*, which is translated "spiritual" (v. 1). This adjective describes those gifts producing spiritual things in those who receive our ministry.

Second, Paul used the word *charismata*, which is translated "gifts" (v. 4). This term tends to emphasize that God gives gifts freely and graciously.

The word *diakonia* is the third term used to describe gifts. This word is translated "ministries" (v. 5) and reveals that our gifts serve others.

Fourth, the word *energema*, translated "activities" (v. 6), suggests gifts are an enduement of God's power or energy.

Finally, the word *phanerosis*, translated "manifestation" (v. 7), reveals that gifts are an evident manifestation of God working through us.

A young lady singing a solo in church is used of God, but everyone knows it is God's work, and not hers, that changes people's lives.

Spiritual gifts are given to Christians for several reasons. First, they equip us with tools for effective outreach ministries (see Eph. 4:12). Second, these same tools equip us to edify, encourage and care for fellow believers (v. 12). They also enable us to contribute practically to the unity of the church (v. 3). Fourth, they provide the means by which we can experience their greatest personal fulfillment in our lives. We find ourselves in ministry by using our gifts effectively (see Rom. 12:4-8). When we understand these principles, we can discover, demonstrate and develop our spiritual giftedness.

The Role of the Timothy Model in Meditation

Understanding our spiritual gifts is an important part of the process of letting God lead in our lives. God is the giver of gifts and He grants them "as He wills" (1 Cor. 12:11). The abilities He gives us are often the prime indicators of the kind of ministry He wants us to have. A person gifted in evangelism will be frustrated doing any ministry that cuts him or her off from sharing the gospel with unsaved people. Just so, a person called to teach must teach.

Beyond discovering our giftedness, we can discover God's will for our ministry in other ways. At least 12 steps will help us gain insight into how we should serve God, and where. When we implement these principles, we will have liberty to say no to the "wrong place" for us (the right place for others). We will have freedom to find the "right place" where God has called us to minister.

The first step in discerning God's will involves yielding ourselves to do God's will. Jesus said, "If anyone is willing to do God's will, that person shall know My doctrine, whether it comes from God or whether I speak on My own authority" (John 7:17, author's translation). The apostle Paul urged, "I beseech you therefore, brethren, by the mercies of God, that you present [yield] your bodies a living sacrifice, holy, acceptable to God, which is your reasonable service" (Rom. 12:1). God does not show His will to those unprepared to do it; He shows His will to those who want to do it.

Second, we can find God's will for our lives by searching the Bible. The psalmist wrote, "Your word is a lamp to my feet and a light to my path" (Ps. 119:105). The Scriptures shed light on the path God calls us to take in life. We study the Bible to understand God, His gifts, His principles for service and the person God uses.

Praying for guidance to apply God's will is the third step in the process. Throughout His teaching ministry, Jesus taught "that men always ought to pray and not lose heart" (Luke 18:1). When we lack wisdom, we are urged to "ask of God, who gives [wisdom] to all liberally and without reproach, and it will be given to him" (Jas. 1:5).

Fourth, we need to make sure our motives are pure when seeking God's will. Jesus reminded His disciples,

> "The lamp of the body is the eye. If therefore your eye is good, your whole body will be full of light. But if your eye is bad, your whole body will be full of darkness. If therefore the light that is in you is darkness, how great is that darkness!" (Matt. 6:22,23).

We need to keep our eyes focused on pleasing God if we would discern His will for our lives.

Fifth, we need to begin doing right. As we wait on God for His direction in life, we need to begin by doing what we know is right. "And do not be conformed to this world, but be transformed by the renewing of your mind, that you may prove what is that good and acceptable and perfect will of God" (Rom. 12:2).

In the sixth place, we need to face our strengths and weaknesses realistically. When God gives us a great ability in a specific area, it is probably God's will for us to use that gift in service to Him. In contrast, if we do not have ability in a specific area, that ministry is probably not God's will for us. This principle is implied in our understanding of how God has gifted us for ministry (see 1 Cor. 12:11). Some Christians do not understand God's gifts to them and complain because they are unable to do something, rather than celebrating what they *can* do for God.

The seventh step involves the results of peace. When we do the will of God, we experience inner peace. "And the peace of God, which surpasses all understanding, will guard your hearts and minds through Christ Jesus" (Phil. 4:7). Paul urged the Colossian Christians, "And let the peace of God rule in your hearts, to which also you were called in one body; and be thankful" (Col. 3:15).

Seeking spiritual counsel from godly people is the eighth step in seeking to understand God's will. "Where there is no counsel, the people fall; but in the multitude of counselors there is safety" (Prov. 11:14).

The ninth step is walking through an open door to find God's will. We need to study circumstances to determine what doors are open to us. Do not forget, some closed doors are God's NO! The open-door principle was one of the ways Paul sought to discern God's direction in his own ministry (see Acts 16:6,7; 1 Cor. 16:9).

In the tenth place, let's not move forward until we know we are following God's leading. This involves confidence or assurance. When we have honestly met every spiritual qualification and we have done everything God has told us to do—and we have confidence—then we need to move forward. "But those who wait on the Lord shall renew their strength; they shall mount up with wings like eagles, they shall run and not be weary, they shall walk and not faint" (Isa. 40:31).

The eleventh step involves the long look, or the eternal look. When making decisions about God's will, it is best to look at circumstances through God's eyes. Even when we experience current difficulties, it may be God's will for the long run. Short-term pain often leads to long-term gain. When Paul considered some of the problems he encountered in life, he concluded,

> For I am persuaded that neither death nor life, nor angels nor principalities nor powers, nor things present nor things to come, nor height nor depth, nor any other created thing, shall be able to separate us from the love of God which is in Christ Jesus our Lord (Rom. 8:38,39).

Finally, we need to be flexible about our past decisions made regarding the will of God. We may have made bad choices, mistakes, wrong turns or whatever. Like Paul, many of us would agree,

> Brethren, I do not count myself to have apprehended; but one thing I do, forgetting those things which are behind and reaching forward to those things which are ahead, I press toward the goal for the prize of the upward call of God in Christ Jesus (Phil. 3:13,14).

Ten Principles to Take Away

Considering our personal needs, it is important to identify some steps to help us follow the example of Timothy in meditation. When we begin thinking about our gifts and calling, we might try some of the following.

1. Tell God YES and yes. We begin the Christian life by saying one big YES when we surrender our lives to Jesus Christ once and for all. Then each day we tell God yes, not in the sense of our first commitment to God, but, every day we again say yes.

2. Read about the call, commitment and obedience of other believers. We will learn about God's call and gifts by studying the experience of others.

3. Sing and meditate using the historic hymns of the Christian faith. These hymns call us to a deeper commitment to Christ. The following list of hymns is derived from several popular church hymnals. As you meditate on the words to these hymns, choose one that best expresses your heart's desire.

Hymns Celebrating the Timothy Model
All for Jesus (Mary D. James)
Dare to be a Daniel (Philip P. Bliss)
Follow On (W. O. Cushing)
Have Thine Own Way, Lord (Adelaide A. Pollard)
His Way with Thee (Cyrus S. Nusbaum)
I Am Resolved (Palmer Hartsough)
I Surrender All (Judson W. VanDeVenter)
Is Your All on the Altar? (Elisha A. Hoffman)
Jesus Calls Us (Cecil F. Alexander)
Jesus, I My Cross Have Taken (Henry F. Lyte)
My Jesus, I Love Thee (William R. Featherstone)
Send the Light (Charles H. Gabriel)
Sweet Will of God (Leila N. Morris)
Take My Life and Let It Be (Frances R. Havergal)
The Call for Reapers (John O. Thompson)
We'll Work Till Jesus Comes (Elizabeth Mills)

We've a Story to Tell to the Nations (H. Ernest Nichol)
Where He Leads I'll Follow (William A. Ogden)
Wherever He Leads I'll Go (B. B. McKinney)
Work for the Night Is Coming (Annie L. Coghill)

4. The new praise and worship choruses will guide your meditation. The following list of popular praise and worship choruses identifies God's call to a deeper commitment to God. Try singing some of these choruses to express your willingness to do God's will as He makes it known.

Choruses Celebrating the Timothy Model
Above All Else (Kevin Walker/Barbara Ross)
Carry the Light (Twila Paris)
Following Jesus (L. Weaver)
Here I Am (Chris A. Bowater)
I Have Decided to Follow Jesus (Source unknown)
Jesus Be the Lord of All (Lanny Wolfe)
Jesus Is Lord of All (Gloria Gaither and
William J. Gaither)
Let God Be God in Me (Walker/Till/Walker/Ross)
My Lord Knows the Way Through the Wilderness
(Sidney E. Cox)
Shine, Jesus Shine (Graham Kendrick)
Song for the Nations (Chris Christensen)
The Greatest Thing (Mark Pendergrass)

5. Learn your spiritual giftedness. Through the years, various writers have discussed several ways we can identify our spiritual gifts. More recently, several people have developed testing instruments that help Christians discover personal areas of potential giftedness. Using a spiritual gift inventory will help you discover how God has given you abilities for ministry.

6. Ask several Christians to help you identify your gift. Educators, counselors and ministers recognize the dangers of making decisions based on limited data. Even when using a spiritual gift inventory, it is best to confirm any preliminary conclusions by using the "two or three witnesses" principle. In the Old Testament, a matter could not be confirmed legally without two or three witnesses agreeing to it (see Deut. 17:6).

7. Ask three revealing questions. These questions will help confirm any initial conclusion from a spiritual gift inventory, or anything someone else may tell you. First ask: Is this consistent with what I know about this gift? It is possible that something in your background or even the way you felt as you completed the inventory may slightly color your answers. Is it possible that a friend or minister is guilty of "gift imposing" (i.e., pushing you to do something for God that is contrary to your giftedness)?

Then ask a second question: Is the presence of this gift evident in my service and evident to other mature Christians I respect? If you possess a gift, it should be apparent at least in embryonic form to mature and spiritual Christians who know you.

The third question is: Is the exercise of this gift effective in ministry? When you use your spiritual gift, you should experience maximum effectiveness with minimum effort. What are the results?

8. Don't wait till you find your spiritual gift before you do something. This is the paralysis of analysis. Just follow your heart and serve God. Just find a need in your church and meet it.

9. Begin demonstrating your gifts. Many churches have a shortage of workers because gifted members are not using their gifts in ministry. It would probably take a single phone call to the church office to learn of several ministry opportunities available in your church that would be ideal for your spiritual gift.

Being involved in ministry will motivate you to develop your gift for greater effectiveness. Every Christian needs to continually learn more about his or her spiritual gift and develop gift-related skills that will increase the ministry.

10. Begin today looking for articles, books, seminars, workshops and other opportunities to develop your spiritual gift. If you have a gift, it can grow in effectiveness or manifestation: "Earnestly desire the best gifts" (1 Cor. 12:31). Paul told the Romans, "For I long to see you, that I may impart to you some spiritual gift" (Rom. 1:11).

As you follow the Timothy example in meditation, be sensitive to what God is attempting to tell you. God still speaks to Christians today, but not always in an audible voice. Rather, God speaks through the Bible (see Heb. 1:1-3), prayer (see Rom. 8:26, 27), circumstances (see Acts 16:6-10) and other believers in the church (see Eph. 4:15,16). God speaks through inner urges or leading (see Acts 16:6; Gal. 5:25). God is always working in our world and will invite us to join Him in His work as we are willing to yield and be sensitive to His leading in our lives.

When God makes His will known, we usually need to make adjustments to do what He invites us to do. Sometimes these changes are comparatively minor. Occasionally, they may involve something major, such as moving to a new community. Regardless of the changes required, yielding to God's revealed will puts us in the center of His blessing. As we yield, we discover that being anywhere with Jesus beats remaining in our comfort zone at the expense of distancing our relationship with God.

Suggested Scripture Passages for Meditating on Your Gifts

Acts 13:1-4	Ephesians 4:7-16
Romans 1:11-16	1 Timothy 4:11-16
Romans 11:29; 12:1-8	2 Timothy 4:1,2
1 Corinthians 12:1-11	

Prayer	Praise
1. That I would grow daily in my ability to serve God.	1. Praise God for calling me to be His child (see 1 Thess. 2:11).
2. That God would lead me to opportunities to use my gifts and serve Him.	2. Praise God for the spiritual gifts He has given me to serve Him (see 1 Cor. 7:7).
3. That I would be willing to do everything I have an opportunity to do.	3. Praise God that He has used me in the past in His service.
4. That God would use my gifts as I attempt to serve Him.	4. Praise God for opportunities to serve Him and a desire to use my gifts.
5. That God would always give me strength to serve Him (see Phil. 4:13).	5. Praise God that He considers me worthy to serve Him in this world.
6. That God would be glorified as I follow His leading and I attempt to use my gifts for Him.	6. Praise God for daily strength to do what He leads me to do.
7.	7.
8.	8.
9.	9.
10.	10.

Journaling

Many ministers keep records of their ministries (i.e., records of marriages, funerals, counseling appointments, etc.). All Christians are ministers of Jesus Christ, but they don't keep those kinds of records. Every believer, however, can assess his or her ministry and serve better by writing and keeping records.

1. Make a list of your strongest spiritual gifts (abilities) and write how you serve in using each ability.
2. Prioritize your list of gifts. Then ask if you are properly using your strongest gift. As you meditate on your strengths, you should grow more confident serving by using these gifts.
3. Make a list of your weakest gifts. These are the ones where you need growth. Assign a verse to each of them, and meditate on how they can grow (see 1 Tim. 4:15).
4. Make a list of the times God has used you in the past. Ask: Why did God use me? Also ask: How did my gifts play a part in God's service? Meditate on God's grace that used you and your gifts.
5. Pray over each of your spiritual gifts, asking God to increase your usefulness (see 1 Cor. 12:31). Meditate on how God can use your gifts in a greater way, and how you can grow your gifts.

Bible Study for Your Calling and Spiritual Gifts

1. None of us can say we have no spiritual gifts. What does this verse say to you personally?

> "But each one has his own gift from God, one in this manner and another in that."—1 Corinthians 7:7

_____
_____
_____
_____

2. What should be our attitude, knowing we are gifted by God?

> "As each one has received a gift, minister it to one another, as good stewards of the manifold grace of God."—1 Peter 4:10

_____
_____
_____
_____

3. We may develop our natural talents, but who gives us our spiritual gifts?

> "There are diversities of gifts, but the same Spirit. There are differences of ministries, but the same Lord. And there are diversities of activities, but it is the same God who works all in all."—1 Corinthians 12:4-6

_____
_____
_____
_____

4. On what basis does God give spiritual gifts or abilities to believers?

> "But one and the same Spirit works all these things, distributing to each one individually as He wills."—1 Corinthians 12:11

_____

_____

_____

_____

5. Many unsaved people have natural talents, but sometimes their abilities appear to be the same as a believer's spiritual gift. What are two ways we can know when our abilities are spiritual gifts?

> "But the manifestation of the Spirit is given to each one for the profit of all."—1 Corinthians 12:7

_____

_____

_____

_____

6. Sometimes believers are afraid to use their spiritual gifts, or for some other reason, they don't use them. What does this verse mean to you?

> "Therefore I remind you to stir up the gift of God which is in you through the laying on of my hands."—2 Timothy 1:6

_____

_____

_____

_____

7. A believer can begin using a spiritual gift that has not manifested itself in his or her life. What does this verse mean to your giftedness?

> "For I long to see you, that I may impart to you some spiritual gift, so that you may be established."—Romans 1:11

_____
_____
_____
_____

8. Part of meditating on your spiritual giftedness is remembering those who were responsible for your conversion. List those who contributed to your salvation.

> "And the things that you have heard from me among many witnesses, commit these to faithful men who will be able to teach others also."—2 Timothy 2:2

_____
_____
_____
_____

9. Four generations are mentioned in this verse. List them.

> "When I call to remembrance the genuine faith that is in you, which dwelt first in your grandmother Lois and your mother Eunice, and I am persuaded is in you also."—2 Timothy 1:5

_____
_____
_____
_____

10. Apparently Timothy received his gift as older servants of God were ministering to him. Who has helped you develop your spiritual gifts?

> "Do not neglect the gift that is in you, which was given to you by prophecy with the laying on of the hands of the eldership."—1 Timothy 4:14

_____

_____

_____

_____

11. You will not lose your gifts, nor will the call of God change. What does this verse mean to you?

"For the gifts and the calling of God are irrevocable."
—Romans 11:29

_____

_____

_____

_____

12. When we become discouraged in serving Christ, what should we remember?

"He who calls you is faithful, who also will do it."
—1 Thessalonians 5:24

_____

_____

_____

_____

Verses to Memorize and Meditate

"For the gifts and the calling of God are irrevocable."
—Romans 11:29

"He who calls you is faithful, who also will do it."
—1 Thessalonians 5:24

"Do not neglect the gift that is in you, which was given to you by prophecy with the laying on of the hands of the eldership."
—1 Timothy 4:14

"And the things that you have heard from me among many witnesses, commit these to faithful men who will be able to teach others also."—2 Timothy 2:2

"Therefore I remind you to stir up the gift of God which is in you through the laying on of my hands."—2 Timothy 1:6

"All Scripture is given by inspiration of God, and is profitable for doctrine, for reproof, for correction, for instruction in righteousness, that the man of God may be complete, thoroughly equipped for every good work."—2 Timothy 3:16,17

"As each one has received a gift, minister it to one another, as good stewards of the manifold grace of God."—1 Peter 4:10

"For I say, through the grace given to me, to everyone who is among you, not to think of himself more highly than he ought to think, but to think soberly, as God has dealt to each one a measure of faith."—Romans 12:3

Photocopy and cut these verses into small cards to carry with you for memorization and meditation.

~ 8 ~

THE HAGGAI
MODEL:
Considering Your Failures

"NOW THEREFORE, THUS SAYS THE LORD
OF HOSTS: 'CONSIDER YOUR WAYS!'"

—*Haggai 1:5*

God's people were standing in the middle of rubble and broken stones from the original Solomon's Temple. They were worshiping God in a trash heap. People were lined up to bring their sacrifices to God; they were sincere, repentant and obedient. The people did exactly what God told them to do. Each father placed his hands on the head of a lamb to confess his sins and the sins of his family. The lamb was killed and the blood was shed for the forgiveness of sins. Because God is faithful, He recognized the faith of those who shed blood for the remission of their sins.

The altar of God was located high on Mount Moriah, the site where Solomon's magnificent Temple had once stood (see 2 Chron. 3:1). Now, nothing but rubble was strewn on the hilltop. Large stones—too big for a group of men to move—were surrounded with weeds and broken columns. Trash was piled together.

The people were obedient to God, but discouraged. They had returned from the Babylonian captivity having high expectations. Darius, King of Persia, had released them from captivity, allowing them to rebuild the altar of God upon their return to their Jewish homeland. They began to dig trenches for the foundation to a second Temple. They wept unashamedly, "Many...old men who had seen the first temple, wept with a loud voice when the foundation of this temple was laid" (Ezra 3:12). They were disappointed because the second Temple was smaller than the first Temple. It wouldn't be like the Temple in the *good ol' days.* "Yet many shouted aloud for joy" (v. 12). They were the younger people who had never seen Solomon's Temple.

Unfortunately, their enemies lied to the king and stopped construction on the Temple.

As Haggai watched the people sacrifice, God spoke to him. As a result, he went to the leadership and delivered five sermons in the fall of 520 B.C. A new king had been installed in Persia who was sympathetic to the cause of rebuilding the Temple. So Haggai motivated the people to seek permission from him to finish rebuilding the Temple.

September 1, 520 B.C.

Haggai went to the Jewish headquarters to ask, "Is it time?" (Hag. 1:4). He preached, "Is it time for you yourselves to dwell in your paneled houses, and this temple to lie in ruins?" (v. 4). Haggai told the people to "consider." His favorite phrase was, "Consider your ways" (v. 5).

David meditated on God the Creator; Joshua meditated on God's Word; but Haggai wanted people to think about their failures, mistakes and sins. Haggai's message was clear:

> "You have planted big crops,
> but harvest only a little.
> You eat all the time,
> but you are not satisfied.

> You drink all the time,
> but don't enjoy it.
> You wear fine tailored clothes,
> but you are not warm.
> You earn money to fill your pocketbook,
> but it has holes.
> Why?
> Because God's house lies in ruins,
> but your homes are beautiful."
> —Haggai 1:4-6, author's translation

September 24, 520 B.C.

Haggai's sermon was a rousing success. Within 24 days, four great things occurred as a result of his sermon. Haggai had asked them to "Consider your ways." Their thoughts about their spiritual poverty and disobedience had led to tremendous results.

First, the sermon worked in the leader's heart. "The Lord stirred up the spirit of Zerubbabel...Joshua...and...the remnant of the people" (Hag. 1:14).

Second, they obeyed God's command through Haggai: "Zerubbabel...Joshua...with all the remnant of the people, obeyed the voice of the Lord their God" (v. 12).

Third, a revival took place. It was not just that the people did what their leaders decided. "The people feared the presence of the Lord" (v. 12). Revival is defined as a time when God's presence lives among His people.

Fourth, the people got busy building God's house. "They came and worked on the house of the Lord of hosts, their God" (v. 14).

October 21, 520 B.C.

Within a month, the people were discouraged again. Some slowed down their work. Others quit. Why is it that some tasks believers begin with great joy, but they quit when they become discouraged in their feelings?

God gave the discouraged people something to think or consider. "The glory of this latter house shall be greater than of the former, saith the Lord of hosts" (Hag. 2:9, *KJV*). The people probably were comparing their work (it was called Zerubbabel's Temple) to Solomon's Temple, and it did not measure up. Solomon's Temple was constructed of stone, gold and beautiful trimmings. This second Temple was just a wooden building.

People always become discouraged building a second-rate thing, especially when they remember the wonderful qualities of the first. However, they had no idea that the glory of the Temple they were building involved Jesus Christ. The glory of their Temple would not be in its construction, but when Jesus would enter their building more than 500 years later, He would bring it glory.

December 24, 520 B.C.

Haggai's fourth and fifth message came in one day (Hag. 2:10-19, and 2:20-23). Haggai again told the people, "Consider..." your sin that causes punishment, "yet you did not turn to Me" (vv. 15,17). So as they occupied the new Temple, Haggai twice used the word "Consider" to warn the people.

> "Consider from the day you dedicate this Temple, that if you want Me to bless you, don't go back to your old ways. Consider this carefully."—Haggai 2:15-18, author's translation

Consider Your Failures

It is not our failures in life that hurt us; it is the way we think about our failures that hurts us. Therefore, the prophet Haggai would tell you today, "Consider your ways." He would tell us to think about our laziness, mistakes and sins.

Separate in your thinking the kind of mistakes you make, because different kinds of mistakes bring different consequences. First come the intentional mistakes; these are the mistakes we plan to make. An example could be the woman who plans to cut corners in cleaning her house to save time. When she is caught by others who notice the dirty house, she is embarrassed. Sometimes in our Christian lives we cut corners—we may stop giving our tithes; we may stop attending church; we may stop separating ourselves from a particular sin.

Second is the unintentional mistake. An example could be when we forget to pick up our clothes from the cleaners. We may have nothing else to wear so we may need to quickly wash something else at home or wear something dirty. We didn't mean to do it, but, nevertheless, we pay the consequences.

Our attitude toward intentional mistakes should be different from our attitude toward unintentional mistakes. Although our attitude is always important, we must begin thinking properly to overcome both mistakes. If we make an intentional mistake, we must confess it (see 1 John 1:9), ask forgiveness, repent, then do the right thing. If we have made unintentional mistakes, we must realize that our hearts were innocent. So we must recognize what we did wrong, pay the consequences, then do the right thing.

Process for Thinking About Your Mistakes

How to Consider Your Mistakes[1]

1. Mess up.
2. Blow up.
3. Cover up.
4. Back up.
5. Slow up.
6. Wake up.
7. Smell the coffee.

1. Mess up. Everyone messes up. This is not the same as sinning. "Mess up" is the human expression, "To err is human." Usually, we mess up early in a problem, and sometimes the things we do to mess up have much larger ramifications than the problem itself. Why? Because of two future problems. First, if we mess up after we have committed a mistake, the problem gets larger. Second, if we mess up once, we will mess up again.

As an example—my opinion is that young couples who are in deep financial trouble don't just need more money to help them get out of debt. Their faulty thinking about money may just put them right back into bankruptcy. They need guidance to help them change their thinking about balancing their budget and about their purchases. Haggai would tell the couple, "Consider your ways."

2. Blow up. After we have made a mistake, we usually get mad (i.e., we get mad at ourselves or we get mad at someone else). We get mad because we have to change a tire in the snow, or we get mad because someone causes us to be late. When we are controlled by emotions, we cannot properly handle our problems.

> Ignorant eyes are blinded by fears,
> Emotional eyes are blinded by tears.

A wife who is mad at her husband for dropping the groceries, and cannot control her anger, may in spite not immediately pick up the plastic milk carton before it is all spilled. A man may be deeply in love with a woman, and as a result can't see her faults. If he can't control his anger after marriage, these faults may ultimately destroy his marriage.

What should you do when you make a mistake? Anger is not a good route, nor is it an alternate route; anger is a terrible route. When you get angry at your mistake, you have blinded yourself to solving the problem. When you blow up, you resort to anger, rationalization, compensation, blaming others, blaming self and/or denying responsibility for the problem. Whatever you do, being angry is the wrong response.

John Maxwell says, "Our reaction to the mistake we make, usually makes the mistake bigger than it initially was."

> When you emotionally react and give up,
> Your mistakes are exaggerated and they blow up.

~ 184 ~

When we make a mistake such as being late, forgetful or we just don't do a good job, we often blame other people. When they hear that we blame them, and they know they are innocent, they get mad at us and break relationship with us. As a result, the original mistake is now compounded—it is twice the size and has twice the consequences.

3. Cover up. When we cover up our mistakes, we usually try to make people think well of us; we don't want them to laugh at us . . . or quit liking us . . . or fire us.

Jerry Falwell has preached that Watergate would have been different if Nixon had handled the problem in a Christian way. Nixon could have simply said he knew about the burglary, but didn't stop it. Falwell has said America would have forgiven Nixon, but because of Nixon's cover-up he lost the presidency.

Recently, a female pilot in the U.S. Air Force was forced to resign because she had a sexual affair with a member of the opposite sex. Many Americans might have forgiven her for the sexual affair, although they are against sexual infidelity. She was forced to resign her commission, though, because she lied about the affair and tried to cover it up. She was not forced out of the Air Force because of her sexual affair, but because of her cover-up.

Usually our mistakes don't sink us; the way we respond to our mistakes puts us under. So when the Bible offers us a new way of thinking, it is not just to think about our new life in Christ. We must think differently about our sins and failures. We must think about God's way to solve them.

4. Back up. Too often after making a mistake we tend to put distance between ourselves and the mistake. Sometimes we turn our backs on the mistake as though it didn't happen. Sometimes we put the mistake out of mind as though it were not there. Other times we walk around the block not to face people involved in our mistake. Whether we are embarrassed because of our mistakes, or whether we can't face them, we hurt ourselves by not confronting the problems.

5. Slow up. When we make mistakes in our churches or businesses, and we will not face up to our problems, we slow up. This means we lose the people's respect who know about it, or we lose loyalty among those who work for us. Our mistakes slow down our incentive to work. When we become "mistake obsessed," we lose our stamina. The people following us also slow down, and like a boat dragging an anchor, our whole life slows down.

If you make a mistake at work, and do not handle it properly, it will kill the momentum in your office. If you make a mistake with your child, and don't handle that mistake properly, it can kill harmony in the home. You might even hurt the spiritual growth of your child.

When a parent makes a mistake with a child, specifically in spiritual areas of life, and then the parent refuses to admit his or her mistake, the child may lose the desire to serve God. The parents did two things wrong: first, they made a mistake, and second, they handled it wrong.

6. Wake up. Haggai tells us to "consider" our faults and sin, then "wake up." Something begins to happen when we think about our problems. We think about the consequences, we think about the people involved and we think about our own spiritual lives. After giving deep thought, we should wake up and do something about it.

When you come to the *wake up* place, it doesn't mean you have overcome your problem, or that you are now on "easy street." Coming to the *wake up* place is simply a fork in the road that points you in two different directions. First, you take the high road and go to a whole new level of living. The rules of the high road involve knowing how to solve problems and knowing how to grow in Christ. The second fork in the road is the low road. We can blame others, deny responsibility or try to ignore the problem, hoping it will go away.

The *wake up* section makes you think differently about your problem. This is where you can make a spiritual breakthrough. The prodigal son came to himself while feeding pigs in the pigpen, and suddenly realized that the servants in his father's house ate better food than he was getting . . . the prodigal son was eating husks along with the pigs. His thinking, or his meditation, brought him to a *spiritual breakthrough*. We can never have a *spiritual break-*

through until we can admit that we have messed up. *Spiritual breakthrough* begins in the mind.

What is a *spiritual breakthrough?* A breakthrough does not happen when you try to justify yourself, exonerate yourself, defend yourself, hide responsibility and deny ownership of a problem. When you take responsibility for a problem, however, others recognize your spirit, and those who love you will rally around you . . . forgive you . . . accept you . . . and work with you.

7. Smell the coffee. The *wake up stage*, which is the fork in the road, will make you or break you. When you get to the *wake up stage*, you either give up or you move up and smell the coffee. You give up when you become overwhelmed by your mistakes. You move up and smell the coffee when you acknowledge your weakness, and confess your sin to God and ask others for forgiveness. According to John Maxwell, the three most difficult words to say are,

> I WAS WRONG.

Learning from Our Mistakes

Everyone makes mistakes. The question remains: Will we learn from our mistakes? The greatest mistake we can make in life is to be afraid of mistakes. This causes us to do nothing because we are afraid we will make mistakes.

> ### Considering Our Mistakes Differently
> Mistakes are friends that help me see myself.
> Mistakes are keys that unlock the door of opportunity.
> Mistakes are windows that help me look at the world.
> Mistakes are prophecies that help me understand
> the future.
> Mistakes are highways that take me where I want to go.
> Mistakes are teachers that give me insight into life.
> Mistakes are poetry that help me see how
> things fit together.
> Mistakes are the paint I use for the portrait of my life.

What is the worst mistake of all? It is not what we do wrong; it is not what we do halfway right—the greatest mistake of all is doing nothing. A baseball player once said, "I never hit a home run with the bat on my shoulder."

When we are afraid to make mistakes, we have paralyzed our life and thinking. The world is full of people who are afraid to make mistakes. The only problem is that they may work for people who are not afraid to make mistakes. We need to develop an attitude of learning from the mistakes of other people. This involves a mind-set that first of all wants to overcome mistakes, and second of all, a mind that is open to methods of learning how to overcome mistakes.

> If I had my life to live over again,
> I would make the same mistakes . . . quicker.
> If I had my life to live over again,
> I would learn from my mistakes . . . sooner.

Someone has said that we should learn from the mistakes of other people. Why? Because we can never live long enough to learn all the mistakes by ourselves.

A child never learns to walk without falling down. As a matter of fact, falling down is part of the process of learning to walk. If you spank a baby because he falls down, he will not want to walk again. If you only "cuddle" the baby because he falls down, he may not want to get up again.

Don't make the same mistake more than once. Bear Bryant said we can do three things with a mistake. First, admit it; second, learn from it; and third, don't repeat it.

John Maxwell says, "There are two types of people in this world you want to avoid. First, the man who never makes a mistake because he is not honest, and second is the man who makes the same mistake twice, because he is not learning."

It is not the size of our mistakes that destroys us. Some people think if they make very few mistakes, or at least make small ones, they might succeed in life. Not necessarily so. Some people have made big mistakes, and made them as many as 10 times, but they knew how to overcome them. Many of today's millionaires have filed for bankruptcy at least once.

> It is not the size of your mistakes that makes you a failure;
> It is the size of your heart that makes you a success.

In the years following Israel's Babylonian captivity, a small remnant returned to the land of promise. They were a beaten, discouraged group called a "remnant." They began rebuilding the Temple to worship God, but times were difficult and the task never really got off the ground. Years later, conditions improved so they built beautiful homes for themselves. The Temple site continued to be covered in the rubble. An obscure prophet named Haggai appeared on the scene repeating three words that changed their lives. "Consider your ways" (Hag. 1:5,7).

When we follow the Haggai Model of meditation, we follow the example of a prophet who motivated people to "consider their ways." This creates a two-fold result: first, it deepens our understanding of God; second, it challenges us to make significant changes in our lives. Meditating about God in abstract ways will produce few results. However, when we follow the Haggai example, God changes us.

How Haggai Practiced Meditation

The message of Haggai was simple and straight to the point: "Consider your ways" (Hag. 1:5,7). He called the people of his day to think about their failures and mistakes. He claimed they would gain insight to change their lives. In its simplicity, the message was really profound. As he spoke to those gathered in Jerusalem, Haggai suggested three areas in which they needed to consider their ways.

First, we need to consider our priorities. The remnant had claimed to value God above all things, but a quick reality check indicated they were spending more money on their homes, while neglecting the place where they worshiped God. While complaining the economy was not good enough to build the Temple, they had managed to raise enough money to provide nice wainscoting for their homes. What they said and what they did were incompatible with each other.

Second, we need to consider our religious community. Again, the remnant claimed their relationship with God was the most important thing in their lives, but they found it easier to entertain family and friends than to find the time to worship God. Now Haggai called them to work together for their God.

Finally, we need to consider our faith context. The remnant was apparently guilty of professing faith, but living selfishly. Each morning they probably recited the Shema, reminding themselves of God's priority. Even a glance, however, revealed that in many areas of their lives God was not the priority.

When Haggai called the remnant to think about the way they were living, he also called them to change. When they recognized inconsistencies between their faith and practice, it was time to change their practice. Haggai's message was not lost on the people. "Then Zerubbabel...and Joshua...with all the remnant of the people, obeyed the voice of the Lord their God, and the words of Haggai the prophet, as the Lord their God had sent him; and the people feared the presence of the Lord" (1:12). Within a month, work on the Temple had begun again.

Ten Steps to Apply the Haggai Model

1. **Consider your failures and make a list of them.** Before you can change your life and overcome your mistakes, you need to know what they are. Repentance remains part of the process of trusting Christ for salvation. Although repentance alone cannot save, faith without repentance is not saving faith. Only as we apply the Haggai example and "consider our ways" will we recognize our need, repent of our sin and trust Christ and His finished work on Calvary for our salvation. Then, as Christians, we need to periodically take inventory and repent of sin we have allowed to creep into our lives.

2. **Ask yourself the three historic questions Haggai asked.** First, ask yourself: What is the purpose of living my life and what are my

core values? Christians are often guilty of expressing one faith with their lips and practicing another kind of faith in the way they live. The person who spends a hundred dollars on the latest video game and complains about spending half that amount for a new study Bible is making a vivid statement about his or her real core values in life.

The second question is: What do my relationships with others tell me about my relationship with God? Christians should allow their relationships with God to spill over into other relationships. Do you spend many hours visiting friends regularly, but can never find time to spend with God in the morning? Do your personal friendships tend to hinder rather than help in your walk with God? Once again, your actions speak loudly.

The third question speaks to the heart of your faith. Are your actions consistent with the faith you profess in God?

3. Read practical books that will teach you principles to solve problems and overcome failures. One of the best tools to help you is learning from the thinking of others.

4. Search for historic hymns. As you read and think about the statements in the hymns listed, they can help guide your thoughts about overcoming problems, mistakes and sins. The following list of hymns is derived from several popular church hymnals.

Hymns Celebrating the Haggai Model
Cleanse Me (J. Edwin Orr)
Grace Greater Than Our Sin (Julia H. Johnston)
I Am Coming, Lord (Lewis Hartsough)
Jesus, I Come (William T. Sleeper)
Jesus Is Calling (Fanny J. Crosby)
Just As I Am (Charlotte Elliott)
Lord, I'm Coming Home (William J. Kirkpatrick)
Pass Me Not (Fanny J. Crosby)
Room at the Cross for You (Ira F. Stanphill)
Softly and Tenderly (Will L. Thompson)
The Cleansing Wave (Phoebe Palmer)
Whiter Than Snow (James Nicholson)

---

5. Search for new praise choruses. The new praise and worship choruses of the church will start you thinking about overcoming problems and sins. The following list identifies many that celebrate what God has done for people. Try singing one or two of these choruses as you "consider" the Haggai Model into your personal meditation.

Choruses Celebrating the Haggai Model

Cares Chorus (Kelly Willard)

Change My Heart, O God (Eddie Espinosa)

Fill My Cup, Lord (Richard Blanchard)

He Is Lord (Traditional)

Here I Am (Chris A. Bowater)

Humble Thyself in the Sight of the Lord (Bob Hudson)

Jesus, Lord to Me (Greg Nelson/Gary McSpadden)

Spirit of the Living God (Daniel Iverson)

Take Me In (Dave Browning)

---

6. Make a list of your biggest mistakes in life. As you think about the mistakes you have made, focus on the lessons you have learned about how God wants you to live. The list might discourage some, so always add a positive ending to each problem you have faced. Write about what you learned from your mistake or problem.

7. Make a list of all the lessons you want to learn. Dreams are easy, but it will be difficult to write down how you want your dream fulfilled. Take each item on that list and break it down into achievable steps. These are the specific things God wants us to "consider."

Maybe your list is large. It will not get any smaller by ignoring it. The only way to reduce the size of your list is to begin doing something. As you review the list, ask yourself which of those things can be done first. Little by little, the task can be completed. As you begin making changes, you will achieve the *spiritual breakthrough* available to those who "consider their ways."

Still, sometimes a long list can be discouraging. When you find yourself tempted to put the list on hold for a while, stop and consider carefully. Perhaps you will hear the distant echo of an obscure old prophet. If you are quiet enough, you can almost identify his words: "Consider your ways!"

8. Questions to "consider." It is always good to ask yourself questions. Don't always ask the easy questions; they won't make you grow. Use the following questions to make you think.

Questions to Think About

1. What was the mistake?
2. Why did I do it?
3. How can I fix it?
4. What did I learn from it?

---

9. Share what you have learned with someone else. Share what you did right so others can learn from you, and share what you did wrong, so you can keep them from making the same mistakes.

10. Read how others overcame failure and problems. Amy Carmichael, one of the greatest hymn writers of all time, was blind. Moses, God's orator who preached the book of Deuteronomy, stuttered. Alexander Graham Bell failed many times before inventing the telephone, so did Thomas Edison before inventing the phonograph. I once wrote a book about how average men had planted successful churches but had no financial support. I named the book, *Getting A Church Started In The Face Of Insurmountable Odds With Limited Resources In Difficult Places.* I knew no one would remember the title of the book, but I also knew they would not forget the concept (i.e., that God planted churches through average men who wouldn't give up). What God has done for others, He can do for you.

Suggested Scripture Passages for Meditation About Problem Solving

---

Haggai 1:3-11	Romans 10:17-21
Haggai 2:14-19	1 Corinthians 5:1-13
Acts 6:1-7	1 John 1:7—2:11
	Acts 15:1-27

Prayer	Praise
1. That I may understand why I make mistakes and fail in life, then accept them without discouragement.	1. Praise God that He has given me a desire to overcome past failures and a desire never to repeat them again.
2. That I may have optimism to look beyond my failures to do everything better in the future.	2. Praise God for His unconditional forgiveness and His constant restoration.
3. That I may develop positive thinking patterns so I can always overcome mistakes.	3. Praise God for all He has taught me through my failures.
4. That I will always seek God's forgiveness for intentional sins and learn from them.	4. Praise God for His faithfulness to punish me when I have gone astray.
5. That God would help me fix everything in life I have broken, help me restore everyone I have offended, and help me victoriously overcome every bad habit that leads to mistakes.	5. Praise God that He has provided a way for me to grow so I don't have to make the same mistakes in the future.
6. That I may share with others the wonderful truths I am learning about His name.	6. Praise God that He has not rejected me for my failures, nor flushed me out of His blessings because of my mistakes.
7.	7.
8.	8.

Journaling

Sometimes it is easy to keep a list of our failures because they hurt so much. Like scars, they are easy to remember. However, we should write about our mistakes and failures—to forget them—just as we should write about our victories—to remember them.

Write some of the following things about your failures/mistakes so you can learn from them and never repeat them.

1. Make a list of your most embarrassing failures/mistakes. Why were they embarrassing at the time? What have you learned? How would you handle the problem today?
2. Make a list of the greatest lessons you have learned from your failures/mistakes. Why are these lessons great? How have you changed inwardly? What changes have people seen in you?
3. How have failures/mistakes changed your thinking? Are you more or less afraid of challenges today? Are you more or less disgusted about your failures/mistakes today?
4. Write down what God is teaching you about the overcoming life of Christian victory.
5. Meditate on God's reaction to your problems. Write what you think God feels, does and thinks. The best way to solve a problem is to write a note to yourself, explaining what God wants you to do to get rid of your problem. Add a P.S. Write down the reasons for God's solutions.

Bible Study for Overcoming Failures/Problems

1. How many people will have problems/failures in their lives?

> "'Yet man is born to trouble, as the sparks fly upward.'"
> —Job 5:7
> "'Man who is born of woman is of few days and full of trouble.'"—Job 14:1

_____
_____
_____
_____

2. We will never have problem-free lives, but we should never worry about problems before they happen. What should be our attitude?

> "'Therefore do not worry about tomorrow, for tomorrow will worry about its own things. Sufficient for the day is its own trouble.'"—Matthew 6:34

_____
_____
_____
_____

3. What can we learn from the trials that come to us?

> "My brethren, count it all joy when you fall into various trials, knowing that the testing of your faith produces patience."—James 1:2,3

_____
_____
_____

4. What should our problems and failures teach us?

> "And not only that, but we also glory in tribulations, knowing that tribulation produces perseverance; and perseverance, character; and character, hope."—Romans 5:3,4

_____

5. What is the first step in developing a problem-solving strategy to handle life?

> "If any of you lacks wisdom, let him ask of God, who gives to all liberally and without reproach, and it will be given to him."—James 1:5

_____

6. We should develop principles to overcome our mistakes. Where can we get help to develop our principles of life?

> "He who walks with wise men will be wise, but the companion of fools will be destroyed."—Proverbs 13:20
> "Plans are established by counsel; by wise counsel wage war."— Proverbs 20:18

_____

7. Several steps can help us develop an approach to problem solving. Write the following in your own words:

- Get all the facts.
- Establish biblical principles.
- Evaluate the facts.
- List the various solutions to your problems.
- Choose the best possible solution.

_____
_____
_____

8. Paul prayed for a problem/trial to be taken away. God did not answer his prayer. How can Paul's response be our response?

"'My grace is sufficient for you, for My strength is made perfect in weakness.'"—2 Corinthians 12:9,10

_____
_____
_____
_____

9. What is one of God's purposes in allowing problems to come into our lives?

"In this you greatly rejoice, though now for a little while, if need be, you have been grieved by various trials, that the genuineness of your faith, being much more precious than gold that perishes, though it is tested by fire, may be found to praise, honor, and glory at the revelation of Jesus Christ."—1 Peter 1:6,7

_____
_____
_____
_____

10. How does God use problems to accomplish His purpose in our lives?

> "And we know that all things work together for good to those who love God, to those who are the called according to His purpose." —Romans 8:28

_____

11. God will not abandon us in our problems. What can we expect from God in our problems?

> "And our hope for you is steadfast, because we know that as you are partakers of the sufferings, so also you will partake of the consolation." —2 Corinthians 1:7

_____

12. Conclude this Bible study with prayer. How will you praise God?

> "I will praise the Lord according to His righteousness, and will sing praise to the name of the Lord Most High." —Psalm 7:17

_____

Note

1. This outline is taken from an *Injoy* audiotape by John Maxwell.

Verses to Memorize and Meditate

"Blessed is the man who endures temptation; for when he has been approved, he will receive the crown of life which the Lord has promised to those who love Him."—James 1:12

"No temptation has overtaken you except such as is common to man; but God is faithful, who will not allow you to be tempted beyond what you are able, but with the temptation will also make the way of escape, that you may be able to bear it."
—1 Corinthians 10:13

"But if we walk in the light as He is in the light, we have fellowship with one another, and the blood of Jesus Christ His Son cleanses us from all sin."—1 John 1:7

"If we confess our sins, He is faithful and just to forgive us our sins and to cleanse us from all unrighteousness."—1 John 1:9

"'Man who is born of woman is of few days and full of trouble.'"—Job 14:1

"Now therefore, thus says the Lord of hosts: 'Consider your ways!'"—Haggai 1:5

"Beloved, do not think it strange concerning the fiery trial which is to try you, as though some strange thing happened to you."—1 Peter 4:12

"That the genuineness of your faith, being much more precious than gold that perishes, though it is tested by fire, may be found to praise, honor, and glory at the revelation of Jesus Christ."
—1 Peter 1:7

Photocopy and cut these verses into small cards to carry with you for memorization and meditation.

~9~

THE ASAPH
MODEL:
Meditating on God's Intervention

"IN THE DAY OF MY TROUBLE I SOUGHT THE
LORD;...AND WAS TROUBLED; I COMPLAINED,
AND MY SPIRIT WAS OVERWHELMED. AND I SAID,
'THIS IS MY ANGUISH; BUT I WILL REMEMBER
THE YEARS OF THE RIGHT HAND OF THE MOST
HIGH.' I WILL ALSO MEDITATE ON ALL YOUR
WORK, AND TALK OF YOUR DEEDS."

—*Psalm 77:2,3,10,12*

A gentle wind brushed the newly erected Tabernacle in Jerusalem. Thousands upon thousands of people were crowded into every possible viewing spot. Multitudes were waiting to see the approach of the Ark of God. God's people had come to Jerusalem from every town, farm and tribe of Israel. Everyone wanted to be there when the Ark of God was brought into the city of God. They were packed on top of the walls, on tops of houses, and sitting on every rock that gave them a view of the highway into Jerusalem.

The crowd was as silent as a still pond of water. The people were instructed not to speak until the Ark of God appeared. They stood silently as the eternal hills quietly wait for the dawn. They waited for the signal to shout.

Every eye was on Asaph, a priest who was lead singer of Israel. Asaph had been appointed by David to lead the musicians because he was loyal to King David when Saul pursued him in the wilderness. Asaph had run through the woods with David as King Saul had tried to murder David. Because of Asaph's loyalty, King David had placed him in charge of the musical celebration. David could depend on Asaph to glorify God with thunderous singing.

Now, more people than Asaph had ever seen in his life were silently watching. Anticipation whispered into Asaph's ear that this was the event for which he was born. Asaph, who had been ostracized from the city of Jerusalem, was now in charge of the people of Jerusalem. Asaph, who had seen suffering, trouble and danger, was now God's singer. Many times he had almost been killed. As Asaph waited for King David's procession to appear on the road below, he thought of the times he had almost been killed.

But as for me, my feet were almost gone,
my steps had almost slipped.
I was envious of those who opposed God,
I saw their prosperity,
I saw they had no danger.
They are not in trouble, as others who have problems,
They are men of pride,
They are men of violence.
Then I understood their end when I went into the
Sanctuary of God,
My enemy's place is slippery,

My enemy will be cast down.
Who have I in heaven, but God my strength,
It is good to draw near to God,
It is good to put trust in Him.
—Palm 73, author's translation

Asaph had suffered sorrow and disappointment. Today, however, multitudes of thousands would praise God, and he would lead them. Asaph had been faithful to David because he knew David was anointed king by God. Because Asaph had been faithful, now he was exalted.

David and the Ark appeared down below in the valley. Priests in white linen were carrying the Ark of God on staves upon their shoulders. David, dressed in a white linen tunic, danced joyfully before the Ark.

Asaph pointed to hundreds of priests—standing at attention upon the walls of Jerusalem—standing in perfect formation. They lifted silver trumpets to their puckered lips, ready to signal the entrance of the Ark of God into the eternal city of peace.

When Asaph struck the cymbal, the trumpets blasted a triumphant note. The Levitical singers lifted their voices. The silent crowd erupted into thunderous praise. The noise erupted out of Jerusalem, over the walls and down the mountainside, like a boiling pot that spills its contents into the fire.

David heard the bombastic greetings. He danced before the Lord all the more.

Asaph never forgot the day the Ark of God was brought into the Temple. At the end of the celebration, and within everyone's view, David turned to Asaph to commission him to minister before the Ark of God. Only Asaph had the privilege to sacrifice morning and evening before the Ark. Thousands of other priests would sacrifice for the hundreds of thousands of worshipers in the Tabernacle, but only Asaph would sacrifice before the Ark of God. This was the greatest privilege in Israel. Asaph wrote a psalm in response:

> For promotion comes neither from the east,
> nor from the west,
> God is the all-knowing Judge,
> God puts one down,
> God puts another up,
> In God's hand is a cup, He pours the same on all,
> The wicked drinks, and is cut off,
> The righteous drinks, and is exalted.
> —Psalm 75, author's translation

From that day on, Asaph lived in the presence of God and supervised the priests of God. He had oversight of singers, musicians and Levites who served God in the Tabernacle. That night as Asaph lay upon his bed, he remembered the cold, lonely days in the open fields, separated from family, home and the Tabernacle of God. Asaph wrote a psalm:

> I remember, in times of trouble, my songs in the night,
> I prayed constantly to the Lord,
> Will you cast me away forever,
> Is your mercy gone forever?
> I remember in infirmity, God's right hand protected me,
> I remembered His past wonders,
> I meditated all night on His works.
> —Psalm 77, author's translation

For the rest of his life, Asaph was faithful to the Lord in service to the Ark of God. Twelve psalms are attributed to Asaph, or to the "Sons of Asaph." He was called the Chief Musician by David and by Solomon in the years of Israel's greatest power. The Sons of Asaph continued to serve after he died, until Jeduthun (see 2 Chron. 35:15). Some historians believe the Sons of Asaph continued into and through the exile. Psalms 74, 79, 81 and 83 could have been written by the Sons of Asaph during the Babylonian captivity. A few think Asaph wrote these psalms by prophecy, perhaps out of his reflection when he and David were exiled from Jerusalem.

The Psalms of Asaph

50 God, Our Mighty Judg

73 Understanding Successful Sinners

74 A Cry for Help

75 The Triumph of the Righteous

76 The Victorious Power of God

77 Remembering God's Mighty Works

78 God's Work on Behalf of Israel

79 Praying for God's Judgments

80 Pleading for God's Favor

81 A Call to Worship

82 God and the Judges

83 A Prayer Against Enemies

It is only natural that past acts of God become our starting point in meditating on God Himself. In good times, celebrate the work of God in your midst. In difficult times, recall the work of God in past generations. It will encourage you to continue trusting in God. In one of Asaph's psalms he confessed, "I have considered the days of old, the years of ancient times. I call to remembrance my song in the night; I meditate within my heart, and my spirit makes diligent search" (Ps. 77:5,6). When you choose an interventional act of God as a starting point in your meditation, you are following the Asaph Model.

How Asaph Practiced Meditation

For Asaph, meditating on the mighty acts of God in Israel's past was a means of overcoming discouragement. He wrote, "'This is my anguish; but I will remember the years of the right hand of the Most High.' I will remember the works of the Lord; surely I will remember Your wonders of old. I will also meditate on all Your work, and talk of Your deeds"(Ps. 77:10-12). His meditation worked so well that he saw it as the key for others to experience a steadfast hope in God. "That they may set their hope in God, and not forget the works of God, but keep His commandments" (78:7).

1. In anxiety turn to God. The Asaph Model often begins from a sense of personal frustration, anxiety and anguish. Asaph realized God knew his heart and God knew how he really felt about the difficult times in which he lived. Although Asaph might be able to hide his personal frustrations from others, he knew he could not hide them from God. Further, he had no good reason to hide his anxiety from God. Perhaps he understood God often gives people a holy dissatisfaction with their circumstance to motivate them to turn to Him. That being the case, Asaph's anguish became a starting point to consider what God had in store for him in the days ahead.

2. Meditate on God's past work. One way to prepare for challenging problems is to meditate on the things God has done through the lives of others who lived before you. As Asaph meditated on "all" the works of God, he gave special attention to at least three specific kinds of work.

First, he described these works as the "years of the right hand of the Most High." The right hand of God usually represents the strength of God as the possessor of heaven and earth. Remember the potential strength God has and what He has the potential to do.

Second, Asaph meditated on the "works of the Lord." These works grew from the unique covenant God had made with Israel. This is the way God providentially blessed Israel.

In the third place, Asaph meditated on His "wonders of old." These included those works or miracles that tended to overwhelm those who saw them, causing them to stand back in wonderment.

Characteristics of God for Meditation

1. The strength of God
2. The providential care of God
3. The past miracles of God

---

3. Obey what is meditated. For Asaph, an important part of meditation involved keeping the commandments of God. Many of the promises of God in Scripture may be described as conditional promises. Although God is always ready and willing to honor His

Word, God has restricted Himself in granting some promises only when His people obey Him. This means certain promises of God have conditions. As Asaph prayed for God to work in and through him, He remembered the commandments that had conditions. Asaph claimed the promise, "Turn us again, O God of hosts, and cause thy face to shine; and we shall be saved" (see Ps. 80:3,7,19, *KJV*). God's promise to shine on Israel was connected to the following: "So will not we go back from thee" (v. 18, *KJV*).

4. Share what is meditated. Meditating on the mighty acts of God in the past helped Asaph recognize God at work in his own life and ministry. Therefore, part of his meditation included a commitment to share with others what God was doing in his life. "So we, Your people and sheep of Your pasture, will give You thanks forever; we will show forth Your praise to all generations" (79:13). This commitment to share his testimony with others was an act of faith because it was made when he had no testimony to share.

The Role of the Asaph Model in Meditation

Although the Asaph Model is named in honor of one psalmist, his model of meditation was widely practiced in Scripture. One reason may have been its many benefits. Using the Asaph Model in our personal meditation may prove to be the key to achieving a spiritual breakthrough in at least seven areas.

First, the Asaph Model is one key to overcoming fear. It will help us trust God in the midst of a challenging situation. Moses reminded Israel as they prepared to enter the Promised Land,

> "If you should say in your heart, 'These nations are greater than I; how can I dispossess them?'—you shall not be afraid of them, but you shall remember well what the Lord your God did to Pharaoh and to all Egypt: the great trials which your eyes saw, the signs and the wonders, the mighty hand and the outstretched arm, by which the Lord your God brought you out. So shall the Lord your God do to all the peoples of whom you are afraid" (Deut. 7:17-19).

The intervention of God on their behalf in the past should have encouraged them that God would do the same in the future. God's mighty acts include not only how He has blessed His people in the past, but also how He has judged them. The promise that many believers claim, "Great is thy faithfulness" (Lam. 3:23, *KJV*), is His faithfulness to punish His people when they sin. Remembering how God has handled sin in the past reminds us how serious God is about our living a holy life.

Second, the Asaph Model is a strong motive to serve God. The prophet Samuel told Israel, "'Only fear the Lord, and serve Him in truth with all your heart; for consider what great things He has done for you'" (1 Sam. 12:24). God's past works demonstrate He is trustworthy and that serving Him has its own rewards.

Third, the Asaph Model results in our having greater confidence in the Scriptures. This principle is emphasized in a verse that occurs twice in Scripture. "Remember His marvelous works which He has done, His wonders, and the judgments of His mouth" (1 Chron. 16:12; Ps. 105:5).

Fourth, the Asaph Model is a call to worship. The psalmist invited worshipers, "Come, behold the works of the Lord, who has made desolations in the earth" (Ps. 46:8). This invitation was then followed by the exhortation, "Be still, and know that I am God; I will be exalted among the nations, I will be exalted in the earth!" (v. 10).

Fifth, meditating on the mighty works of God also gives us greater insight into the character of God. "He has made His wonderful works to be remembered; the Lord is gracious and full of compassion" (Ps. 111:4). Asaph had trouble understanding some things in his life, "Until I went into the sanctuary of God; then I understood" (73:17).

Sixth, the Asaph Model gives us insight into the Scriptures. The psalmist recognized this relationship when he prayed, "Make me understand the way of Your precepts; so shall I meditate on Your wonderful works" (Ps. 119:27).

Ultimately, thinking about the way God has worked in your past stimulates you to a personal thirst for God. "I remember the days of old; I meditate on all Your works; I muse on the work of Your hands. I spread out my hands to You; my soul longs for You like a thirsty land. Selah" (Ps. 143:5,6). Perhaps the greatest value in using the works of God as a starting point in our meditation is that it creates this hunger for a deeper relationship with God Himself.

Ten Steps to Apply the Asaph Model

1. Read how God has intervened in history. Much of the Bible is written to record the normal events in the history of God's people. God, however, also intervened by preparing special works for His purpose and glory. When the churches in Galatia began to wander from the simplicity of the gospel, Paul devoted two chapters in the brief Epistle to the Galatians to remind them of the Jerusalem controversy so they could understand the history of the problem they were causing (see Gal. 1—2). A history of the Early Church was written to show how God intervened time and again to glorify Himself (see Acts).

Recording history has continued to be the practice of Christians throughout the centuries. The oldest extant history of the Church was produced by the church father Eusebius, who recorded the work of God in the Early Church. In this sense, history becomes His Story.

Some recorded histories tell the story of God working in very dark hours of the Christian Church. Perhaps the best known is John Foxe's *Book of Martyrs*, recording the persecution of Christians for the cause of Christ. This is a record of the dying grace they received from God at their moment of need.

2. Read magazines, journals, letters and other written accounts. Both home and foreign missionaries, as well as other ministers of God, tell how God has intervened in their lives. Books such as the *Journal* of David Brainard have been used to promote revival in communities where they were widely read. As some read the stories of growing churches, they have practiced the same principles and built new churches. The same has happened as people describe answers to prayer; it motivates to further prayer.

3. Biographies and testimonial accounts of Christian leaders also motivate people to meditate on God. Many of these books describe the struggles of men and women to trust God in terms you can identify. As you read how God used others, you are encouraged to believe that God may have something special He wants to do in and through your life.

4. Historic hymns tell of God's intervention. As you read and sing the statements in the listed hymns, you are reminded not only of the experience of the hymn writer, but also of your own experience with God. The following hymns are derived from several church hymnals in hopes that several may be included in your worship of God.

Hymns Celebrating the Asaph Model

All That Thrills My Soul (Thoro Harris)

All the Way My Savior Leads Me (Fanny J. Crosby)

Amazing Grace (John Newton)

At Calvary (William R. Newell)

Blessed Assurance (Fanny J. Crosby)

Fill My Cup, Lord (Richard Blanchard)

He Keeps Me Singing (Luther B. Bridgers)

He Leadeth Me (Joseph Gilmore)

Heaven Came Down (John W. Peterson)

In My Heart There Rings a Melody (Elton M. Roth)

It Is Well with My Soul (Horatio G. Spafford)

Love Lifted Me (James Rowe)

Since I Have Been Redeemed (Edwin O. Excell)

The Way of the Cross Leads Home
(Jessie B. Pounds)

---

5. Sing the modern praise choruses. This Asaph Model is not only celebrated in the historic hymns, but is also a common theme in many of the new praise and worship choruses. Because of the nature of this music, new songs that tell what God is doing in people's lives are released daily. As you consider the following list, other choruses may come to mind that may be more familiar to you. Try singing one or two of these choruses as you follow the Asaph Model in your personal meditation time.

Choruses Celebrating the Asaph Model
Be Bold, Be Strong (Morris Chapman)
Because He Lives (William J. Gaither and Gloria Gaither)
I Am Crucified with Christ (John G. Elliott)
I Will Sing of the Mercies (Psalm 89:1)
My Life Is in You, Lord (Daniel Gardner)
My Tribute (To God Be the Glory) (Andraé Crouch)
Oh, How He Loves You and Me (Kurt Kaiser)
The Joy of the Lord (Alliene G. Vale)
We Celebrate (Paula Till/Robert Till/Sammy Davenport)

---

6. Honestly express your feelings to God about your anxieties. When the angel of the Lord greeted Gideon, Gideon's response was, "'If the Lord is with us, why then has all this happened to us? And where are all His miracles which our fathers told us about, saying, "Did not the Lord bring us up from Egypt?" But now the Lord has forsaken us and delivered us into the hands of the Midianites'" (Judg. 6:13). Rather than being rebuked for expressing his anxiety, Gideon was commended for his honesty (see v. 14).

7. Focus your meditation on what God has done for you. A dissatisfaction in your life is often the starting point in thinking how God can work in your behalf. Think back to when God has demonstrated His power as the possessor of heaven and earth? What has He done for you that demonstrates you are indeed part of His family? Can you recall times when God moved in such a way you were simply overwhelmed by what He did?

8. Think through verses of promises and claim them. As you think about God's promises, do not be surprised when verses come to mind that emphasize what God can do. When this happens, often our first impulse is to set the thought aside because we are discouraged. Before doing that, ask yourself an important question: Is this really God's attempt to change my focus? Perhaps some commandment is not being kept. Failure to meet the conditions of God's blessing in our lives hinders God from granting the blessing He wants to give.

> **Basis for Meditation**
> Is there a commandment to obey?
> Is there a promise to claim?
> Is there a sin to forsake?
> Is there an example to follow?
> Is there an error to avoid?
> Is there a duty to fulfill?
> Is there a prayer to pray?

9. Write a personal testimony to share with others. As you experience a spiritual breakthrough and see what God is doing in your life, be sure to share God's power with others. This may involve taking time to write down your personal testimony to ensure the work of God is clearly communicated to others. They may be challenged and/or encouraged by it.

As you prepare your personal testimony, begin by praying for wisdom and divine guidance (see Jas. 1:5,6). Ask God to help you view your testimony from His perspective and in the context of how He can use it in the lives of others.

On three occasions in the Acts, the apostle Paul gave his personal testimony (see Acts 22:1-21; 24:10,11; 26:2-23). In comparing each account, it is apparent Paul had developed or prepared his testimony to share with others. He began first by briefly describing his life before his conversion. Second, he told his listeners how he was converted. Then he described the difference his conversion had made in his life. That three-point outline is a good guide for preparing your personal testimony.

Often it is best to focus on a single theme in preparing your testimony rather than addressing several topics. When you describe your experience in the context of loneliness, forgiveness, a pursuit of happiness or a search for personal fulfillment, people who have similar needs will readily identify with your experience. If you try to prepare a testimony that speaks to all the things God has done in your life, those who hear it may become confused and/or overwhelmed.

10. Keep a written record of God's intervention in your life. Christianity differs from many of the world's religions in that Christians believe God is willing to become involved in their lives. Because God wants to become involved in your life and He has done so in the past, keep a written record. Then you can share with others what God has done in your life. Some keep journals; others keep a record of answered prayers. I still have my prayer request sheet from January 1951 when I asked my wife for our first date. I also have my prayer request sheet for September 1951 when I asked her to marry me. In case you are wondering, she said "yes" both times.

Suggested Scripture Passages for Meditating on God's Intervention

Psalm 3	Psalm 82
Psalm 50	Psalm 90
Psalm 77	Acts 9:20-25
Psalm 79	

Prayer	Praise
1. That I may never get so discouraged that I will not turn to God, or be able to remember His powerful ability to intervene in my life.	1. Praise God for His plan and power to work all things for good in my life.
2. That I may understand God's methods to turn frustration into hope, and I may always be able to apply them.	2. Praise God for His past deliverance for me and others from the crises of life.
3. That I may worship God for His wisdom and power to intervene in frustrating problems.	3. Praise God for His love and care and that He comes to me in times of distress and intervenes for me.
4. That I may grow in grace because of the valleys of vexation I experience.	4. Praise God for His perfect leadership in my life, both in and out of times of trouble.
5. That I may praise and worship God better because I have learned how He intervenes.	5. Praise God for His daily provision for all my needs.
6. That I may help others who have difficulties understanding how God can intervene for them.	6. Praise God that I understand He has a plan for me in my distressing valleys and that He delivers me.
7.	7.
8.	8.
9.	9.

Journaling

Two benefits can be derived from writing down the works of God. First, it helps you understand what God is doing in your life at the present time, because you clarify your thinking when you write down what God is doing through your experience. A second benefit is that when you return to read past events, it helps you remember and understand what God did in the past. Both benefits lead to better meditation because they are accurately based on how God intervened in your life.

Suggestions

1. Make a list of the obvious ways God has intervened in your personal life.
2. Make a list of the intervening acts of God in your church or ministry.
3. Keep a daily record/diary/journal of what God does for you. You will also want to write down what God is teaching you, as well as the thoughts about God you want to remember.
4. Write down the various ways God intervenes for others.
5. Write down the verses that promise God's intervention.

Bible Study of God's Intervention

1. What is God's promise that He will intervene when problems come?

> "Call upon Me in the day of trouble; I will deliver you, and you shall glorify Me." —Psalm 50:15

_____
_____
_____
_____

2. What is the natural reaction of most people when they get into trouble?

> "O God, why have You cast us off forever? Why does Your anger smoke against the sheep of Your pasture?" —Psalm 74:1

_____
_____
_____
_____

3. What should be your first step when troubles come?

> "And I said, 'This is my anguish; But I will remember the years of the right hand of the Most High.' I will remember the works of the Lord; surely I will remember Your wonders of old." —Psalm 77:10,11

_____
_____
_____
_____

4. Why does trouble come to *some* people? (Remember, this is not the only reason problems come.)

> "Because they did not believe in God, and did not trust in His salvation. In spite of this they still sinned, and did not believe in His wondrous works."—Psalm 78:22,32

_____
_____
_____
_____

5. Some people get impatient with God for a variety of reasons. Note what Asaph said, and list several reasons some believers have a hard time waiting on God.

> "How long, Lord? Will You be angry forever? Will Your jealousy burn like fire?—Psalm 79:5

_____
_____
_____
_____

6. What prayer can we pray when waiting for God's intervention?

> "Restore us, O God; cause Your face to shine, and we shall be saved!"—Psalm 80:3

_____
_____
_____
_____

7. Why are some people blind to the interventions of God?

> "I am the Lord your God, who brought you out of the land of Egypt; open your mouth wide, and I will fill it. But My people would not heed My voice, and Israel would have none of Me. So I gave them over to their own stubborn heart, to walk in their own counsels."—Psalm 81:10-12

_____
_____
_____
_____

8. The following verses suggest ways in which God intervened for His children. Write a summary of each thing God did.

"He divided the sea and caused them to pass through; and He made the waters stand up like a heap."—Psalm 78:13

_____
_____
_____
_____

"In the daytime also He led them with the cloud, and all the night with a light of fire."—Psalm 78:14

_____
_____
_____
_____

"He also brought streams out of the rock, and caused waters to run down like rivers."—Psalm 78:16

_____
_____
_____
_____

"Had rained down manna on them to eat, and given them of the bread of heaven."—Psalm 78:24

_____
_____
_____
_____

Verses to Memorize and Meditate

"Lord, You have been our dwelling place in all generations."
—Psalm 90:1

"And we know that all things work together for good to those who love God, to those who are the called according to His purpose."—Romans 8:28

"The days of our lives are seventy years; and if by reason of strength they are eighty years, yet their boast is only labor and sorrow; for it is soon cut off, and we fly away. Who knows the power of Your anger? For as the fear of You, so is Your wrath."—Psalm 90:10,11

"The Lord is my light and my salvation; whom shall I fear? The Lord is the strength of my life; of whom shall I be afraid?"
—Psalm 27:1

"For to me, to live is Christ, and to die is gain."—Philippians 1:21

"But those who wait on the Lord shall renew their strength; they shall mount up with wings like eagles, they shall run and not be weary, they shall walk and not faint."—Isaiah 40:31

"No grave trouble will overtake the righteous, but the wicked shall be filled with evil."—Proverbs 12:21

"The Lord shall preserve your going out and your coming in from this time forth, and even forevermore."—Psalm 121:8

Photocopy and cut these verses into small cards to carry with you for memorization and meditation.

~ *10* ~

THE MALACHI MODEL:
Meditating on God's Name

"THEN THOSE WHO FEARED THE LORD SPOKE TO
ONE ANOTHER, AND THE LORD LISTENED AND
HEARD THEM; SO A BOOK OF REMEMBRANCE WAS
WRITTEN BEFORE HIM FOR THOSE WHO FEAR THE
LORD AND WHO MEDITATE ON HIS NAME."

—*Malachi 3:16*

Malachi walked into the Temple of God and everything seemed in order—at least outwardly. People were praying, priests were sacrificing and the voices of the Levitical singers were joined in a psalm. Yet Malachi was disturbed because he had received a message from God to the people: God's people were complacent and he had to shake them up.

"I have a message from God," Malachi's voice thundered across the courtyard. "My message is a burden from God."

Some priests ran to hush up the prophet; he was in their

Temple, which was their turf. They wanted Malachi silenced, but Malachi could not be silenced. He thundered,

"The Lord says He loves you!" (1:2, author's translation).

The people listened politely to the scruffy prophet, yet they did not respect him or heed his sermon. They only tolerated Malachi. So with a snicker, or even worse, with polite sarcasm, they answered,

"In what way has the Lord loved us?" (v. 2, author's translation).

Malachi told them God had demonstrated His love by choosing Israel, leading Israel and protecting Israel. Malachi told them God wanted to be honored in His Temple. He challenged his audience,

"Where is God's honor?" (v. 6).

Malachi told the crowd of listeners that a son honors his father, but they had not honored God. A slave reverences his master, but they had not reverenced God. The people continued to protest,

"In what way have we not honored God's name?" (v. 7, author's translation).

Malachi told them they had offered sheep that were maimed, blind or sick. They gave God "second best." They had brought rotten food to the altar. Malachi accused the people of the sin of compromising their families with the sin of divorce. "For the Lord God of Israel says that He hates divorce" (2:16). Malachi accused them of profaning the holy institution of marriage, "which He loves" (v. 11).

The people answered that God was indifferent to the injustice they were suffering. They wanted God to perform a miracle and punish the armies that invaded Israel; but God did nothing. They wanted God to punish Persia for the extreme taxation they paid; but God did nothing. They witnessed evil nations about them flourish, but they were oppressed. The people cried out,

"'Where is the God of justice?'" (v. 17).

Malachi was trying to prepare the people of Israel for a new way of life. David's kingdom was gone; the day of miracles was past. The old kingdom way was not coming back. Malachi had to teach Israel how to live for God even when He didn't immediately punish every transgression. The people of Israel had to learn to live for God even when He allowed them to be captured by their enemy. Malachi promised that the Messiah, their Deliverer was coming. He promised,

"The Lord, whom you seek, will suddenly come to His temple'" (3:1).

Malachi called for the people to repent in their hearts and return to the Lord. He told them God wanted religion of the heart and mind, not outward conformity. People who compromise are blind; they don't see their compromise. The people said to Malachi,

"In what way shall we return?'" (v. 7).

Malachi told them they needed to give their tithes to God. He accused the people of robbing God by refusing to pay their tithes. He preached,

"Bring all the tithes into the storehouse, that there may be food in My house, and try Me now in this, says the Lord of hosts, 'If I will not open for you the windows of heaven and pour out for you such blessing that there will not be room enough to receive it'" (Mal. 3:10).

The people of Israel wanted an outward kingdom; they didn't understand God's inward kingdom. They wanted a return of David to the throne and Jewish soldiers to protect them. The people were complaining that they served God, and got nothing out of it. They said,

"What profit is it that we have kept His ordinance?" (v. 14).

The people of Malachi's day are not different from people today. People want outward Christianity, not inward faith. They are more interested in outward physical miracles than in the One who has power to change them inwardly. They want money in answer to their prayers more than they want the One who can satisfy all their needs. They want a tangible blessing from God more than they want God Himself. Malachi's answer was inward faith; he wanted their hearts changed and he wanted them to think correctly about God. He wanted them to meditate on God.

"Then those who feared the Lord spoke to one another, and the Lord listened and heard them; so a book of

> remembrance was written before Him for those who fear
> the Lord and who meditate on His name."
>
> —Malachi 3:16

The popular New Age and Hindu expressions of meditation widely practiced in our society invite people to look deep within themselves. One of the distinguishing marks of Christian meditation, however, is that it causes us to look beyond ourselves to God Himself. The Scriptures describe a place deep within ourselves where our sin nature lives. Rather than looking at our flawed nature, Christian meditation invites us to look at God, who is without flaw. When we meditate as Christians, we meditate on God Himself.

Results of the Malachi Meditation

"Then those who feared the Lord spoke to one another, and the Lord listened and heard them; so a book of remembrance was written before Him for those who fear the Lord and who meditate on His name" (Mal. 3:16). This verse describes the discipline closely associated with the Malachi Model.

The first discipline is *reverence*. In Scripture, the name of God represents the very essence of who God is. His name reveals aspects of His personality. His name is as close as we will ever get to actually seeing God this side of heaven. Those who understand His name would never consider using the name of God without a deep reverence for God Himself. "Thou shalt not take the name of the Lord thy God in vain" (Exod. 20:7, *KJV*).

The second discipline associated with Malachi's example is *prayer*. Prayer is the means by which we talk with God. As we understand more about God through meditating on His name, it will be most natural for us to want to talk with Him, expressing praise and thanksgiving for showing us this aspect of who He is. Our greater understanding of who God is may also become the basis for making requests to God in prayer. Jesus taught us to use

His "name" when we pray: "'In this manner, therefore, pray: Our Father'" (Matt. 6:9). He also taught, "'Whatever you ask in My name, that I will do'" (John 14:13).

A third discipline in meditating on God's name is that He will *value* His relationship with you. "'They shall be Mine,'" says the Lord of Hosts, "'On that day that I make them My jewels'" (Mal. 3:17). Of course, we value our relationship with God, but Malachi suggests God feels the same way about us. God calls us "My jewels." Think of a woman talking about "my diamond," then realize how much God values you.

Fourth, God promises to especially *protect* those who meditate on His name. "And I will spare them as a man spares his own son who serves him" (v. 17). A good father always takes care of his children. Our parental instincts motivate us to protect our children from danger. God apparently feels the same way about us. In the New Testament Paul asks, "He who did not spare His own Son, but delivered Him up for us all, how shall He not with Him also freely give us all things?" (Rom. 8:32).

Fifth, the Malachi Model helps us gain greater *discernment* about life. "'Then you shall again discern between the righteous and the wicked, between one who serves God and one who does not serve Him'" (Mal. 3:18). Just as bank employees learn to identify counterfeit money by working with the real thing, so our meditation on the name of God helps us discern that which is not right in life around us.

A sixth discipline of meditating on God's names is our *growth and maturity*. Those who think about God's names are protected and fed by God. Malachi likens them to special calves protected in the stall of the barn, not left out to face the dangers of the pasture.

> "But to you who fear my name the Sun
> of Righteousness shall arise with healing in His wings;
> and you shall go out and grow like fat stall-fed calves."
> —Malachi 4:2

Those who meditate on God's names will immediately recognize one name for Jesus Christ; He is called "The Sun of Righteousness" in this verse. Jesus, the Son of God, gives us warmth, strength and life, just as the sun in heaven.

Why Think About God's Names?

By using these various disciplines of meditation, we gain unique insights into the character of God. Following any one of these disciplines alone, however, is like trying to complete a jigsaw puzzle without the picture on the box to show us how all the pieces fit together. We may catch glimpses of beauty in one piece of the puzzle as we try to solve how some pieces fit together, but will fail to recognize the whole picture because we are looking only at scattered parts. How can we gain a fuller picture of who God is?

Moses was interested in gaining a fuller picture of God. As a child, he was probably taught the stories of how God had worked among his people. He learned enough to choose to identify with the people of God, although it meant turning his back on the comfortable life of Egypt. He had personally witnessed God in a burning bush and had heard God's voice audibly. Later still, he met with God in a thick cloud and talked with God as one friend talks with another. Still, Moses wanted more: "'Please, show me Your glory,'" he pleaded (Exod. 33:18).

God chose to honor Moses' request in an unusual way. It was not possible for Moses to look directly on God. Fallen human beings could never survive that experience. God chose to reveal Himself to Moses in the most complete way He could without destroying Moses. He placed Moses in a split rock where he would be safe. "Now the Lord descended in the cloud and stood with him there, and proclaimed the name of the Lord" (34:5). God used His name to reveal Himself most fully to Moses.

Meditating on the name of God is the key to the jigsaw. The Malachi Model of meditation is thinking about the names of God, and all who do so are promised a special blessing of God. As we follow the Malachi Model, we will discover significant insights into the very nature of God and our relationship with Him.

The psalmist identified meditating on the name of God as the basis for a growing faith. He wrote, "Some trust in chariots, and some in horses; but we will remember the name of the Lord our God" (Ps. 20:7). When we use the Malachi Model, we gain new insight into God. Hudson Taylor was once asked about the secret to his great faith in God. Taylor objected, saying, "I do not have great faith. I have a little faith in a great God." As our understanding of God increases, our ability to trust Him appears to grow also.

Although the word "Trinity" is not used in Scripture, the Bible describes God in three persons. Each person of the Trinity is further revealed in His names. As noted earlier in this book, more than a thousand different names of God are revealed in Scripture. The author has listed these names in three other books he has written about the names of the Father, Son and Holy Spirit. The three charts following list some of the principal names of each Person of the Godhead. As you study these names, consider how a better understanding of that aspect of God's personality might help you trust Him more.

The Names of God in Scripture

Elohim (God)

YHWH or Jehovah (Lord)

Adonai (Lord)

El Shaddai (Almighty/All Sufficient God)

El Elyon (God Most High)

El Olam (The Everlasting God)

El Gibbor (Mighty God)

Jehovah-Sabaoth (The Lord of hosts)

Jehovah-Jireh (The Lord will Provide)

Jehovah-Rapha (The Lord that Heals)

Jehovah-Nissi (The Lord our Banner)

Jehovah-Shalom (The Lord our Peace)

Jehovah-Tsidkenu (The Lord our Righteousness)

Jehovah-Shammah (The Lord is there)

The Names of Jesus in Scripture
The Word (Logos)
The Seed of the Woman
The Rising Star
The Captain of the Lord's Hosts
The Angel of the Lord
The Desire of Israel
The Son of David
A Light to the Gentiles
The Righteous Branch
Jesus Christ our Lord
Our Great God and Savior
King of Kings and Lord of Lords

The Names of the Holy Spirit in Scripture
The Comforter (Helper)
The Reprover
The Restrainer
The Spirit of Life
The Spirit of Sanctification
The Baptizer
The Seal of God
The Fullness of God
The Spirit of Revelation
The Holy Spirit

Meditating on the names of God in Scripture is also the basis for effective evangelism. This was recognized by the most evangelical of all the Old Testament prophets, Isaiah. He wrote,

"O Zion, You who bring good tidings, get up into the high mountain; O Jerusalem, You who bring good tidings, lift up your voice with strength, lift it up, be not afraid; say to the cities of Judah, 'Behold Your God!'" (Isa. 40:9).

As people are invited to carefully consider who God is, they will be drawn to Him like a moth to a burning light. Jesus expressed this thought when He told His disciples, "'And I, if I am lifted up from the earth, will draw all peoples to Myself'" (John 12:32).

In Old Testament times, the Jewish scribes believed the name of God was equivalent to God's presence or God's person. To misuse His name was to misuse God. The name of the Lord (*Jehovah*) was specially connected with the altar or the holy of holies, which was viewed as the localized presence of God on earth. So precious was the name *Jehovah* that the people were not even to take the names of false gods on their lips, lest they blaspheme God's name by allowing both names to come out of the same mouth (see Exod. 23:13; Josh. 23:7).

At first, the name of God was used in greeting (i.e., "The Lord bless you" [Ruth 2:4]), but later that changed. Rabbis came to view the name *Jehovah* as too holy to pronounce. After a period of time, the name *Jehovah* was pronounced only by the priest in the Temple when blessing the people (see Num. 6:23-27).

During the Maccabean Revolt in the second century B.C., the Temple was destroyed and the priests ceased to pronounce the name *Jehovah* completely. After a period of time, Jewish doctrines arose that forbade speaking the name of God. It was widely believed that those who spoke the name of God would be barred from the world to come. At least one rabbi taught that pronouncing the name of God was a capital crime.

All kinds of practices developed about writing the name *Jehovah*. When a scribe copying the Scriptures came to the sacred name, he would lay aside his quill and get a new one with which to write *Jehovah*. Then he would break the new pen so that no other name would ever flow from it again, ensuring that the scribe could not be charged with blaspheming God's holy name.

When Jesus taught His disciples to pray to the Father, He taught them to pray, "'Hallowed be Your name'" (Matt. 6:9). At least two practical Christian applications flow from knowing and hallowing the name of God in our lives.

First, hallowing the name of God is usually viewed as a prohibition against cursing. This is consistent with the commandment, "'You shall not take the name of the Lord your God in vain'" (Exod. 20:7).

Second, we hallow God's name when we seek Him by faith. Believing in His name is the way we become part of the family of God. "But as many as received Him, to them He gave the right to become children of God, to those who believe in His name" (John 1:12). The apostles preached that salvation was exclusively found in the name of Christ. "'Nor is there salvation in any other, for there is no other name under heaven given among men by which we must be saved'" (Acts 4:12).

Biblical Hebrew contained no journalistic differences in type styles to allow for capitals, italics, etc. in writing the Scriptures. The use of capital letters and the capitalization of God's name was introduced by Sebastian Munster of Basel, Switzerland, in a Latin version published in 1534. The example was followed in several other translations, such as the *Geneva Bible* (1560), and the *Bishops' Bible* (1568). The most extensive use of special type styles appeared in the *Authorized* or *King James Version* (1611), in which the translators used various combinations of capital letters to communicate the different meanings and interpretations of the names of God. (For a full explanation of the capitalization of God's many names, see Appendix B of the author's book *My Father's Names*, Regal Books, 1991.)

Ten Steps to Apply the Malachi Model

As we incorporate the Malachi Model into our personal discipline of meditation, we should try to apply some of the following suggestions.

1. **Reverence God's name in speaking and writing.** This begins with a spirit of reverence for God who has revealed Himself to us in His names. Make sure to capitalize God's names when writing them. Do not use abbreviations, but write out His names in full.

Spell His names correctly. When you speak, do not use God's name in jest or without due reverence.

2. Do not curse using God's name or take His name in vain. Although the third Commandment states, "'You shall not take the name of the Lord your God in vain'" (Exod. 20:7), many still do. Be careful! There is a consequence for those who use His name irreverently, "'The Lord will not hold him guiltless who take His name in vain'" (v. 7).

3. Use the historic hymns of the Christian faith to celebrate the names of God. As you read and think about the great hymns, they can help guide your thoughts as you meditate on God. The following list of hymns is derived from several popular church hymnals.

Hymns Celebrating the Malachi Model

All Hail the Power of Jesus' Name (Edward Perronet)

At the Name of Jesus (Caroline M. Noel)

Blessed Be the Name (William H. Clark/Ralph E. Hudson)

Crown Him with Many Crowns (Matthew Bridges)

Freely, Freely (Carol Owens)

Glory to His Name (Elisha A. Hoffman)

He Keeps Me Singing (Luther B. Bridgers)

Hear Now the Name (Jack W. Hayford)

How Sweet the Name of Jesus Sounds (John Newton)

Join All the Glorious Names (Isaac Watts)

Praise Him! Praise Him! (Fanny J. Crosby)

O Come, O Come, Emmanuel (Latin Hymn)

Take the Name of Jesus with You (Lydia Baxter)

We Bless the Name of Christ, the Lord
(Samuel F. Coffman)

What a Wonderful Savior! (Elisha A. Hoffman)

---

4. Learn the new praise and worship choruses. The following list of popular praise and worship choruses identifies many ways to celebrate God's name. Try singing one or two of these choruses as you meditate on God.

Choruses Celebrating the Malachi Model
Abba Father (Steve Fry)
All Hail, King Jesus (Dave Moody)
At the Name of Jesus (Dennis L. Jernigan)
Bless His Holy Name (Andraé Crouch)
Blessed Be the Lord God Almighty (Bob Fitts)
Blessed Be the Name of the Lord (Don Moen)
Emmanuel (Bob McGee)
Glorify Thy Name (Donna Adkins)
Hallowed Be Thy Name (Babbie Mason/Robert Lawson)
His Name Is Wonderful (Audrey Mieir)
How Excellent Is Thy Name (Paul Smith/Melodie Tunney)
How Majestic Is Your Name (Michael W. Smith)
Jesus Is the Sweetest Name I Know (Lela Long)
Jesus, Name Above All Names (Nadia Hearn)
No Other Name (Robert Gay)
Praise the Name of Jesus (Roy Hicks, Jr.)
The Sweetest Name of All (Tom Coomes)
There's Something About That Name
(William J. Gaither and Gloria Gaither)

5. Memorize a list of names for each person of the Trinity. A suggested list was given earlier. For a complete list of more than 1,000 names of the Father, Son and the Holy Spirit, see appendices 1-8 of the author's book *The Names of the Holy Spirit* (Regal Books, 1994). This book was awarded the Gold Medallion Award by the Christian Booksellers Association for literary merit, and I personally believe it was because it honored all the names of God.

6. Spend much time in prayer using God's many names. Jesus taught His disciples to pray, "'Hallowed be Your name'" (Matt. 6:9). Ask God to set apart His name in your own life, then meditate on each name of God as you use each name in prayer. It will change you.

8. Use God's name in confession and repentance. When we recognize the name of Jesus is the authority of Jesus, we realize our sins are forgiven by His name.

9. Recognize the uses of God's name. The name of God is as powerful as the person of God, for His name represents His character. Use the following in meditation:

> Believe in His name, John 1:12
> Baptized in His name, Matthew 28:19
> Call on His name, Romans 10:13
> Ask in His name, John 14:13
> Walk in His name, Acts 3:6
> Made strong through His name, Acts 3:16
> No other name, Acts 4:12
> Teach in His name, Acts 5:28
> Suffer for His name, Acts 5:41
> Demons come out in His name, Acts 16:18
> Sing unto His name, Romans 15:9
> Gather in His name, 1 Corinthians 5:4
> Justified in His name, 1 Corinthians 6:11
> Giving thanks in His name, Ephesians 5:20
> Every knee bows at His name, Philippians 2:10

10. Make a list of what you want to do through the power of God's name. Meditating on the name of God will stretch your vision of what God wants to do in and through you. "'The people who know their God shall be strong, and carry out great exploits'" (Dan. 11:32). As you meditate on the name of God, make a list of the things you believe God is calling you to do. Then continue thinking about God to motivate you to accomplish each of these tasks. If the task seems beyond you, remember. "It is God who works in you both to will and to do for His good pleasure" (Phil. 2:13).

Suggested Scripture Passages for the Malachi Model of Meditation

Exodus 3:14,15	Psalm 138:1-8	Matthew 6:9-13
Exodus 33:18—34:8	Malachi 3:16—4:2	John 4:19-26
	1 John 2:12	

Prayer	Praise
1. That God would remove spiritual blindness so I can understand the meaning of His many names.	1. Praise God that I have been born again (see John 3:1-8) and have God's Spirit to lead me into truth.
2. That I may understand His plan and purpose in my life.	2. Praise God that He has revealed so much about Himself through His names.
3. That I may worship God in a greater way through using His many names.	3. Hallowed be Thy name in my study and meditation.
4. That I may grow as a believer in character and spiritual strength.	4. Thank you that I can ask anything in Jesus' name and receive it (see John 14:13,14).
5. That my meditation may focus more on God and His glory and less on me and my needs.	5. Praise Father, Son and Holy Spirit for living in me (see John 14:20-27).
6. That I may share with others the wonderful truths I am learning about His name.	6. Thank You for a good mind to understand You and a spirit to learn about You.
7.	7.
8.	8.
9.	9.
10.	10.

Journaling

Write down what you learn about God so you will retain your thoughts. One person who meditated on the Bible claimed his mind was like a sieve; he couldn't remember everything so he meditated on God's Word each day. He said, "The Bible is the water of life, it keeps my mind clean." Although that picture is very true, we can keep our thoughts focused in two ways:

Why Write Down Your Meditation?
- We remember what we write
- We can review what we forget

---

1. Write as many names as you can remember of the Father, Son and Holy Spirit. After you have finished your list, consult a concordance to add to your list.
2. I have many names/titles. I am father, husband, grandfather, dean, professor, reverend, doctor, Sunday School teacher, boss, etc. Each name suggests a different task or relationship in my life. After you have written the names of God, go back and write the task or relationship each suggests.
3. Write down your prayer of worship and thanksgiving for the different names of God. Writing a prayer does not make it more appealing to God—He looks at your heart. Writing a prayer, however, will help you become more exact in your meditation of God and in your understanding of His nature.
4. Write your feelings as you meditate on God's names.
5. Write what God is saying to you in your meditation to know and to do.

Bible Study to Focus on God's Names

1. A person's name reflects his or her task and character. What can you learn about God from His name?

> "Now the Lord descended in the cloud and stood with him there, and proclaimed the name of the Lord."
> —Exodus 34:5

_____

_____

_____

_____

2. What does it mean to you to not take God's name in vain?

> "'You shall not take the name of the Lord your God in vain, for the Lord will not hold him guiltless who takes His name in vain.'"—Exodus 20:7

_____

_____

_____

_____

3. What is God's first name in the Old Testament?

> "In the beginning God created the heavens and the earth."
> —Genesis 1:1

_____

_____

_____

4. What is God's second name (actually a compound name) used in Scriptures?

> "And the Lord God formed man of the dust of the ground, and breathed into his nostrils the breath of life; and man became a living being."—Genesis 2:7

_____
_____
_____
_____

5. When God's Son was born, what name was given to Him? What does this name mean? How did this name characterize His life and death?

> "'And she will bring forth a Son, and you shall call His name Jesus, for He will save His people from their sins.'"—Matthew 1:21

_____
_____
_____
_____

6. What name did Jesus tell us to use when we pray to God?

> "'In this manner, therefore, pray: Our Father in heaven, hallowed be Your name.'"—Matthew 6:9

_____
_____
_____
_____

7. How did Jesus want us to use His name when we pray?

> "'And whatever you ask in My name, that I will do, that the Father may be glorified in the Son. If you ask anything in My name, I will do it.'"—John 14:13,14

_____
_____
_____
_____

8. Why is it important for a person to believe in Jesus' name to be saved?

> "But as many as received Him, to them He gave the right to become children of God, to those who believe in His name."—John 1:12

_____
_____
_____
_____

9. To be saved, a person must believe in the name of Jesus. What does it mean to believe in His name?

> "But these are written that you may believe that Jesus is the Christ, the Son of God, and that believing you may have life in His name."—John 20:31

_____
_____
_____
_____

10. What happens to those who reject the name of Jesus?

> "Nor is there salvation in any other, for there is no other name under heaven given among men by which we must be saved."—Acts 4:12

_____
_____
_____
_____

11. If we believe in Jesus' name, what else may we be called to do?

> "So they departed from the presence of the council, rejoicing that they were counted worthy to suffer shame for His name."—Acts 5:41

_____
_____
_____
_____

12. How important will the name of Jesus become in the future?

> "Therefore God also has highly exalted Him and given Him the name which is above every name, that at the name of Jesus every knee should bow, of those in heaven, and of those on earth, and of those under the earth."—Philippians 2:9,10

_____
_____
_____
_____

Verses to Memorize and Meditate

"Then those who feared the Lord spoke to one another, and the Lord listened and heard them; so a book of remembrance was written before Him for those who fear the Lord and who meditate on His name."—Malachi 3:16

"But to you who fear My name the Sun of Righteousness shall arise with healing in His wings; and you shall go out and grow fat like stall-fed calves."—Malachi 4:2

"Nor is there salvation in any other, for there is no other name under heaven given among men by which we must be saved."
—Acts 4:12

"But as many as received Him, to them He gave the right to become children of God, to those who believe in His name."—
John 1:12

"But these are written that you may believe that Jesus is the Christ, the Son of God, and that believing you may have life in His name."—John 20:31

"For whoever calls on the name of the Lord shall be saved."
—Romans 10:13

"'You shall not take the name of the Lord your God in vain.'"
—Exodus 20:7

"'And whatever you ask in My name, that I will do, that the Father may be glorified in the Son.'"—John 14:13

Photocopy and cut these verses into small cards to carry with you for memorization and meditation.

—

THE KORAH MODEL:

Contemplating Intimacy with God

"WE HAVE THOUGHT, O GOD, ON YOUR
LOVINGKINDNESS, IN THE MIDST OF YOUR TEMPLE."

—*Psalm 48:9*

Two priests walked through the Golden Gate into Jerusalem; they were heading toward Solomon's Temple. To them, Jerusalem was the most beautiful city in the world, and the gates of Jerusalem were its glory. Molten gold had been poured over the heavy cedar gate; visitors first seeing the gold immediately felt the splendor of the Eternal City. The first priest broke into a psalm:

> "The Lord loves the gates of Zion, more than any other
> dwelling. Glorious things are spoken of you Zion,
> city of our God."
> —Psalm 87:3, author's translation

More beautiful than the city, however, was Solomon's Temple; it was the jewel. The city was the crown, but the Temple was the sparkle to Jerusalem's gold. The Temple was not large, but was unusually beautiful.

The two priests were Sons of Korah, members of an elite family of Levites. David had appointed them "over the work of the service, keepers of the gates of the tabernacle: and their fathers, being over the host of the Lord, were [spiritual] keepers of the [city]" (1 Chron. 9:19, *KJV*).

The two priests were returning from Zebulon where they had been conducting business. They had not see the Temple for three months, nor had they sacrificed to the Lord during that time. Their empty hearts wanted to worship the Lord in His Temple. The second priest remembered as he was coming through the countryside; he broke into a psalm:

> "As a young deer, running through the woods
> looking for water,
> So pants my soul after thee, O God,
> My soul is thirsty for God.
> I have been away from thy Temple,
> now I want to worship my God,
> I want to appear in the presence of God,
> I want to pour out my soul to God.
> They saw my discouragement and said,
> where is your God?
> As deep calls to deep, I call to God,
> I will go up with worshipers this day."
> —Psalm 42, author's translation

As the two priests approached the Temple, other priests bowed their heads in reverence, for the Sons of Korah were influential. They assigned the priests their duties, and they made sure each did his task impeccably. Although the Sons of Korah had power over others, they were godly men. They went into the Temple to pray for themselves, not just as a task to pray for others.

Solomon's Temple was built on an expansive nine-foot-high platform. The priests climbed the 10 golden stairs—a dramatic entrance into God's presence. Two tall pillars called Jachin and Boaz (see 1 Kings 7:15-22) stood on either side as they made their entrance into the *Ulam*, or porch.

They saw the altar of burnt offerings at the head of the court-yard, made of brass; it stood on a great rock (covered today by the Dome of the Rock, *Harom el Sherif*). Smoke lazily ascended into heaven from burning flesh on the grate. The first priest sang to God:

> "O send out your light, the truth that shines,
> Let your light lead me to You,
> Let it bring me to Your holy hill,
> Then will I come to God, I come to the altar of God,
> I come to God my exceeding joy,
> I praise you with sacrifice, my God."
> —Psalm 43, author's translation

Next, the priest saw the giant bowl, called the sea or laver, made of copper alloy. It glistened, some seven and a half feet tall, taller than a man, and 15 feet across (see 1 Kings 7:23-26; 2 Chron. 4:2-6). The laver was a reservoir of 10,000 gallons of pure water, but was not used for ceremonial washings. Ten smaller lavers (see 2 Chron. 4:6) were placed around the room for daily cleansing.

The two priests walked across the courtyard. They saw other priests doing their duties. One priest held a new baby to the heavens in the act of dedication. Another priest instructed a man to lay hands on the head of a lamb and confess the sins of his family. Clusters of worshipers could be seen everywhere, each standing with their priests. Some worshipers were bringing their tithes, others were praying and still others were preparing the peace offering . . . a sacrifice that priests and worshipers would eat together.

The two priests entered through the two cypress doors into the *Hekhal*, the first chamber. The cypress doors were carved with cherubim, palm trees and open flowers (see 1 Kings 6:18,32,35) and inlaid with gold. Once inside, the noise of the courtyard was shut out. The chamber was as quiet as God.

The first priest dropped to his knees to pray:

> "How amiable is your Temple, O Lord God of hosts,
> My soul longs for your courts,
> My heart cries out for the living God.
> Yes, the sparrow must find a house for its young,
> My home is with my God,
> Even with your altar my God.
> Blessed are all who desire to dwell in Your house,
> They go from strength to strength.
> Every one to appear before God.
> I would rather be in your court one day, than any other place one thousand,
> I would rather be a doorkeeper in God's house,
> Than be rich in the tents of wickedness.
> God protect me, be my sun and shield,
> Lord give me grace and glory,
> Don't keep any good thing from me."
> —Psalm 84, author's translation

Inside the chamber, the two Sons of Korah saw 12 tables holding 12 loaves of shewbread. The bread symbolized the strength of God. Ten golden lampstands (see 1 Kings 7:49) symbolized God as our light and wisdom.

In the next room—the *Devir*, the holy of holies—stood the Ark of God, a gold-covered box that symbolized the presence of God. In this room, God Himself visited when Solomon dedicated the Temple.

> "Indeed it came to pass, when the trumpeters and singers were as one, to make one sound to be heard in praising and thanking the Lord, and when they lifted up their

voice with the trumpets and cymbals and instruments of
music, and praised the Lord, saying: 'For He is good, for
His mercy endures forever,' that the house, the house of
the Lord, was filled with a cloud, so that the priests could
not continue ministering because of the cloud; for the
glory of the Lord filled the house of God."
—2 Chronicles 5:13,14

Keeping the gate meant more than taking tickets at a sporting
event, or policemen guarding a border crossing to keep out illegals.
The Sons of Korah sat in the Temple gate, as city fathers sat in the
gate of the city, which meant they made laws and settled disputes
about the Temple, the same as is done by the board members of a
modern-city church.

Because the Sons of Korah knew the importance of God's
House, it is only natural they composed psalms about the Temple
gates, altars, courts and worship.

The Sons of Korah wrote 12 psalms, none ascribed to an individual author. Their authorship was attributed to the Sons of Korah
in general, rather than to a specific person. There is an intriguing
reason why they didn't put a name on their psalms. Originally,
Korah was the family leader in Egypt, in the line of Levi (see Exod.
6:24)—that meant Korah was a priest who sacrificed to God. Moses
and Aaron, however, also Levites, became leaders of God's people.
Korah was jealous. Korah, along with two companions, resisted the
leadership of Moses (see Num. 16; 26:9-11; 27:3; Jude 11). Because
Korah refused to appear before God as commanded, Korah, Datham
and Abirom and their followers were swallowed up by the earth in
an earthquake. The children of Korah, however, were spared (see
Num. 26:11).

The Sons of Korah were ashamed of their father's rebellion and
stiffneckedness. In repentance, they followed a meek and selfless
lifestyle. Never again did a Son of Korah become a prideful leader,
but in humility they served without recognition or fanfare. Thus,
they did not put their individual names on their works, but
ascribed their writings to the Sons of Korah.

The Psalms of the Sons of Korah

42 Longing for God
43 Hoping in God
44 A Prayer for the Distressed
45 The Beauty of the King
46 Our Refuge and Strength in God
47 Celebrating the Lord God Most High
48 The Beauty of the City of Zion
49 Discerning Real Value in Life
84 Enjoying the House of God
85 The Prayer of the Returned Exiles
87 Zion, the City of God
88 A Lament over Affliction

The theme of the Sons of Korah is knowing God intimately. They wanted to know God and walk with God. A recurring theme in their psalms is the altar of God, perhaps because they remembered the sin of their family namesake. By staying close to the altar, they stayed close to cleansing and purity. Maybe at the altar they were kept from temptation.

Knowing God

As a young child sat at his desk working with crayons and paper, his teacher came by to check on his progress.

"What are you drawing today?" she asked to begin the conversation.

"I am drawing a picture," he responded as he continued drawing.

"I see," the teacher agreed, and asked, "And what are you drawing?"

"I am drawing a picture of God."

"But, no one knows what God looks like," the teacher pointed out.

Her statement caused the child to stop his work temporarily. After a moment's thought he continued his work. "They will after I finish my picture," the budding artist concluded.

What is God like? It is a question that puzzles the child and the theologian. We have no portraits of God. Even the earliest pictures of Jesus were made four centuries after His death. The face of Jesus has been drawn by artists around the world, and each one reflects the race and culture of the artist. Because we don't know what Jesus looks like, He can only be seen in the heart of the beholder. It is almost certain Jesus had neither the blond hair nor blue eyes common in Western portraits of Christ. However, would the Orientals, Africans or Hispanics see Jesus as clearly in their hearts if they could not picture Him cross-culturally? Most people picture Christ as having characteristics of their particular culture.

God, by His very nature, may be described as "unknowable." Concepts such as *infinity*, *eternality* and *immensity* are used to describe Him. Words such as *finite* and *mortal* are used to describe us. How can we, in our limited minds, comprehend all there is to know about God? We can only conclude that many things about God we will never know.

> "'The secret things belong to the Lord our God, but those things which are revealed belong to us and to our children forever, that we may do all the words of this law.'"
> —Deuteronomy 29:29

Many other things about God, however, we *can* know. By worshiping God, we can celebrate His attributes and learn about Him. The Sons of Korah focused on the attributes of God for their meditation and worship. "We have thought, O God, on Your lovingkindness, in the midst of Your temple" (Ps. 48:9). The example of the Sons of Korah encourages us to use the attributes of God as the starting point in our meditation about who God is and how we can know Him today.

How Korah Practiced Meditation

The forty-eighth psalm, a hymn attributed to the Sons of Korah, encouraged worshipers to celebrate two attributes of God: His *greatness* and *loving-kindness.* The 14 verses of the psalm appear to be divided into two stanzas separated by the word "selah" in verse 8.

> ### Psalm 48: Two Sections
> Section One: God's Greatness
> "It is forever." SELAH (v. 8)
> Section Two: God's Loving-kindness
> "Forever and ever." (v. 14)

Bible teachers are unsure of the exact meaning of the word "selah." It appears to have been some kind of notation related to the technical performance of singing. Some believe the music became louder when the selah appeared. Others claim the music became softer. Still others like to think of the selah as a kind of pause or break in the song. Whatever the exact meaning of the term, Bible teachers agree about the ultimate effect of the selah. It drew attention to the words being sung, not the meter or melody. Selah encouraged the worshiper to "stop and think" about the words he or she had been singing. Some Bible teachers prefer to translate the word "selah" into the expression, "think on that." It could be, "Time out to meditate!"

In this psalm, the Sons of Korah are thinking about God. More particularly, they are thinking about two specific attributes of God (i.e., His greatness and loving-kindness). Each stanza focuses on one of two attributes being celebrated. Because no attribute of God stands alone, even in this psalm where only two are emphasized, realize God's greatness is expressed in His loving-kindness to people. Because people are the apex of His creation, it is only natural to see God's power and might as He shows love to His people.

> Because God is great, how has He revealed
> His power to us?
> Because God is great, how has He expressed
> His loving-kindness toward us?

The Sons of Korah saw the greatness of God in Jerusalem and in the Temple: they worshiped His greatness. "Great is the Lord,...in the city of our God, in His holy mountain" (Ps. 48:1). They saw God's greatness in Jerusalem. "The joy of the whole earth, is Mount Zion...the city of the great King" (v. 2). Jerusalem was the place of "palaces"; it was a place "where kings passed by." It was "the city of the Lord of hosts...the city of our God" (v. 8). The Korah Model is active meditation, not passive. As we engage in biblical meditation, we cannot help but move into an active worship of God.

Every truth about God is related to the way we live our lives. If God really is great, the Sons of Korah concluded they could have confidence in His ability to accomplish what He had promised. "As we have heard, so we have seen in the city of the Lord of hosts, in the city of our God: God will establish it forever" (v. 8). They understood God's loving-kindness and saw it manifested toward them, "For this is God, our God forever and ever; He will be our guide even to death" (v. 14).

Meditating on Intimacy

"But we all, with unveiled face, beholding as in a mirror the glory of the Lord, are being transformed into the same image from glory to glory, just as by the Spirit of the Lord."—2 Corinthians 3:18

This verse identifies six principles that show how to meditate on our intimacy with God. First, Paul assured the Church that becoming like Christ was not a spiritual discipline reserved for just a few, but was applicable to all. Rather than be discouraged about what we *cannot* know about God, Paul encourages us to meditate on what we *can* know about Christ. Although some may understand the attributes of God better than others, all of us can gain better insight into knowing Christ.

Second, Paul describes meditating as with an "unveiled face." This suggests taking steps to get rid of anything in our lives that may hinder our view of Christ. Paul addresses this problem further in the next chapter, when he writes,

> But even if our gospel is veiled, it is veiled to those who are perishing, whose minds the god of this age has blinded, who do not believe, lest the light of the gospel of the glory of Christ, who is the image of God, should shine on them (2 Cor. 4:3,4).

Before we were converted, we were blinded to spiritual truth. Even after our conversion, blindness will continue if we tolerate sin in our lives. Sin has a blinding effect on our minds. "If we confess our sins, He is faithful and just to forgive us our sins and to cleanse us from all unrighteousness" (1 John 1:9). When we are in fellowship with Christ, He gives us light to see spiritual truth and to understand His plan for our lives.

The third step involves focusing on a specific attribute of God. Earlier, I said no attribute of God stands alone, but when we isolate one attribute for the purpose of study, it becomes an effective tool to help us gain insight into God. Paul told us to begin meditating on "the glory of the Lord." There are many other attributes than His glory, but beginning there is a good start. One hymn writer suggested God has "thousands" of attributes. Charles Wesley said His attributes are "glorious all and limitless." Most Bible teachers, however, suggest a number substantially lower. One popular list of God's attributes is found in the Westminster Catechism's definition of God.

Who Is God?
"God is a Spirit infinite, eternal and unchangeable in His being, wisdom, power, holiness, justice, goodness and truth."—Westminster Catechism

---

The fourth step is "beholding as in a mirror." This suggests looking at the attributes of God indirectly. No one has ever seen God. Therefore, no one has ever seen an attribute of God directly. No one has ever seen the wind either, but by studying the effects of the wind, we can learn much about it. Paul here is calling on the Corinthians to follow the example of the Sons of Korah and study the attributes of God.

The fifth step is being "transformed into the same image." God has revealed His glory to us to challenge us to become like Him. This principle is stated in Scripture in the context of several specific attributes of God. "'Be holy, for I am holy'" (1 Pet. 1:16). "Beloved, if God so loved us, we also ought to love one another" (1 John 4:11). "'Therefore you shall be perfect, just as your Father in heaven is perfect'" (Matt. 5:48). As we meditate on the attributes of God, we should look for ways to apply those attributes to our own lives.

The sixth step in the Korah Model is to yield to the Spirit's will and power to change us. Ultimately, the transformation in our lives is accomplished "by the Spirit of God." While the Holy Spirit conducts His work of changing us, we need to cooperate with Him by yielding our lives to His control. Sometimes He will bring experiences and circumstances into our lives as part of that process. How we respond to those experiences and circumstances will often determine how effectively His purposes are accomplished.

Throughout history, two groups of people meditated on God. The first group was the medieval mystics, many of whom were monks who spent long hours daily meditating on God's attributes. Unfortunately, most of these mystics only meditated on God; they didn't put their thoughts into action.

An example of clearheaded meditation can be found in the Puritans who came to New England. Unlike the mystics, the Puritans not only wanted to know God, but they also looked for practical ways to apply what they had learned. Though sometimes ridiculed by contemporary writers for their commitment to family and Protestant-Puritan values, the Puritans greatly enhanced the way Americans lived their lives. New England became a leader of the new nation. Certainly the Puritans were not perfect, but they sought a better life for themselves and their children. They committed themselves to a government based upon covenantal relationships and commitment to the common good. They learned about God and they knew God. They built a nation out of a wilderness with nothing but a belief that God was leading them. They built a nation that has done more good, for more people of the world, than any other, all coming as a result of their relationship with God.

Ten Steps to Apply the Korah Model

Your growth in the Christian life involves growing in your ability to understand God. As you learn about the attributes of God, you can then learn the person of God. You *can* know God. Paul's great passion was, "That I may know Him" (Phil. 3:10). Paul rebuked the Corinthians because he "could not speak to you as to spiritual people but as to carnal, as to babes in Christ" (1 Cor. 3:1). The Hebrew Christians were also urged to leave "the discussion of the elementary principles of Christ" and go on to greater maturity in Christ (Heb. 6:1-3).

> As you learn the nature of God,
> You know God.
> As you learn to know God,
> You grow in God.

1. **Study the doctrine of God to know God.** Study the following truths about God to know more about God.

> God is Creator, Genesis 1:1-27; Romans 1:19-20
> God is Spirit, John 4:24
> God is changeless, Hebrews 1:12; Revelation 1:8
> God is all powerful, Genesis 17:1; 18:14; Isaiah 40:27-31
> God is all knowing, Job 38—39; Romans 11:33-36
> God is everywhere, Psalm 139:7-12
> God is eternal, 2 Peter 3:8; Revelation 1:8
> God is holy, Isaiah 6:1-3
> God is righteous, Deuteronomy 32:4; Romans 2:6-16
> God is love, John 3:16; 1 John 3:1
> God is truth, John 14:6
> God is wise, 1 Timothy 1:17

2. Look up verses for one attribute of God. Meditate on one aspect of God by looking up the word (i.e., the attribute) in a concordance. Isolating a single attribute is one way to gain more value in applying the Korah Model to your meditation. If the love of God seems too large to consider, why not consider how that love is manifested in the covenants of God, or the life of a particular biblical character, or even in the last six months in your own life.

3. Write down the biblical passages for one attribute of God. Meditate on a specific attribute of God. It may be helpful to compile and/or write down the Scripture verses describing that attribute. You will want to take several steps in compiling this list. First, search a concordance for key words relating to that attribute. Then consult a good topical Bible under the heading of the attribute being considered. Many good study Bibles include a cross-reference section of the Bible (or the center column of most Bibles) designed to lead you through a study of an attribute of God.

4. Write down everything you know about one aspect of God. Write in your own words a particular aspect of God. As you read a verse about God, ask yourself what this verse tells you about the way God manifests this attribute. How does this attribute relate to other known attributes of God? Have there been times in your own life when God has responded to you in similar ways?

As you think about the things you are discovering about God, try to arrange them in some sort of logical order. This will assist you in remembering the information you have been studying. Sometimes it may be helpful to use an acrostic to describe your attribute. Many Bible teachers describe God's grace as "God's Riches At Christ's Expense." As you sort and arrange your ideas, do so in a way that helps you remember what God is like.

> **Grace**
> **G**od's
> **R**iches
> **A**t
> **C**hrist's
> **E**xpense

When you have compiled your insights, take time to evaluate them. One of your objectives in this step is to harmonize any apparent contradictions. Review key texts involved in apparent contradictions to ensure you have not tried to make a verse say more than it means. If a conflict remains, a couple of principles will help you resolve it. first, where two verses appear to say different things, the more recent verse probably is the fuller revelation of that truth. Give priority to the New Testament over the Old Testament. Second, where one verse appears to say something different than several others, the consistent teaching of many verses is your norm. Does something about the context of the odd verse explain why it is expressed that way? By checking the context more closely, the problem presented in the verse often disappears.

5. Make a list of life changes that come from your meditation. The purpose of meditating on God is not simply to catalogue new facts about God. How we meditate on God should affect our relationship to Him. In light of new insights, how is your relationship to God likely to change? Often, asking this question leads us to want to worship Him.

6. Use the great hymns of the past to meditate on God. You can benefit from meditation through the rich heritage of great hymns that celebrate God. The following list of hymns is derived from several popular church hymnals. As you sing and meditate on what these hymns tell you about God, they can help guide you into deeper worship.

Hymns Celebrating the Korah Model

All People That on Earth Do Dwell (William Kethe)
God of Grace and God of Glory (Harry Emerson Fosdick)
God the Omnipotent (Henry F. Chorley)
The Hallelujah Chorus (George Frederick Handel)
Holy, Holy (Jimmy Owens)
Holy, Holy, Holy (Reginald Heber)
Immortal, Invisible (Walter Chalmers Smith)
King of Heaven, Lord Most High
(Niles Borop and Dwight Liles)

Praise, My Soul, the King of Heaven (Henry F. Lyte)
Sing Praise to God Who Reigns Above (Johann J. Schütz)
We Praise Thee, O God, Our Redeemer (Julia Cady Cory)

7. Use the new praise choruses to worship God. Worship is a common theme in many of the new praise and worship choruses. Because of the growing reception of this music, new songs are being released daily. The following list of popular praise and worship choruses identifies many that celebrate what God has done in creation. As you consider this list, other choruses may come to mind that may be more familiar to you. Try singing one or two of these choruses as you meditate on God.

Choruses Celebrating the Korah Model
Awesome God (Rich Mullins)
Be Exalted, O God (Brent Chambers)
El Shaddai (Michael Card and John Thompson)
God Is So Good (Traditional)
Holy Ground (Christopher Beatty)
Holy Ground (Geron Davis)
Holy Is He (Claire Cloninger)
Holy Lord (Gerald S. Henderson)
Worthy, You Are Worthy (Don Moen)
You Have Been Good (Twila Paris)

8. Write prayers of adoration/praise. Sometimes our prayer time is simply asking for things. Try praise or adoration of God. If this is difficult, or you find your praise list is short, write down your prayers that focus on God. Make a list of all the things for which you are thankful . . . a list of things for which you praise God . . . a list of things in God you want to magnify.

9. Read devotional books. Some people have difficulty putting their feelings into words. If this is your problem, let others do it for you. Read some of the great classics, such as *My Utmost for His Highest* by Oswald Chambers.

10. Begin a journal/diary. Some have difficulty expressing their feelings in writing. Don't worry about what you write . . . just write. Begin writing a few thoughts. If you continue, you will become more expressive. Then when you read something you wrote earlier, you will be surprised at your growth in knowing God, and your growth in expression.

> Thoughts disentangle themselves
> Over lips and fingertips.

Suggested Scripture Passages for Meditating on the Intimacy of God

Psalm 42	John 15:1-7
Psalm 46:1-11	John 17:1-26
Psalm 84	1 John 2:1-18
Matthew 6:1-34	1 John 4:7-21

Prayer	Praise
1. That I may become more intimate with God through daily Bible reading, prayer and worship.	1. Praise God that He has given me the capacity to know and love Him.
2. That I may learn about God's nature so I will understand how He relates to me.	2. Praise God for the way He makes Himself known to me.
3. That my feelings may grow in proper response to God.	3. Praise God for his unconditional love for me.
4. That I may worship and praise God in a greater way because I have learned more about Him.	4. Praise God that I am in Christ and He lives in me.
5. That knowing God more intimately may make me more practical and effective in my everyday life.	5. Praise God for growth in my understanding of God.
6. That I may know God intimately.	6. Praise God for His plan and purpose for me to know Christ and make Him known.

Prayer:
To know Christ and make Him known.

Prayer	Praise
7.	7.
8.	8.
9.	9.
10.	10.

Journaling

You can become more intimate with God if you will discipline your thoughts in your daily quiet time. By writing down your thoughts, you will better focus on God and will grow in your fellowship with Him. Write down your thoughts in several areas:

1. Write what God is telling you through Bible study.
2. List the areas where you praise God.
3. Write what you learn about the character of God.
4. Write your prayers of adoration or worship of God. (These prayers never get old, for you will return many times to make the same prayers.)
5. Write your devotional thoughts about God.

Bible Study for Successful Living

1. What is the twofold basis of knowing God/Christ? (Besides the printed verse, study John 15:1-7.)

> "'At that day you will know that I am in My Father, and you in Me, and I in you.'"—John 14:20

_____

_____

_____

_____

2. What was the lifelong passion of Paul? What were the three results Paul wanted from knowing Christ?

> "That I may know Him and the power of His resurrection, and the fellowship of His sufferings, being conformed to His death."—Philippians 3:10

_____

_____

_____

_____

3. Paul wanted to know more about Christ. What was he willing to do to gain more knowledge about Christ?

> "Yet indeed I also count all things loss for the excellence of the knowledge of Christ Jesus my Lord, for whom I have suffered the loss of all things, and count them as rubbish, that I may gain Christ."—Philippians 3:8

_____

_____

_____

_____

4. When Paul wanted to know Christ, it was not to become more pious. What kind of piety/godliness did Paul desire?

> "And be found in Him, not having my own righteousness, which is from the law, but that which is through faith in Christ, the righteousness which is from God by faith." —Philippians 3:9

_____
_____
_____
_____

5. What were the spiritual riches Paul wanted?

> "To them God willed to make known what are the riches of the glory of this mystery among the Gentiles: which is Christ in you, the hope of glory."—Colossians 1:27

_____
_____
_____
_____

6. Christ dwells in the believer's life. What did Paul want the indwelling Christ to do for believers?

> "That Christ may dwell in your hearts through faith; that you, being rooted and grounded in love, may be able to comprehend with all the saints what is the width and length and depth and height—to know the love of Christ which passes knowledge; that you may be filled with all the fullness of God."—Ephesians 3:17-19

_____
_____
_____
_____

7. Not only Christ dwells in the believer, but the Father also dwells in the believer. What are the results of Their dwelling in your life?

"'If anyone loves Me, he will keep My word; and My Father will love him, and We will come to him and make Our home with him.'"—John 14:23

_____

_____

_____

_____

8. After the Father and Son indwell believers, the Holy Spirit also comes into their lives. What does the Holy Spirit do when He enters a person's life?

"'If anyone thirsts, let him come to Me and drink. He who believes in Me, as the Scripture has said, out of his heart will flow rivers of living water.' But this He spoke concerning the Spirit, whom those believing in Him would receive; for the Holy Spirit was not yet given, because Jesus was not yet glorified."—John 7:37-39

_____

_____

_____

_____

9. The indwelling Christ also strengthens your faith. How does He do this?

"'I have been crucified with Christ; it is no longer I who live, but Christ lives in me; and the life which I now live in the flesh I live by faith in the Son of God, who loved me and gave Himself for me.'"—Galatians 2:20

_____

_____

_____

10. We are to meditate on our intimacy with Christ. What is the topic of our thoughts?

> "If then you were raised with Christ, seek those things which are above, where Christ is, sitting at the right hand of God. Set your mind on things above, not on things on the earth. For you died, and your life is hidden with Christ in God."—Colossians 3:1-3

_____

_____

_____

_____

11. The Christian life is not just struggling and disciplining ourselves. How are our lives with Christ described?

> "'The thief does not come except to steal, and to kill, and to destroy. I have come that they may have life, and that they may have it more abundantly.'"—John 10:10

_____

_____

_____

_____

12. What is the result of intimacy with God?

> "You will show me the path of life; in Your presence is fullness of joy; at Your right hand are pleasures forevermore."
> —Psalm 16:11

_____

_____

_____

_____

Verses to Memorize

"My soul longs, yes, even faints for the courts of the Lord; my heart and my flesh cry out for the living God."—Psalm 84:2

"For a day in Your courts is better than a thousand. I would rather be a doorkeeper in the house of my God than dwell in the tents of wickedness."—Psalm 84:10

"'If anyone loves Me, he will keep My word; and My Father will love him, and We will come to him and make Our home with him.'"—John 14:23

"As the deer pants for the water brooks, so pants my soul for You, O God. My soul thirsts for God, for the living God. When shall I come and appear before God?"—Psalm 42:1,2

"'The thief does not come except to steal, and to kill, and to destroy. I have come that they may have life, and that they may have it more abundantly.'"—John 10:10

"You will show me the path of life; in Your presence is fullness of joy; at Your right hand are pleasures forevermore."
—Psalm 16:11

"That I may know Him and the power of His resurrection, and the fellowship of His sufferings, being conformed to His death."—Philippians 3:10

"And have put on the new man who is renewed in knowledge according to the image of Him who created him."
—Colossians 3:10

Photocopy and cut these verses into small cards to carry with you for memorization and meditation.

~ Epilogue ~

Throughout this book, we have looked at many ways to meditate on God.

- Following the David Model, we used God's created world as a means of discovering new truth about God.
- Mary gave us the example of pondering the person of Christ.
- In the Saint Paul Model, we considered Christ, our standard of excellence.
- The Saint John example helps us focus on what God has accomplished for us in the atoning death of Christ.
- The Timothy Model invites us to meditate on His call and gifting in our lives.
- By following the Joshua Model, we gain new insights into God's principles for living.
- Haggai provides a model to look at our failures and overcome them.
- The Asaph Model invites us to remember how God intervenes for us.
- Malachi taught us to meditate on His name when we think we can't see outward results.
- The Korah example leads us to contemplate the very character of God.

> ## Differences in Meditation
> 1. Different motivations
> 2. Different thought processes
> 3. Different rules for contemplation
> 4. Different things to think about
> 5. Different results in our lives

Although each meditation model has a different face, a different color and different clothes, there is a similarity in all of them and each of them. God Himself is the source.

God is always in the thoughts of His children; God is not in the thoughts of the unsaved. It is said about them, "God is not in all [their] thoughts" (Ps. 10:4, *KJV*).

So meditating on God is not futile, nor is it just talking to ourselves. When we meditate on God, we can be sure, "Thou [God] understandest my thought afar off" (Ps. 139:2, *KJV*).

How does God think or meditate on us? God said about us, "For I know the thoughts that I think toward you, saith the Lord, thoughts of peace, and not of evil" (Jer. 29:11, *KJV*).

~ *Appendix A* ~
—

MEDITATION THAT IS NOT CHRISTIAN

Meditation is practiced by sects within most of the world's major religions. Such meditating is associated with breath control, visualization, dress, food supplements (diets), drugs, mind control or other physical paraphernalia. The adherents meditate to become one with God, to purge their spirits, to gain peace, to seek nirvana, or karma, or merge themselves into the eternal spirit. Some meditate for physical health. Some meditative movements are separationist movements, and it is even reflected in their names. The Sufi movement within Islam took its name from the Arabic word for "wool," describing the material worn by the original aesthetics and mystics within that movement, in contrast to the fine linens worn by leaders of more mainstream Islam.

Most meditative movements in the West find their origins within the mystical traditions of Eastern religions such as Hinduism, Taoism and Buddhism. Because these worldviews differ radically from a Christian worldview, their discipline of meditation also differs significantly from the way Christians meditate.

Contrast*

Eastern Mystical Meditation	Christian Meditation
1. *Empty* the mind.	1. *Fill* the mind with Scripture.
2. Leads to *passive* lifestyle.	2. Leads to *active* lifestyle.
3. Focus within *yourself*.	3. Focus on *Christ*.
4. *Process* of meditation is important.	4. *Results* of meditation is important.
5. *Self-development*.	5. Worship *God*.
6. Makes the person *isolated* from people.	6. Prepares to *live* with people.
7. Leads *away* from historic Christianity.	7. *Grounded* in historic Christianity.

*These are generalizations to give the big picture of each position.

Expressions of Eastern Mysticism

The practice of meditation has been widely advocated in the West for health, therapeutic and spiritual reasons within recent decades. Although it would be impossible to identify every organization promoting meditation in this brief section, it may be helpful to identify some major approaches to meditation as widely practiced in the United States today. The following paragraphs summarize the emphasis of some popular meditative movements. No attempt has been made to rate the popularity of these movements, as significant changes can occur on relatively short notice. Rather, these approaches to meditation have been listed in alphabetical order and represent various other similar movements growing out of Eastern religions.

Chi Kung. Chi Kung is a discipline developed in China by Taoist monks that uses various breath control, visualization and meditative techniques. Advocates of this approach claim it serves to strengthen a person's internal body energy, resulting in improved health (the result of a bolstered immune system), increased strength, a stabilized heart and a calm mind. Practitioners also tend to believe in the curative powers of certain foods, especially Chinese herbal supplements and the value of various martial arts as complementary tools to achieve a common goal.

Kabbalah: Jewish Mystical Meditation. A once secret practice of Judaism called Kabbalah is gaining popularity as a path to self-understanding and self-improvement. It was popular in the Middle Ages when the practice was passed on to men over the age of 40 who were deemed to have maturity and primitive spirituality so they could handle mysticism's power. Its followers claimed that by studying the Hebrew text, they could attain a more intimate relationship with God. Once they attain the level, its followers can understand hidden meanings in the Torah and can call on God to alter nature on their behalf.

Today, Kabbalah centers are appearing that are open without regard to age or sex. The services involve lighting candles, some traditional Jewish practices, meditation and faith healing. Traditional Orthodox Jews dismiss the movement as a New Age fad. Some of this criticism is true: The walls of Kabbalah centers are decorated with symbols of Buddhism and Hinduism, and some contain Christian crucifixes and Jewish stars.

The word "Kabbalah" means "to receive." The term is used to honor the culture that preserved the understanding of the Jews. To the followers, though, the truth in Kabbalah is the blueprint to understanding everything in the universe. The truth is unlocked by meditation.

Some teach that carrying around books of Kabbalah's 29-volume primary text, *The Zohar,* will bring them good luck and prosperity. Most people can't read the Hebrew text, however, because the books have not been translated into English. Among the Jewish community members, this mysticism once dismissed as irrational is now being embraced by some. Expressions of meditation are growing in the Jewish community.

Krishna Consciousness. Brought to New York City by A. C. Bhaktivedanta Swami Prabhupada in 1965, the International Society for Krishna Consciousness is probably the most recognizable form

of Hinduism in the United States today. His followers are easily recognized in their saffron robes or saris, soliciting funds, selling society publications and chanting the Krishna mantra in public places.
Members of this movement, now based in Los Angeles, build their
devotional lives around the constant chanting of and meditation on
the name of their deity, Krishna. This chanting is perceived to
achieve two desirable results. First, in the temple, Krishna is believed
to come and be present in his image as a result of chanting. Those
who chant also view this as a means of ultimately achieving nirvana
and becoming one with Krishna.

Transcendental Meditation. Introduced to the West in the 1960s,
Transcendental Meditation is an adaptation of an Eastern Yoga technique built around the repetition of a Sanskrit word called a *mantra.*
The mantra is assigned to the practitioner by his or her instructor
and is generally viewed as a word having special power uniquely
fitted to the one using it. Normally, the mantra is the name of some
Hindu deity and the practitioner chants his or her mantra twice
daily for periods of 20 minutes. Constant repetition of the mantra in
a meditative and contemplative state is believed to produce an
altered state of consciousness.

Yoga. Yoga is widely practiced as a health and relaxation technique in North America and is taught on many college campuses
and elsewhere. It is practiced within eight expressions, including
(1) abstentions, (2) obligations, (3) postures, (4) breath control, (5)
abstraction, (6) concentration, (7) meditation and (8) absorption.
Those who practice this discipline believe it will secure them from
the disabilities associated with aging, disease and death, including
those inherited from previous lives. They further believe the practice itself rejuvenates the body and enables the practitioner to
resist all temptation. The ultimate goal of the process is to achieve
a state of oneness with cosmic reality.

Zen. Zen is perhaps the most popular expression of Japanese
Buddhism in the United States, having been practiced in major
American centers throughout the last half of the twentieth century.
Although originally a tool to achieve the disciplined life required of
the practicing Buddhist, Zen came to be closely associated with the

free-love emphasis of the hippie movement in the 1960s, especially in California. Although many expressions of Zen are practiced in the United States today, the basic concept involves isolating words and images from their normal usage in language to gain deeper insights into the perceived reality around one particular one. It is often viewed as a self-development and/or self-realization technique.

The Uniqueness of Christianity

Each of these meditation movements are born out of mysticism radically different from the basic beliefs of the Christian faith. Christianity stands unique from Eastern religions in several areas. Because personal spirituality grows out of a person's theological beliefs, these unique differences of meditation are not variations of Christianity, nor should they be practiced by a believer in Jesus Christ. Christian meditation has different practices, a different objective and produces different results.

The foundation of Christianity is the incarnation of Christ. "And the Word became flesh and dwelt among us, and we beheld His glory, the glory as of the only begotten of the Father, full of grace and truth" (John 1:14). The idea of God taking on human flesh is unthinkable in most other faiths because they believe the human body is evil. Jesus was virgin born, however, which means He did not inherit a sinful nature. Jesus lived without sin (see 2 Cor. 5:21; Heb. 4:15; 1 Pet. 2:21; 1 John 3:5). Jesus died for the sins of the world (see 1 John 4:10) and offers salvation to all. Jesus said, "'I am the way, the truth, and the life. No one comes to the Father except through Me'" (John 14:6). Those who accept Jesus' statement at face value must necessarily reject the claims to deity found in all Eastern and other religions. Their gods are not true and their desire to become one with God through meditation is wrongly based; it is false.

The Trinity is a second unique feature of Christianity. Admittedly, the doctrine of the Trinity is one of the more difficult doctrines of the Christian faith to comprehend, yet it has from biblical times been a mark of orthodoxy. God exists in three Persons—

Father, Son and Holy Spirit—yet is one in nature. The three persons of the Godhead are equal in nature, separate in person, yet submissive in duties (i.e., the Father sends the Son, and together They send the Holy Spirit).

One of the implications of the Trinity is that God is by nature a personal God. Jesus instructed His disciples to pray, "'Our Father'" (Matt. 6:9). This kind of intimacy with God would have been unthinkable even in monotheistic Judaism. Jesus said, "'If anyone loves Me, he will keep My words; and My Father will love him, and We will come to him and make Our home with him'" (John 14:23).

In this intimacy, the believer retains his or her personality and God retains His personality, yet God lives in the believer. In Eastern meditation, the individual loses his or her identity and personality in god. In Christianity, the believer grows and becomes stronger as a result of meditation on Christ and His Word. The Eastern religions and even the prophets of Islam did not advocate such a personal view of God. The doctrine of the Trinity stands in contrast with other faith groups.

The Scriptures are the third unique emphasis of Christianity. Admittedly, all the world's major religions adhere to their own sacred writings, and each religion claims some measure of authority over its adherents. The Christian Scriptures differ both in nature and degree of authority. The Christian Scriptures reveal the uniquely Christian view of God as a Trinity and Christ as the Son of God and God the Son. The Christian Bible is "given by inspiration of God, and is profitable for doctrine, for reproof, for correction, for instruction in righteousness, that the man of God may be complete, thoroughly equipped for every good work" (2 Tim. 3:16,17). Inspiration means the "out breathing" of God's Spirit into the words of Scripture. This results in two things.

First, the Bible is accurate, down to the accounting of every word in the original autographs. Second, the Spirit of God gives life to the words of Scripture, and those who read, memorize and meditate on the words of God receive the Spirit's life (see John 6:63; Heb. 4:12; 1 Pet. 1:22,23; 2 Pet. 1:20,21). Although similar claims are made in some other religious books, in practice it is usually the interpretations of those "scriptures" by a particular religious leader that bears their ultimate authority.

In Christianity, communion with God is viewed as possible. It is the realization of a person's fellowship with God granted through repentance of sin and saving faith in the finished work of Christ on Calvary. The conversion/regeneration experience brings a person into an intimate relationship with God. Jesus said, "'You in Me and I in you'" (John 14:20). This means believers ask Christ to come into their lives when they become Christians, also described as "receiving Christ" (see John 1:12). This experience describes "I in you." A believer does not lose personal identity, nor consciousness, but the believer has the spiritual presence of Jesus Christ in his or her life, and all the spiritual benefits of Christ are available to the believer. By meditating on the indwelling Christ, the believer acquires these benefits for him or herself. Neither Christ nor the believer loses themselves or their consciousness in the other.

There is a second aspect of Christ's promise. He said, "You in Me." That means that in a mystical way the believer was united with Jesus when He died on Calvary and was in the same position with Christ at the resurrection. All the legal benefits of the atonement and resurrection come to the believer because of what Christ said, "You in Me." Just as a child legally is rich because of an inheritance written on paper, so the Christian is rich because of what Christ has done for him or her. This aspect is not an experimental feeling that comes by meditation; it happened historically and becomes ours legally when we are saved. As we meditate on the death of Christ, however, we understand our new position in Christ and can now claim His promises.

Distinctively Christian Meditation

In simplistic terms, meditation as commonly practiced within Eastern mystical traditions involves becoming divorced from external realities and looking within. The primary tool used to achieve this goal is a mantra, usually the name of a god or other symbol having significance within the faith. Through prolonged meditation, a person ultimately hopes to achieve a state of ecstasy and oneness with god.

Christian meditation, in contrast, grows out of the realization that we have Christ experientially in our hearts, and positionally, we are in Christ. Along with the apostle Paul, all Christians can affirm, "'I have been crucified with Christ; it is no longer I who live, but Christ lives in me; and the life which I now live in the flesh I live by faith in the Son of God, who loved me and gave Himself for me'" (Gal. 2:20). Because the Scriptures are God's unique revelation of Himself and how He relates to us, the Bible becomes an important focus during times of Christian meditation.

Ultimately, Christian meditation produces thoughts of God in all His majesty. As a result, we become like God, we modify our lives to God's standards and we let the power of God work through us. This results not in our becoming "ONE" with God, but in our realization of how distant we are from Him in character. The knowledge that we already have a relationship with God encourages us to repent and cooperate with the Holy Spirit in effecting change within our lives so we might be more closely conformed to the image of Christ.

> "And the veil has been removed from us, so we can see and understand Christ. Now we can reflect the glory of the Lord. We daily look at Christ through the mirror of Scriptures, and we become more and more like Him as we meditate on what we see, then we reflect His glory even more."
> —2 Corinthians 3:18, author's translation

WHAT CHRISTIAN LEADERS SAY ABOUT MEDITATION

Jesus Christ will bring those who believe to the contemplation of God, where is the end of all good actions, and everlasting rest, and joy that never will be taken from us. A similitude of this joy Mary prefigured, sitting at the feet of the Lord, and intent on His words; resting, that is, from all action, and intent on the truth in such wise as this life is capable of, whereby she prefigured what is to be in eternity. For while her sister, Martha, was occupied about things that had to be done, good indeed and useful, but destined to pass away when rest succeeds them, she was resting on the word of the Lord. And when Martha complained, He said, not that what she was doing was a bad part, but that Mary's was the best, which should not be taken away. For that which lies in ministering to want, when want is no more, is taken away. And abiding rest is the reward of a transient good work. In that contemplation God will be all in all; because nought else will be sought from Him, but it will suffice to be illumined by Him and to enjoy Him (i.20).

Augustine (354-396)

It is by consideration that we first have recourse to the memory and from thence take those heavenly doctrines which we intend to make the subject of our meditation—such as promises of eternal life, descriptions of the saints' glory, the resurrection, etc. We then present them to our judgement that it may deliberately view them over and take an exact survey and determine uprightly concerning the perfection of our celestial happiness, against all the dictates of flesh and sense, and so as to magnify the Lord in our hearts till we are filled with a holy admiration—but the principal thing is to exercise, not merely our judgement, but our faith in the truth of the everlasting rest; by which I mean both the truth of the promises and of our own personal interest in them. If we did really and firmly believe that there is such a glory and that within a few days our eyes shall behold it, O what passions would it raise with in us! What love, what longing would it excite within us. O how it would actuate every affection!

Richard Baxter (1649)

Contemplation is concerned with the certainty of things, consideration with their investigation. Accordingly contemplation may be defined as the soul's true and certain intuition of a thing, or as the unhesitating apprehension of truth. Consideration is thought earnestly directed to investigation, or the application of the mind searching for the truth.

Bernard of Clairvaux (1090-1153)

Once, as I rode out into the woods for my health, in 1737, having alighted from my horse in a retired place, as my manner commonly had been to walk for divine contemplation and prayer, I had a view that for me was extraordinary, of the glory of the Son of God, as Mediator between God and man, and his wonderful, great, full, pure and sweet grace and love, and meek and gentle condescension. This grace that appeared so calm and sweet, appeared also great above the heavens. The person of Christ appeared ineffably excellent with an excellency great enough to swallow up all thought and conception...which continued near as I can judge, about an hour; which kept me the greater part of the time in a flood of tears and weeping aloud. I felt an ardency of soul to be, what I know not otherwise how to express, emptied and annihilated; to lie in the dust, and to be full of Christ alone; to love him with a holy and pure love; to trust in him; to live upon him; to serve and follow him; and to be perfectly sanctified and made pure, with a divine and heavenly purity. I have, several other times, had views very much of the same nature, and which have had the same effect.

Jonathan Edwards (1746)

Meditation is a spiritual act as definite and purposeful as a business engagement, a pledge of friendship, or a solemn undertaking. In it we apply spiritual facts and principles to ourselves as individuals and as citizens of the Kingdom of God. Having pondered them, we seek to appropriate their value by an outgoing of our loving desires toward God, and by exercising our will in the formation of resolutions. No meditation is really valid unless it leaves us with something to which we can return during the day's business and find it helpful there.

Bridgid E. Herman (19th Century)

You should meditate not only in your heart but also out-wardly, repeating and comparing the actual, literal words in the book, reading and re-reading them with careful attention and thought as to what the Holy Spirit means by them.

Martin Luther (1539)

To be spiritually minded is, not to have the notion and knowledge of spiritual things in our minds; it is not to be constant, no, nor to abound, in the performance of duties: both which may be where there is no grace in the heart at all. It is to have our minds really exercised with delight about heavenly things, the things that are above, especially Christ himself as at the right hand of God.

John Owen (1681)

The lack of meditation is a great want in our modern religious life.

W. L. Walker (1929)

~ *Appendix C* ~

—

A TOPICAL INDEX OF SCRIPTURES ABOUT MEDITATION

Benefits of Meditation: Blessing of God

"'And you shall remember the Lord your God, for it is He who gives you power to get wealth, that He may establish His covenant which He swore to your fathers, as it is this day.'"—Deuteronomy 8:18

"Let Your tender mercies come to me, that I may live; for Your law is my delight."—Psalm 119:77

"Let not mercy and truth forsake you; bind them around your neck, write them on the tablet of your heart, and so find favor and high esteem in the sight of God and man."
—Proverbs 3:3,4

Benefits of Meditation: Divine Protection

"He who dwells in the secret place of the Most High shall abide under the shadow of the Almighty."—Psalm 91:1

Benefits of Meditation: Heart's Desire

"Delight yourself also in the Lord, and He shall give you the desires of your heart."—Psalm 37:4

Benefits of Meditation: Joy of the Lord
"May my meditation be sweet to Him; I will be glad in the Lord.
—Psalm 104:34

Benefits of Meditation: Peace of God
"You will keep him in perfect peace, whose mind is stayed
on You, because he trusts in You."
—Isaiah 26:3

Benefits of Meditation: Overcoming Anger
"Be angry, and do not sin. Meditate within your heart on your bed,
and be still. Selah."—Psalm 4:4

Benefits of Meditation: Overcoming Fear
"'If you should say in your heart, "These nations are greater than I;
how can I dispossess them?"—you shall not be afraid of them, but
you shall remember well what the Lord your God did to Pharaoh
and to all Egypt: the great trials which your eyes saw, the signs
and wonders, the mighty hand and the outstretched arm, by which
the Lord your God brought you out. So shall the Lord your God
do to all the peoples of whom you are afraid.'"
—Deuteronomy 7:17-19

Benefits of Meditation: Overcoming Sin
"Your word I have hidden in my heart, that I might
not sin against You."—Psalm 119:11

"Incline my heart to Your testimonies, and not to covetousness."
—Psalm 119:36

"Turn away my eyes from looking at worthless things,
and revive me in Your way."—Psalm 119:37

Benefits of Meditation: Renewed Mind
"And do not be conformed to this world, but be transformed
by the renewing of your mind, that you may prove what is
that good and acceptable and perfect will of God."
—Romans 12:2

Benefits of Meditation: Stability

"The law of his God is in his heart; none of his steps shall slide."
—Psalm 37:31

"My heart is steadfast, O God, my heart is steadfast;
I will sing and give praise."—Psalm 57:7

"Ponder the path of your feet, and let all your ways be established."
—Proverbs 4:26

Benefits of Meditation: Wisdom

"My mouth shall speak wisdom, and the meditation of my heart shall
give understanding."—Psalm 49:3

"So teach us to number our days, that we may gain a
heart of wisdom."—Psalm 90:12

"You, through Your commandments, make me wiser than my
enemies; for they are ever with me. I have more understanding than all
my teachers, for Your testimonies are my meditation."—Psalm 119:98,99

"My son, if you receive my words, and treasure my commands
within you, so that you incline your ear to wisdom, and apply your
heart to understanding; Then you will understand the fear of the Lord,
and find the knowledge of God."—Proverbs 2:1,2,5

"Apply your heart to instruction, and your ears to
words of knowledge."—Proverbs 23:12

"When I saw it, I considered it well; I looked on it
and received instruction."—Proverbs 24:32

Examples of Meditation

"And Abraham went early in the morning to the place where he had
stood before the Lord. Then he looked toward Sodom and Gomorrah,
and toward all the land of the plain; and he saw, and behold, the smoke
of the land which went up like the smoke of a furnace."
—Genesis 19:27,28

"And Isaac went out to meditate in the field in the evening; and he lifted his eyes and looked, and there, the camels were coming."
—Genesis 24:63

"My heart was hot within me; while I was musing, the fire burned. Then I spoke with my tongue."—Psalm 39:3

"But while he thought about these things, behold, an angel of the Lord appeared to him in a dream, saying, 'Joseph, son of David, do not be afraid to take to you Mary your wife, for that which is conceived in her is of the Holy Spirit.'"—Matthew 1:20

"But when she saw him, she was troubled at his saying, and considered what manner of greeting this was."—Luke 1:29

"But Mary kept all these things and pondered them in her heart."
—Luke 2:19

"These were more fair-minded than those in Thessalonica, in that they received the word with all readiness, and searched the Scriptures daily to find out whether these things were so."—Acts 17:11

Motive for Meditation: Overcoming Evil Thoughts
"Then the Lord saw that the wickedness of man was great in the earth, and that every intent of the thoughts of his heart was only evil continually."—Genesis 6:5

"'Speak to the children of Israel: Tell them to make tassels on the corners of their garments throughout their generations, and to put a blue thread in the tassels of the corners. And you shall have the tassel, that you may look upon it and remember all the commandments of the Lord and do them, and that you may not follow the harlotry to which your own heart and your own eyes are inclined, and that you may remember and do all My commandments, and be holy for your God.'"
—Numbers 15:38-40

"Why do the nations rage, and the people plot a vain thing?"
—Psalm 2:1

Motive for Meditation: Seeking God's Blessing

"'But from there you will seek the Lord your God, and you will find Him if you seek Him with all your heart and with all your soul.'" —Deuteronomy 4:29

Motive for Meditation: Spiritual Insight

"One thing I have desired of the Lord, that will I seek: that I may dwell in the house of the Lord all the days of my life, to behold the beauty of the Lord, and to inquire in His temple."—Psalm 27:4

Role of the Holy Spirit in Meditation

"'But the Helper, the Holy Spirit, whom the Father will send in My name, He will teach you all things, and bring to your remembrance all things that I said to you.'"—John 14:26

Spiritual Disciplines Associated with Meditation: Admonishing One Another

"Let the word of Christ dwell in you richly in all wisdom, teaching and admonishing one another in psalms and hymns and spiritual songs, singing with grace in your hearts to the Lord."—Colossians 3:16

Spiritual Disciplines Associated with Meditation: Giving to God

"'Moreover, because I have set my affection on the house of my God, I have given to the house of my God, over and above all that I have prepared for the holy house, my own special treasure of gold and silver.'"—1 Chronicles 29:3

"So let each one give as he purposes in his heart, not grudgingly or of necessity; for God loves a cheerful giver."—2 Corinthians 9:7

Spiritual Disciplines Associated with Meditation: Moral Purity

"'I have made a covenant with my eyes; why then should I look upon a young woman?'"—Job 31:1

Spiritual Disciplines Associated with Meditation: Prayer

"Give ear to my words, O Lord, consider my meditation."—Psalm 5:1

"Let the words of my mouth and the meditation of my heart be acceptable in Your sight, O Lord, my strength and my redeemer."—Psalm 19:14

Spiritual Disciplines Associated
with Meditation: Repentance

"'Because he considers and turns away from all the transgressions which he committed, he shall surely live; he shall not die.'"
—Ezekiel 18:28

"A second time the rooster crowed. Then Peter called to mind the word that Jesus had said to him, 'Before the rooster crows twice, you will deny Me three times.' And when he thought about it, he wept."
—Mark 14:72

"And the Lord turned and looked at Peter. Then Peter remembered the word of the Lord, how He had said to him, 'Before the rooster crows, you will deny Me three times.' So Peter went out and wept bitterly."
—Luke 22:61,62

"'Remember therefore from where you have fallen; repent and do the first works, or else I will come to you quickly and remove your lampstand from its place—unless you repent.'"—Revelation 2:5

"Therefore lay aside all filthiness and overflow of wickedness, and receive with meekness the implanted word, which is able to save your souls."—James 1:21

Spiritual Disciplines Associated with
Meditation: Teaching One Another

"Let the word of Christ dwell in you richly in all wisdom, teaching and admonishing one another in psalms and hymns and spiritual songs, singing with grace in your hearts to the Lord."
—Colossians 3:16

Spiritual Disciplines Associated
with Meditation: Worship

"In God we boast all day long, and praise Your name forever. Selah."
—Psalm 44:8

"My heart is steadfast, O God, my heart is steadfast; I will
sing and give praise."—Psalm 57:7

"Bless the Lord, O my soul, and forget not all His benefits."
—Psalm 103:2

"Let the word of Christ dwell in you richly in all wisdom, teaching and
admonishing one another in psalms and hymns and spiritual songs,
singing with grace in your hearts to the Lord."—Colossians 3:16

Subject of Meditation: Attributes of God
"We have thought, O God, on Your lovingkindness, in the midst of
Your temple."—Psalm 48:9

"And the Word became flesh and dwelt among us, and we beheld His
glory, the glory as of the only begotten of the Father,
full of grace and truth."—John 1:14

"But we all, with unveiled face, beholding as in a mirror the
glory of the Lord, are being transformed into the same image from
glory to glory, just as by the Spirit of the Lord."—2 Corinthians 3:18

"And consider that the longsuffering of our Lord is salvation
—as also our beloved brother Paul, according to the wisdom
given to him, has written to you."—2 Peter 3:15

Subject of Meditation: Blessings of God
"Bless the Lord, O my soul, and forget not all His benefits."
—Psalm 103:2

Subject of Meditation: Christ
"And the Word became flesh and dwelt among us, and we beheld His
glory, the glory as of the only begotten of the Father,
full of grace and truth."—John 1:14

"Therefore, holy brethren, partakers of the heavenly calling, consider
the Apostle and High Priest of our confession, Christ Jesus."
—Hebrews 3:1

"For consider Him who endured such hostility from sinners against
Himself, lest you become weary and discouraged
in your souls."—Hebrews 12:3

Subject of Meditation: Covenant
"Remember His covenant forever, the word which He commanded, for
a thousand generations."—1 Chronicles 16:15

Subject of Meditation: Cross of Christ
"But God forbid that I should boast except in the cross of our Lord
Jesus Christ, by whom the world has been crucified to me,
and I to the world."—Galatians 6:14

"Behold what manner of love the Father has bestowed on us, that we
should be called children of God! Therefore the world does not know
us, because it did not know Him."—1 John 3:1

Subject of Meditation: God Himself
"'Therefore know this day, and consider it in your heart, that the Lord
Himself is God in heaven above and on the earth beneath;
there is no other.'"—Deuteronomy 4:39

"'And you shall remember the Lord your God, for it is He who gives
you power to get wealth, that He may establish His covenant which
He swore to your fathers, as it is this day.'"
—Deuteronomy 8:18

"My soul shall make its boast in the Lord; the humble shall
hear of it and be glad."—Psalm 34:2

"Delight yourself also in the Lord, and He shall give you the desires of
your heart."—Psalm 37:4

"In God we boast all day long, and praise Your name forever. Selah."
—Psalm 44:8

"Be still, and know that I am God; I will be exalted among the nations,
I will be exalted in the earth!"—Psalm 46:10

"Remember now your Creator in the days of your youth, before the difficult days come, and the years draw near when you say, 'I have no pleasure in them.'"—Ecclesiastes 12:1

"You will keep him in perfect peace, whose mind is stayed on You, because he trusts in You."—Isaiah 26:3

"And the Word became flesh and dwelt among us, and we beheld His glory, the glory as of the only begotten of the Father, full of grace and truth."—John 1:14

Subject of Meditation: House of God

"'Moreover, because I have set my affection on the house of my God, I have given to the house of my God, over and above all that I have prepared for the holy house, my own special treasure of gold and silver.'"
—1 Chronicles 29:3

Subject of Meditation: Interventional Work of God

"And Moses said to the people: 'Remember this day in which you went out of Egypt, out of the house of bondage; for by strength of hand the Lord brought you out of this place. No leavened bread shall be eaten.'"—Exodus 13:3

"'If you should say in your heart, "These nations are greater than I; how can I dispossess them?"—you shall not be afraid of them, but you shall remember well what the Lord your God did to Pharaoh and to all Egypt: the great trials which your eyes saw, the signs and wonders, the mighty hand and the outstretched arm, by which the Lord your God brought you out. So shall the Lord your God do to all the peoples of whom you are afraid.'"—Deuteronomy 7:17-19

"'And you shall remember that the Lord your God led you all the way these forty years in the wilderness, to humble you and test you, to know what was in your heart, whether you would keep His commandments or not.'"—Deuteronomy 8:2

"'Remember what the Lord your God did to Miriam on the way when you came out of Egypt!'"—Deuteronomy 24:9

"'Remember what Amalek did to you on the way as you were coming out of Egypt.'"—Deuteronomy 25:17

"'Remember the days of old, consider the years of many generations. Ask your father, and he will show you; your elders, and they will tell you.'"—Deuteronomy 32:7

"Only fear the Lord, and serve Him in truth with all your heart; for consider what great things He has done for you."—1 Samuel 12:24

"Remember His marvelous works which He has done, His wonders, and the judgments of His mouth."
—1 Chronicles 16:12

"'Listen to this, O Job; stand still and consider the wondrous works of God.'"—Job 37:14

"Come, behold the works of the Lord, who has made desolations in the earth."—Psalm 46:8

"I have considered the days of old, the years of ancient times. I call to remembrance my song in the night; I meditate within my heart, and my spirit makes diligent search."
—Psalm 77:5,6

"And I said, 'This is my anguish; but I will remember the years of the right hand of the Most High.' I will remember the works of the Lord; surely I will remember Your wonders of old. I will also meditate on all Your work, and talk of Your deeds."—Psalm 77:10-12

"That they may set their hope in God, and not forget the works of God, but keep His commandments."—Psalm 78:7

"Remember His marvelous works which He has done, His wonders, and the judgments of His mouth."—Psalm 105:5

"He has made His wonderful works to be remembered; the Lord is gracious and full of compassion."—Psalm 111:4

"Make me understand the way of Your precepts; so shall I meditate on Your wonderful works."—Psalm 119:27

"I remember the days of old; I meditate on all Your works; I muse on the work of Your hands. I spread out my hands to You; my soul longs for You like a thirsty land. Selah."—Psalm 143:5,6

"Consider the work of God; for who can make straight what He has made crooked?"—Ecclesiastes 7:13

"Remember the former things of old, for I am God, and there is no other; I am God, and there is none like Me."—Isaiah 46:9

Subject of Meditation: Latter End
"'Oh, that they were wise, that they understood this, that they would consider their latter end!'"—Deuteronomy 32:29

"When I thought how to understand this, it was too painful for me—until I went into the sanctuary of God; then I understood their end."
—Psalm 73:16,17

Subject of Meditation: Mind of Christ
"Let this mind be in you which was also in Christ Jesus."
—Philippians 2:5

"Finally, brethren, whatever things are true, whatever things are noble, whatever things are just, whatever things are pure, whatever things are lovely, whatever things are of good report, if there is any virtue and if there is anything praiseworthy—meditate on these things."
—Philippians 4:8

"If then you were raised with Christ, seek those things which are above, where Christ is, sitting at the right hand of God. Set your mind on things above, not on things on the earth."—Colossians 3:1,2

Subject of Meditation: Name of God
"Some trust in chariots, and some in horses; but we will remember the name of the Lord our God."—Psalm 20:7

"O Zion, You who bring good tidings, get up into the high mountain;
O Jerusalem, You who bring good tidings, lift up your voice
with strength, lift it up, be not afraid; say to the cities of Judah,
'Behold your God!'"—Isaiah 40:9

"Remember the former things of old, for I am God, and there
is no other; I am God, and there is none like Me."
—Isaiah 46:9

"Then those who feared the Lord spoke to one another, and the Lord
listened and heard them; so a book of remembrance was written before
Him for those who fear the Lord and who meditate on His name."
—Malachi 3:16

Subject of Meditation: Nature

"'But now ask the beasts, and they will teach you; and the birds of the
air, and they will tell you; or speak to the earth, and it will teach you;
and the fish of the sea will explain to you. Who among all these does
not know that the hand of the Lord has done this, in whose hand is
the life of every living thing, and the breath of all mankind?'"
—Job 12:7-10

"When I consider Your heavens, the work of Your fingers, the moon
and the stars, which You have ordained, what is man that You are
mindful of him, and the son of man that You visit him?"—Psalm 8:3,4

"Go to the ant, you sluggard! Consider her ways and be wise."
—Proverbs 6:6

"'Look at the birds of the air, for they neither sow nor reap
nor gather into barns; yet your heavenly Father feeds them.
Are you not of more value than they?'"
—Matthew 6:26

"'So why do you worry about clothing? Consider the lilies of the field,
how they grow: they neither toil nor spin; and yet I say to you that
even Solomon in all his glory was not arrayed like one of these.'"
—Matthew 6:28,29

"'Consider the ravens, for they neither sow nor reap, which have
neither storehouse nor barn; and God feeds them. Of how
much more value are you than the birds?'"—Luke 12:24

"'Consider the lilies, how they grow: they neither toil nor spin;
and yet I say to you, even Solomon in all his glory was not arrayed
like one of these.'"—Luke 12:27

Subject of Meditation: Personal Lifestyle
"I thought about my ways, and turned my feet to
Your testimonies."—Psalm 119:59

"Ponder the path of your feet, and let all your ways be established."
—Proverbs 4:26

"Now therefore, thus says the Lord of hosts: 'Consider your ways!'"
—Haggai 1:5

"Thus says the Lord of hosts: 'Consider your ways!'"—Haggai 1:7

"Brethren, if a man is overtaken in any trespass, you who are spiritual
restore such a one in a spirit of gentleness, considering yourself lest
you also be tempted."—Galatians 6:1

"Look to yourselves, that we do not lose those things we worked for,
but that we may receive a full reward."—2 John 8

Subject of Meditation: Personal Responsibilities
"Do not neglect the gift that is in you, which was given to you by
prophecy with the laying on of the hands of the eldership. Meditate on
these things; give yourself entirely to them, that your progress may be
evident to all."—1 Timothy 4:14,15

"Consider what I say, and may the Lord give you understanding
in all things."—2 Timothy 2:7

"Look to yourselves, that we do not lose those things we worked for,
but that we may receive a full reward."—2 John 8

Subject of Meditation: Scriptures

"'Speak to the children of Israel: Tell them to make tassels on the corners of their garments throughout their generations, and to put a blue thread in the tassels of the corners. And you shall have the tassel, that you may look upon it and remember all the commandments of the Lord and do them, and that you may not follow the harlotry to which your own heart and your own eyes are inclined, and that you may remember and do all My commandments, and be holy for your God.'"—Numbers 15:38-40

"'And these words which I command you today shall be in your heart.'"—Deuteronomy 6:6

"'Therefore you shall lay up these words of mine in your heart and in your soul, and bind them as a sign on your hand, and they shall be as frontlets between your eyes.'"—Deuteronomy 11:18

"'This Book of the Law shall not depart from your mouth, but you shall meditate in it day and night, that you may observe to do according to all that is written in it. For then you will make your way prosperous, and then you will have good success.'"
—Joshua 1:8

"'Remember the word which Moses the servant of the Lord commanded you, saying, "The Lord your God is giving you rest and is giving you this land."'"—Joshua 1:13

"Remember His marvelous works which He has done, His wonders, and the judgments of His mouth."—1 Chronicles 16:12

"But his delight is in the law of the Lord, and in His law he meditates day and night."—Psalm 1:2

"The law of his God is in his heart; none of his steps shall slide."
—Psalm 37:31

"I delight to do Your will, O my God, and Your law is within my heart."—Psalm 40:8

"But the mercy of the Lord is from everlasting to everlasting on those who fear Him, and His righteousness to children's children, to such as keep His covenant, and to those who remember His commandments to do them."—Psalm 103:17,18

"Praise the Lord! Blessed is the man who fears the Lord, who delights greatly in His commandments."—Psalm 112:1

"Your word I have hidden in my heart, that I might not sin against You."—Psalm 119:11

"I will meditate on Your precepts, and contemplate Your ways." —Psalm 119:15

"I will delight myself in Your statutes; I will not forget Your word." —Psalm 119:16

"Open my eyes, that I may see wondrous things from Your law." —Psalm 119:18

"Princes also sit and speak against me, but Your servant meditates on Your statutes."—Psalm 119:23

"Your testimonies also are my delight and my counselors." —Psalm 119:24

"Make me understand the way of Your precepts; so shall I meditate on Your wonderful works."—Psalm 119:27

"Make me walk in the path of Your commandments, for I delight in it."—Psalm 119:35

"Incline my heart to Your testimonies, and not to covetousness." —Psalm 119:36

"And I will delight myself in Your commandments, which I love. My hands also I will lift up to Your commandments, which I love, and I will meditate on Your statutes."—Psalm 119:47,48

"I thought about my ways, and turned my feet to
Your testimonies."—Psalm 119:59

"Their heart is as fat as grease, but I delight in Your law."—Psalm 119:70

"Let Your tender mercies come to me, that I may live;
for Your law is my delight."—Psalm 119:77

"Let the proud be ashamed, for they treated me wrongfully with
falsehood; but I will meditate on Your precepts."—Psalm 119:78

"I will never forget Your precepts, for by them
You have given me life."—Psalm 119:93

"The wicked wait for me to destroy me, but I will consider
Your testimonies."—Psalm 119:95

"Oh, how I love Your law! It is my meditation all the day."
—Psalm 119:97

"You, through Your commandments, make me wiser than my enemies;
for they are ever with me. I have more understanding than all my
teachers, for Your testimonies are my meditation."—Psalm 119:98,99

"My life is continually in my hand, yet I do not forget Your law."
—Psalm 119:109

"I am small and despised, yet I do not forget Your precepts."
—Psalm 119:141

"My eyes are awake through the night watches, that I
may meditate on Your word."—Psalm 119:148

"Consider my affliction and deliver me, for I do
not forget Your law."—Psalm 119:153

"Consider how I love Your precepts; revive me, O Lord, according to
Your lovingkindness."—Psalm 119:159

"Princes persecute me without a cause, but my heart
stands in awe of Your word."—Psalm 119:161

"I long for Your salvation, O Lord, and Your law is my delight."
—Psalm 119:174

"I have gone astray like a lost sheep; seek Your servant, for I do not
forget Your commandments."—Psalm 119:176

"How precious also are Your thoughts to me, O God!
How great is the sum of them!"—Psalm 139:17

"My son, if you receive my words, and treasure my commands within
you, so that you incline your ear to wisdom, and apply your heart to
understanding; Then you will understand the fear of the Lord,
and find the knowledge of God."—Proverbs 2:1,2,5

"Let not mercy and truth forsake you; bind them around your neck,
write them on the tablet of your heart, and so find favor and high
esteem in the sight of God and man."—Proverbs 3:3,4

"He also taught me, and said to me: 'Let your heart retain my words;
keep my commands, and live.'"—Proverbs 4:4

"My son, give attention to my words; incline your ear to my sayings.
Do not let them depart from your eyes; keep them in the midst
of your heart."—Proverbs 4:20,21

"My son, keep my words, and treasure my commands within you. Keep
my commands and live, and my law as the apple of your eye. Bind
them on your fingers; write them on the tablet of your heart."
—Proverbs 7:1-3

"'Remember the Law of Moses, My servant, which I commanded him in
Horeb for all Israel, with the statutes and judgments.'"—Malachi 4:4

"For I delight in the law of God according to the inward man."
—Romans 7:22

"Let the word of Christ dwell in you richly in all wisdom, teaching and
admonishing one another in psalms and hymns and spiritual songs,
singing with grace in your hearts to the Lord."
—Colossians 3:16

"But you, beloved, remember the words which were spoken
before by the apostles of our Lord Jesus Christ."
—Jude 17

Subject of Meditation: Salvation Experience
"'And remember that you were a slave in the land of Egypt, and the
Lord your God brought you out from there by a mighty hand and by
an outstretched arm; therefore the Lord your God commanded
you to keep the Sabbath day.'"—Deuteronomy 5:15

"'You shall remember that you were a slave in the land of Egypt,
and the Lord your God redeemed you; therefore I command
you this thing today.'"—Deuteronomy 15:15

"'And you shall remember that you were a slave in Egypt, and you shall
be careful to observe these statutes.'"—Deuteronomy 16:12

"'But you shall remember that you were a slave in Egypt, and the Lord
your God redeemed you from there; therefore I command you to do
this thing.'"—Deuteronomy 24:18

Subject of Meditation: Ways of God
"I will meditate on Your precepts, and contemplate Your ways."
—Psalm 119:15

Times of Meditation: Day
"Oh, how I love Your law! It is my meditation all the day."
—Psalm 119:97

Times of Meditation: Early in Life
"Remember now your Creator in the days of your youth, before
the difficult days come, and the years draw near when you say,
'I have no pleasure in them.'"—Ecclesiastes 12:1

Times of Meditation: Night

"When I remember You on my bed, I meditate on You
in the night watches."—Psalm 63:6

"I have considered the days of old, the years of ancient times. I call to
remembrance my song in the night; I meditate within my heart, and
my spirit makes diligent search."—Psalm 77:5,6

"My eyes are awake through the night watches, that I may
meditate on Your word."—Psalm 119:148

Times of Meditation: Sabbath

"'Remember the Sabbath day, to keep it holy.'"—Exodus 20:8

Tools of Meditation: Clothing

"'Speak to the children of Israel: Tell them to make tassels on the
corners of their garments throughout their generations, and to
put a blue thread in the tassels of the corners. And you shall
have the tassel, that you may look upon it and remember
all the commandments of the Lord and do them, and that you
may not follow the harlotry to which your own heart and your
own eyes are inclined, and that you may remember and do all My
commandments, and be holy for your God.'"—Numbers 15:38-40

Tools of Meditation: Religious Celebrations

"'Remember the Sabbath day, to keep it holy.'"—Exodus 20:8

"You shall eat no leavened bread with it; seven days you shall eat
unleavened bread with it, that is, the bread of affliction (for you came
out of the land of Egypt in haste), that you may remember
the day in which you came out of the land of Egypt all the days
of your life."—Deuteronomy 16:3

"And when He had given thanks, He broke it and said, 'Take, eat; this is
My body which is broken for you; do this in remembrance of Me.' In
the same manner He also took the cup after supper, saying, 'This cup is
the new covenant in My blood. This do, as often as you drink it, in
remembrance of Me.'"—1 Corinthians 11:24,25

Warnings Against Forgetting God

"'Only take heed to yourself, and diligently keep yourself,
lest you forget the things your eyes have seen, and lest they
depart from your heart all the days of your life. And teach them
to your children and your grandchildren, especially concerning
the day you stood before the Lord your God in Horeb,
when the Lord said to me, "Gather the people to Me,
and I will let them hear My words, that they may learn
to fear Me all the days they live on the earth,
and that they may teach their children."'"
—Deuteronomy 4:9,10

"'Take heed to yourselves, lest you forget the covenant
of the Lord your God which He made with you, and make
for yourselves a carved image in the form of anything which
the Lord your God has forbidden you.'"
—Deuteronomy 4:23

"'Remember! Do not forget how you provoked the Lord your
God to wrath in the wilderness. From the day that you
departed from the land of Egypt until you came to this place,
you have been rebellious against the Lord.'"
—Deuteronomy 9:7

"'But they and our fathers acted proudly, hardened their necks, and did
not heed Your commandments. They refused to obey, and they were
not mindful of Your wonders that You did among them. But they
hardened their necks, and in their rebellion they appointed a leader
to return to their bondage. But You are God, ready to pardon, gracious
and merciful, slow to anger, abundant in kindness, and did not
forsake them.'"—Nehemiah 9:16,17

"So are the paths of all who forget God; and the hope of
the hypocrite shall perish."—Job 8:13